BEYOND THE BIG LIE

BEYOND THE BIG LIE

THE EPIDEMIC OF POLITICAL LYING, WHY REPUBLICANS DO IT MORE, AND HOW IT COULD BURN DOWN OUR DEMOCRACY

BILL ADAIR

ATRIA BOOKS

New York London Toronto Sydney New Delhi

An Imprint of Simon & Schuster, LLC
1230 Avenue of the Americas
New York, NY 10020

First Atria Books hardcover edition October 2024

ATRIA BOOKS and colophon are trademarks of Simon & Schuster, LLC.

Simon & Schuster: Celebrating 100 Years of Publishing in 2024

For information about special discounts for bulk purchases, please contact Simon & Schuster Special Sales at 1-866-506-1949 or business@simonandschuster.com.

The Simon & Schuster Speakers Bureau can bring authors to your live event. For more information or to book an event, contact the Simon & Schuster Speakers Bureau at 1-866-248-3049 or visit our website at www.simonspeakers.com.

Manufactured in the United States of America

1 3 5 7 9 10 8 6 4 2

Library of Congress Cataloging-in-Publication Data

Names: Adair, Bill (Professor of Journalism), author.
Title: Beyond the big lie : the epidemic of political lying, why Republicans do it more, and how it could burn down our democracy / Bill Adair.
Description: First Atria Books hardcover edition. | New York : Atria Books, 2024. | Includes bibliographical references and index.
Identifiers: LCCN 2024019300 | ISBN 9781668050705 (hardcover) | ISBN 9781668050712 (paperback) | ISBN 9781668050729 (ebook)
Subjects: LCSH: Truthfulness and falsehood—Political aspects. | Political culture—United States. | United States—Social conditions—21st century. | United States.—Politics and government—21st century.
Classification: LCC JA79 .A325 2024 | DDC 306.20973—dc23/eng/20240626
LC record available at https://lccn.loc.gov/2024019300

ISBN 978-1-6680-5070-5
ISBN 978-1-6680-5072-9 (ebook)

For Katherine

Lies are often much more plausible, more appealing to reason, than reality, since the liar has the great advantage of knowing beforehand what the audience wishes or expects to hear.

—Hannah Arendt

Contents

PROLOGUE

My Lie to Brian from Michigan

Under the glare of the lights in the C-SPAN studio, I lied about lying.

I was there for a live interview on *Washington Journal*, the sober morning show on the public affairs network. The program was an oasis of calm in the daily shoutfest of political television, a place where I could explain PolitiFact, the fact-checking site I edited, and our latest work on the 2012 presidential campaign.

I appeared frequently on radio and television back then because producers liked PolitiFact's mix of substance and pizazz. We researched factual claims by politicians and political groups and rated their accuracy. I was on CNN, MSNBC, and ABC so often that I occasionally got recognized ("You're the Truth-O-Meter guy!"). The C-SPAN interviews were my favorite because the segments ran thirty minutes long, which gave me lots of time to explain our process for researching and rating claims. And C-SPAN shows were always unpredictable because I got to take live questions from the audience at home.

On this day, the first was Richard from New York on the Republican line. He asked a convoluted question about Ron Paul's military contributions, the delegate count, and how some guy with a prosthetic hip had been thrown to the ground during a Louisiana GOP convention. I couldn't say anything about the guy with the prosthetic hip, but I quickly pulled up our fact-check on Paul's military contributions on my iPad and explained our conclusion: *Yes, Paul had the most contributions.*

Next up was a caller on the Democratic line, Brian from Michigan, who wanted to know about fact-checkers' ratings of the parties. He had read in *The Nation* that PolitiFact and the *Washington Post* gave Republicans a lot more False ratings than Democrats—and that Democratic lies were "smaller."

"Isn't that true?" he asked.

"I can honestly say I do not keep score," I said, "and asking me that question is almost like asking an umpire who is out at home more, the Yankees or the Red Sox."

I was lying. Actually, we did keep score. That was one of my proudest innovations when I created PolitiFact: You could look at a scorecard for Barack Obama or Mitt Romney or Newt Gingrich and see how many times their claims had been rated True or False, or our lowest rating, Pants on Fire. We did not publicly tally the ratings by party for reasons I'll explain later in this book, but the patterns were readily apparent if you just browsed our report cards for officials from each party. And I knew better than anyone: The pattern, then and now, is that Republicans simply lied more. *A lot more.*

That truth has haunted me for years. I've avoided discussing it publicly even as it crippled our political discourse, enabled the rise of a destructive band of Republican leaders, and fueled a deadly mob attack on our Capitol.

It's time for me to speak up.

Introduction

It hurts to admit that I lied to Brian. I became a fact-checker because I believed journalists weren't doing enough to tell people about the lies in political campaigns. In 1985, as a political science student at Arizona State University, I crafted my own independent study course to examine the ads and news coverage in a statewide ballot initiative that sought to reduce health care costs. Hospitals opposed the proposal and ran a bunch of false ads claiming that it would hurt the quality of care that people could receive. The campaign was a classic political tug-of-war, with hundreds of thousands of dollars spent on advertising for and against the proposal.

The *Arizona Republic*, the largest newspaper in the state, did a few fact-checks of the ads, but its coverage was no match for all the money spent by the health care industry. My report concluded that journalists should ramp up their fact-checking, particularly for TV ads.

Fifteen years later, after spending most of the 1990s as a reporter covering transportation for the *St. Petersburg Times* (now the *Tampa Bay Times*), I got my chance to cover politics and try a few fact-checks when I took a job in the newspaper's Washington bureau. My first beat was to cover Congress, which, in the late 1990s, was still functional. There was some typical theater—party leaders would come to the microphones and exaggerate their outrage with the other side, but they'd often make a deal. Over time, though, I saw things deteriorate as partisanship became more important than progress. And I began to notice the lies.

One of the first lies I encountered was the "death tax," a politicized rebranding of the estate tax, which at the time affected less than 2 percent of the people who died. The less-than-sexy reality was that only heirs to the wealthiest of the wealthy had to pay. In 1997, Republicans wanted to change the rules so that even fewer wealthy people were affected. To hide that reality, they smartly called it the death tax, and they uttered sound bites such as "death should not be a taxable event," which made it seem like the law applied to everyone. It was a classic falsehood about policy, a category that gets some of the craftiest lies.

My motivation for becoming a fact-checker was not partisan. Like a typical Washington reporter, I was more interested in catching politicians of either party screwing up than I was in favoring any of them. But it was difficult for any honest reporter to miss the pattern: Republicans took shortcuts to craft a good talking point, while Democrats were more careful to be accurate. That didn't mean Democrats never lied—I did cover Bill Clinton's denial of his sexual relationship with Monica Lewinsky, after all. And for decades, Democrats distorted the supposedly imminent threat of Republicans taking away Social Security and Medicare. Although Republicans tried to be fiscally responsible by limiting the benefits in future years, Democrats made it sound like the actions would be immediate, and Granny would lose her monthly check if she voted for the GOP. But the overall pattern was that Republicans simply used more falsehoods, both in Congress and on the campaign trail.

In 2004, for example, Republicans were worried that Sen. John Kerry, the Democratic nominee for president, might peel away military and veteran support from President George W. Bush because Kerry had served valiantly in the Vietnam War while Bush had missed combat as a member of the Texas Air National Guard. Conveniently, a group of veterans emerged to raise doubts about whether Kerry really deserved the acclaim he had earned for his military service. Swift Boat Veterans for Truth, a political group funded by Republican donors, produced a series of ads that claimed Kerry had lied about his war record and did not deserve the medals he won for his combat service. But it turned out the Republican-funded group was lying. When journalists investigated the claims against Kerry, they didn't hold up. (Appropriately, this kind of underhanded tactic has since become known as "swiftboating.")

That same year at the Republican National Convention in New York, I saw a speech by Sen. Zell Miller that was so full of distortions and half-truths it ultimately led me to start PolitiFact. Miller, a senator from Georgia, was the most prominent Democrat to endorse President Bush in 2004. He gave a fiery speech that portrayed Kerry as "weak" and "wobbly," a leader who would put the nation's security at risk.

Miller, a former Marine with an appealing southern drawl, cited many examples of military aircraft and weapons systems that he said were critical in the ongoing war in Iraq but had been opposed by Kerry. He said the Massachusetts senator had been against the B-1 and B-2 bombers, F-14A Tomcats, the Apache helicopter, and the Patriot and Trident missiles, among others. "This is the man who wants to be the commander in chief of our U.S. armed forces!?" Miller said, his voice heavy with sarcasm. "Armed with what? Spitballs?"

Watching his speech on-site from the media center at Madison Square Garden, I knew Miller was twisting the facts. I didn't immediately check the details, but I knew that Kerry, then a four-term senator, was not the clueless peacenik that Miller portrayed. And worse, I didn't do anything. Instead, I turned my attention to writing a routine article about another speech that night and I didn't bother to change course. I, like so many others in the media, let Miller's half-truths go unchallenged.

That night stuck with me. The more I thought about it, the more guilty I felt that I hadn't thrown up a red flag. The day-to-day discourse in Washington didn't get much fact-checking by any news organization, including mine. Instead, coverage of the daily fight in D.C. followed a simple recipe: Take 1 serving of Republican talking points, stir in 1 serving from Democrats, and *voilà!* Balanced journalism! I began to feel that I wasn't providing the real nutrition that people needed.

The backdrop for this was Bush's false justification of the Iraq War. He said the United States should go to war because his intelligence agencies had discovered that Iraqi leader Saddam Hussein possessed—or at least was *seeking*—weapons of mass destruction. Ultimately, though, no such weapons were found. Bush would later claim he was simply acting on the intelligence reports available at the time and never had any larger regrets about invading the country, but the war left a lasting impression on the public's faith in the government—and on the media as a check on that government.

At that point, I was the bureau chief for the *St. Petersburg Times* and had lots of freedom to write a wide range of stories, from occasional fact-checks (I checked claims by climate change deniers) to investigative projects. With the Bush-Kerry race behind us, the Miller speech a persistent bug in my ear, and the next presidential campaign coming up, I went to my editors with an unusual idea.

* * *

I'd never liked ordinary approaches to the news. Although there's a glamor to covering Congress (I never got tired of seeing the Capitol dome) and the White House (I still have the seating cards that I stole from my flights on Air Force One), the stories you write on those beats lean toward the routine. A friend who covered the White House said the only good thing about the job was telling people he had it.

In Florida and Washington and wherever I was sent, I gravitated to offbeat stories. As a transportation reporter, I wrote about whether red cars got more speeding tickets (answer: slightly more). As a congressional reporter, I showed how people beg for money from the chairman of the Appropriations Committee and how House members wrestled with the pressures of parenthood. When I covered the White House,

I spent a week with the president's advance team to reveal how they staged a picture-perfect campaign rally.

I wanted to bring that offbeat approach to fact-checking.

Other news organizations had tried it since the movement began in the early 1990s, but many of the stories had gotten wishy-washy. The reporters, fearful of being called biased by Republicans, had retreated to a familiar on-the-one-hand, on-the-other-hand approach. Their stories weren't really fact-checks because there were no conclusions about what was accurate. I told my editors that we should avoid this squishiness and should rate the claims on a scale from True to False.

The idea of a regional newspaper from Florida doing a national fact-checking project—and my even grander idea, a visual representation of honesty (and lack thereof) called the Truth-O-Meter—struck many of my journalism colleagues as, well, weird. *Shouldn't you be writing about the Everglades? Why are you guys doing this?* We had partnered with *Congressional Quarterly*, a magazine and news service that focused on policy, to give our effort some cred, but the concept still seemed awfully ambitious to a lot of Washington traditionalists.

Yup. That was the whole idea.

* * *

People like to joke about lying—*How do you know a politician is lying? His lips are moving*—but it can have grave consequences. The lies about the Vietnam War and weapons of mass destruction in Iraq led to thousands of unnecessary deaths. In her famous essay about the Pentagon Papers, "Lying in Politics," Hannah Arendt wrote that lies infect everyone, even the people who tell them. "The more successful a liar is, the more people he has convinced, the more likely it is that he will end by believing his own lies."

Lying matters because it destabilizes our social fabric. It makes people distrust government, the mainstream media, and our educational system. Their interactions with government at all levels begin with skepticism and evolve to vitriol. Many people now reject facts unless the facts support their preconceived notions. Edelman, the global communications firm, summed up the bleak situation in a recent annual report on the decline of trust around the world. "Distrust," the report said, "is now society's default emotion."

Lying matters because it threatens our democracy. After Joe Biden won the 2020 election, many Americans hoped the firestorm of falsehoods of the Trump era would fade away. But a new storm emerged, one that was so large and potent it became known simply as the Big Lie, the set of groundless claims that Trump won the election. As Arendt warned, it seems to have infected a large share of the Republican Party.

Lying matters because it endangers our health. Lies about COVID-19, which heightened vaccine skepticism and enabled fraudsters to peddle ridiculous treatments, led to thousands of unnecessary deaths. A Yale study found that after the vaccine was introduced, Republican counties in Ohio and Florida had 43 percent higher excess deaths than Democratic counties. In the fall of 2023, Florida governor Ron DeSantis was still promoting vaccine skepticism as a presidential candidate.

Lying matters because it cripples our discourse. With such an imbalance of falsehoods, our political parties and elected officials are unable to have adult conversations about the critical issues of our time. They can't agree on facts because one side denies the truth.

Jeff Jackson, then a Democratic congressman from Charlotte, North Carolina, told me in an interview that lying has caused an insurmountable divide on many issues. "It's just impossible to reach a compromise on anything. I'm of the opinion that we actually know roughly what the policy solution is to most of the problems our country faces. But if any of those solutions involve any compromise, it becomes politically impossible because you just can't sell compromise in an echo chamber."

Our media ecosystem provides fertile ground for lies to sprout. The analog age had friction that slowed or stopped falsehoods, and people had a clearer understanding about trusted news sources. But the friction is gone, and consumers often can't distinguish a trustworthy site from a bogus one. Kevin Madden, a veteran political operative who worked for prominent Republicans before leaving the party, told me the way people consumed false content forty years ago indicated they were aware of its provenance. Back then, misinformation

> never really made its way past the checkout counter at the supermarket. It was *News of the World* or *The Enquirer*, and it kind of stopped there. I remember when I was a kid, my mom would read those in line and then put them back because she never really wanted to be associated with that sort of thing. It was kind of like, "I want to get my fix here, leave it here, have my moment with all that crap." There was a reputational issue if you ever actually put that in your bag and walked out of the store with it. And now [Madden held up his phone] that's the new checkout counter, right? It's with you in your pocket.

Indeed, the cell phone, the tablet, the laptop, and twenty-four-hour cable television have made it easier than ever to get the news (and the lies) that we want. And as weaponized gerrymandering further exaggerates our partisan divide, we're left with ever more extreme politicians who mindlessly utter party talking points with no shame whatsoever.

That has made political lying feel inevitable. *Everybody does it!* But lying is no longer just the background noise of our politics, nor is it a seasonal problem confined to election years. It has crippled our discourse and made it impossible for us to have a serious discussion on the vital issues of our day—the climate crisis, public health, or the future of Social Security and Medicare.

* * *

My response to Brian was a lie not only because we did, in fact, keep a count, but also because I had seen the unmistakable pattern before PolitiFact, since I'd been writing about politics in the late 1990s. And it had grown more pronounced in the digital age.

Yes, Brian, Republicans lie more.

The score wasn't *completely* lopsided. We caught Democrats in plenty of exaggerations and falsehoods, particularly when they were targeting senior citizens to scare them about what Republicans would do to their Medicare and Social Security. But Democrats didn't lie nearly as often, and a fair number of their mistakes were what I would call misdemeanors. They would get the name of a state wrong or modestly exaggerate a statistic. And then they would do something that few Republicans would ever do: apologize for their mistake.

Republicans lied far more often, and they were ruthless and repetitive. Their lies often came directly from party talking points, the scripted lines that elected officials use in speeches and media appearances. Our PolitiFact fact-checkers would notice the same lines used over and over, in cookie-cutter campaigns in Wisconsin and Ohio and Florida and Georgia and throughout the country.

As a longtime political reporter, I found Republicans had more effective talking points than Democrats and used them more often, with far better discipline than Democrats did. That also was true for their falsehoods. They just kept repeating them until people believed they were true.

What saddened me was how many of the lies preyed on old people. Faced with a shrinking constituency of their aging white base, GOP officials tried scaring them with an avalanche of falsehoods about crime and immigration. I saw this in a discovery by Ciara O'Rourke, a PolitiFact Texas reporter, that a state politician had started claiming that Phoenix had become the number two kidnapping capital of the world. The talking point was soon echoed by other Republicans, including John McCain. It was based on an ABC news segment, so they seemed to have some basis for it, but when O'Rourke checked it out, ABC did not back up the story, and the basis for the claim fell apart. But that didn't matter anymore. The message had already spread far and wide: *The Mexicans are coming to kidnap you.* The Republicans loved to scare their supporters about immigrants, falsely portraying them as criminals and even as carrying disease.

The party disparity could be seen in PolitiFact's unique individual scorecards, which revealed a tally for each person or group being fact-checked. They showed how a politician scored on the Truth-O-Meter—how many True, Half True, False, et cetera, ratings they had received. The tallies were a product of journalism, not social science (the fact-checked claims were selected based on what was newsworthy and what we believed people were curious about), but I found they still reflected a politician's general attitude about getting facts right. Barack Obama's record was heavily weighted toward True ratings; Sarah Palin's had a lot of False and Pants on Fire ratings.

Because PolitiFact was a simple database, we could easily have provided overall tallies comparing the parties, which of course would have revealed that Republicans had the most falsehoods. I knew what would happen: Republicans would cry selection bias and say we cherry-picked claims to run up the score against them. They would claim we had no credibility and tell people not to trust our work.

I wasn't afraid of taking heat for individual fact-checks, but I felt it was important to show we were nonpartisan, and I believed revealing the party totals would undermine that. I felt our commitment to objectivity was more important than telling which side lied more. The result was a paradox of the journalistic goal of objectivity. By trying to show we treated each side fairly, we denied our audience the critical knowledge we gained from that commitment.

I lied on C-SPAN because I was trying to show my fairness as a fact-checker and political journalist. I'd used a similar maneuver many times, more of a dodge than a lie, in other TV and radio interviews, in Q&A sessions after speeches. I had avoided telling the truth in all the writing I've done about political fact-checking. I loved the umpire analogy, which could disarm the peskiest Brians.

I, like most Washington journalists, was afraid the Republicans would call me biased. My job was difficult enough because of the nature of fact-checking, a challenging job in which we declared what was true and what was false. I didn't want to make it more difficult with a blunt statement that Republicans were the bigger liars. It was best to leave that math to the *Nation* magazine and let Brian tell people about it.

* * *

Fact-checkers were ready for the Big Lie, the collection of falsehoods ranging from uncounted ballots to problems with Sharpies that supposedly meant Donald Trump really won the 2020 election. Throughout the campaign, they had seen the signs that he and his followers were preemptively building a case that Trump would be "robbed" in the election. For months he complained that mail-in voting was "rigged" to favor the Democrats and that the system was so shaky it couldn't be trusted. That odd strategy had the unwanted effect of discouraging Republicans from voting early, but it also helped build a future case that the election was stolen.

After the polls closed—and after Trump halfheartedly declared victory in a largely forgotten speech at 2:00 a.m.—fact-checkers and other U.S. news organizations mobilized. In the next two months, they did an extraordinary job debunking the ridiculous falsehoods that kept popping up on social media and conservative websites. They quickly disproved the allegations of a magical increase in votes in Michigan, of a voting machine company with close ties to Venezuela and antifa, as well as ballots being burned in Virginia Beach, among many others. For a brief moment, I thought the truth might win.

But the traditional ways of asserting the facts were no match for a tidal wave of falsehoods. The foundation for the Big Lie had been laid years earlier, and a bunch of fact-checkers (liberal journalists!) were not going to persuade Republicans of the truth. All the debunking in the world could not change the minds of Trump supporters who were determined to cling to the false belief that the election was stolen. Three years after the election, more than one-third of Americans do not believe Biden won.

* * *

This is not a book about Donald Trump. Although he is mentioned in many of the chapters, in researching and writing *Beyond the Big Lie*, I found he is as much a symptom as a cause. Lying in politics began long before Trump and will be around long after he's gone. This book focuses primarily on lying by politicians and their supporters in the media. There are some excellent books on the broader problem of misinformation and how it's being spread, but I decided to keep my spotlight on political lies, the tactics used in spreading them, and the people who are victimized by them.

In 2019, I gave the commencement address at Warren Wilson College in North Carolina and talked a lot about black bears, which are common on the school's mountainside campus. I said that while many people fear them, they are generally peaceable, solitary, and of little concern to their human neighbors. That fear, I noted, comes from the fact that people don't know much about them. A real black bear, outside the confines of a picture book or nature documentary, is a wholly foreign concept to 99 percent of the population. But when there aren't enough facts at hand, misinformation about anything (bears, politics, and so on) can fester. After my speech, a parent thanked me for my fact-checking work and said misinformation was the most serious problem facing our world.

I hadn't thought of the phenomenon in those bold terms, but I think he's right. I've come to realize the magnitude of the problem. The Big Lie, denialism about climate change, and skepticism about COVID vaccines all show how lies have fooled millions of people. It's time to think more deeply about who peddles the lies, who falls for them, who those lies can hurt, and how we can address the problem.

I am hopeful that somehow Brian from Michigan finds this book and sees me finally admit it. He was right.

CHAPTER 1

The Ministry of Truth

APRIL 27, 2022: ANNOUNCEMENT DAY

The day began bright and promising for Nina Jankowicz. Shortly before 7:00 a.m., *Politico*'s *Playbook* newsletter broke the news she had been waiting for: The Department of Homeland Security was launching an organization to coordinate its efforts to combat disinformation . . . and she had been named executive director. The three-sentence scoop ("FIRST IN PLAYBOOK") said the group would be "focused specifically on irregular migration and Russia." It had a big, clunky name: the Disinformation Governance Board.

That was the extent of the DHS announcement. There was no news release, no fact sheet, no website, and no briefing for members or staff on Capitol Hill, the usual protocol for announcing a significant organization like this one. Jankowicz, who had experience in communications from her work with an NGO and a fellowship in Ukraine, would have expected that. She had recommended a more elaborate announcement, but her bosses had rejected her plan in favor of simply leaking the news to the *Politico* newsletter, a longtime Washington strategy to curry favor with journalists.

Still, she was happy the news was out. She'd waited her whole life for this moment—from her days as a nerdy teen in New Jersey who won a Model Congress award for her portrayal of Joe Biden, as a student at Bryn Mawr College who became fascinated with foreign affairs and Russia, and then as an expert who had authored two books on misinformation and online attacks. Now, in this new role, she could really do something to fight the lies.

She was thirty-three and relied on a wry sense of humor to get her through stressful days. She'd been meeting with officials inside the department for about eight weeks to prepare for the launch. She'd worked some days from home and other days from a creepy, sterile office in a government complex that had once been a psychiatric facility, and she had been unable to say much about what was underway. Now she was able to tell the world.

She was a prolific Twitter user (thirty-nine hundred tweets since she joined in 2012), so she revealed the news there, with a link to the *Politico* article: "Cat's out of the bag: here's what I've been up to the past two months, and why I've been a bit quiet on here. Honored to be serving in the Biden Administration @DHSgov and helping shape our counter-disinformation efforts." She also posted a new photo of herself, with a slight smile below her warm blue eyes, stationed in front of the DHS and American flags. "Here's my official portrait to grab your attention," she wrote. "Now that I've got it: a HUGE focus of our work, and indeed, one of the key reasons the Board was established, is to maintain the Dept's commitment to protecting free speech, privacy, civil rights, & civil liberties."

Later that morning, Homeland Security Secretary Alejandro N. Mayorkas testified before Congress about his department's budget request for the coming year. It would have been an ideal opportunity to give a detailed explanation of the new group in the context of his department's larger goals of combating misinformation and, most importantly, to emphasize that the organization would not limit free speech. But during his two-hour appearance, he mentioned the Disinformation Governance Board only briefly in response to a question about election security—and he mangled its name, calling it the "Mis- and Disinformation Governance Board."

Jankowicz, working from her Arlington, Virginia, home that day, was not watching his testimony, but she was pleased with the early reactions to her appointment from friends and colleagues online. She got congratulations from a Ukrainian diplomat, a Scottish politician, and the prominent misinformation researcher Joan Donovan. By early afternoon, she decided to lie down in bed. She was eight months pregnant and sometimes needed a little rest. Lying there, scrolling through her phone, she saw a tweet from Jack Posobiec, a well-known conservative influencer:

> *BREAKING: Biden Admin Department of Homeland Security to create a "Disinformation Governance Board" dedicated to "countering misinformation"*

Posobiec followed it with tweets that showed he—or someone he knew—had spent some time digging into Jankowicz's background and personal life: that she "once claimed militarized Trump supporters would show up to the polls with weapons to intimidate voters," that she worked as an adviser to the Ukrainian government under a Fulbright-Clinton Fellowship, that she tweeted about the Hunter Biden laptop in 2020, and even that she was known "for forming a Harry Potter 'wizard rock band' known as the Moaning Myrtles."

In less than sixty seconds after his first tweet, two anonymous accounts replied to Posobiec with a reference to the powerful propaganda agency in George Orwell's *1984*. "Ministry of Truth," they said.

Jankowicz realized immediately that her day—and really, her foreseeable future—had changed. Posobiec was a powerhouse in conservative circles, a senior editor at Human Events, a site that railed against China, "woke ideology," and Big Tech. In a profile in *The New Yorker*, he was quoted saying that he practiced "4-D journalism," which he said meant he was "willing to walk into an anti-Trump march and start chanting anti-Clinton stuff—to make something happen, and then cover what happens." He had been a Pizzagate conspiracy theorist and had authored

Citizens for Trump: The Inside Story of the People's Movement to Take Back America. He was, some Republican operatives would tell the news site Semafor, the new George Will.

What worried Jankowicz was that Posobiec had a huge audience not just through Human Events but also through social media (1.7 million Twitter followers at the time) and podcasts. She rushed to her computer and fired off an email to her DHS colleagues. "I've gotten a lot of positive notes today, which are always nice to read," she wrote to DHS communications and public affairs officials. She noted that she'd gotten some blowback calling the agency "The Ministry of Truth," and "some abuse— which I expected and am used to. However, given the tenor of the discourse and those that are sharing it, I wanted to make everyone aware there is a fair possibility this could escalate and end up on a hostile TV network in the coming days." She again urged her colleagues to say more and said she was "happy to jump on a call if you'd like."

She wrote with the pretend calm of a DHS bureaucrat, but her message was clear: The right-wing outrage machine had roared into action. This soon would be on Fox. Jankowicz knew how these guys played the game. She had authored *How to Be a Woman Online: Surviving Abuse and Harassment, and How to Fight Back*, which, coincidentally, had just been published a week earlier. It offered practical advice for women who get attacked online, including which documents to collect when reporting the harassment to law enforcement. Another section encouraged women to find humor in the absurdity of the attacks. *Kirkus Reviews* praised her for being "forthright [and] sometimes blisteringly witty."

The right-wing outrage machine—Fox, talk radio, conservative websites, and Republican politicians—was always ready to be mad, always ready to distort. Because the DHS had said virtually nothing about what the board would actually do (and not do), prominent members of the Republican Party and their supporters in the media began filling the void with lies and exaggerations. And DHS had tossed them red meat: a new government agency with an Orwellian name, headed by a smart young woman whose past was easy to distort.

"Just revealed: Biden's DHS is creating a 'Disinformation Governance Board' dedicated to 'countering misinformation,'" tweeted Eric Schmitt, then the Missouri attorney general and a Republican candidate for U.S. Senate. "The same people who lied about COVID, Trump, the Laptop from Hell and the Russia Hoax will now be creating a real Ministry Of Truth. No way."

The right wing also zeroed in on a 2020 tweet she made during a presidential debate about one of their favorite points of attack, Hunter Biden's stolen laptop, which they believed contained emails that showed corruption by President Biden. She had written:

> Back on the "laptop from hell," apparently- Biden notes 50 former natsec officials and 5 former CIA heads that believe the laptop is a Russian influence op. . . . Trump says "Russia, Russia, Russia."

That tweet and others prompted criticism that she was peddling her own misinformation and was "a Hunter laptop denier."

Conservative media was just revving its engines. At 6:00 p.m. the *Daily Mail* published an article that cherry-picked tweets and interviews from Jankowicz to make her appear to be an overzealous censor. The article grabbed a quote from an NPR interview in which the host asked her about "free speech absolutists who are often online trolls themselves" and often have great wealth to be able to protect themselves. Jankowicz gave a detailed and nuanced reply about the danger of online harassment, but the *Daily Mail* left out that context and framed it strictly around Elon Musk buying Twitter.

After it was published, *Daily Mail* editors continued to juice up the published article to make it more negative. According to an analysis by Advance Democracy, Inc., a group that conducts research into the spread of political disinformation, over the next twenty-four hours, the editors altered the first-paragraph description of Jankowicz from "a woman who questioned the validity of Hunter Biden's laptop and criticized Elon Musk's takeover of Twitter" to "a woke so-called expert who's against free speech and tried to pour cold water on the Hunter laptop scandal."

The criticism mounted quickly. At 7:00 p.m., Rep. Andrew Clyde, a Republican from Georgia, went to the floor of the House and attacked the new DHS board that he said "will be led by political hack Nina Jankowicz. This is nothing more than a blatant attempt to install a Ministry of Truth in order to push Biden's propaganda, lies, and radical agenda."

In the first week after the *Politico* announcement, Jankowicz was mentioned in more than 140,000 tweets—and 56,000 of them also mentioned "Ministry of Truth" or "Minister of Truth." In the early hours and continuing over the coming weeks, the overwhelming majority of the comments attacked the board and Jankowicz. That included tens of thousands of tweets, Facebook posts, and other articles and blog posts.

The narrative had been set, a string of distortions and lies that took root before the Department of Homeland Security could get its act together to explain that the board was really just an internal coordinating council. The narrative was that the Biden administration set up the board to be a national censor, to protect political pals and coddle the tech companies—all run by a lefty woman who couldn't be trusted and wanted to silence free speech.

The officials running DHS, a group of seasoned veterans who were *LAUNCHING AN ORGANIZATION ABOUT DISINFORMATION*, spent the announcement day utterly unprepared for the disinformation their poor planning had generated. Unaware of the urgency of the moment, they exchanged a series of sleepy, acronym-filled emails that indicate they were still confused about how to describe the board. It turns out they had, in fact, drafted a fact sheet, but it was going to be provided to reporters "on background," meaning the full document would not be posted on a website—a strategy of the analog age and another early blunder in failing to define a group that needed defining. For no good reason, they were limiting who could learn the facts about a group that was now being defined by lies.

Jankowicz grew frustrated with the impotent response of her colleagues and took it upon herself to speak up. She sought to clarify the facts about her "laptop from hell" comment: "For those who believe this tweet is a key to all my views," she wrote on Twitter, "it is simply a direct quote from both candidates during the final presidential debate. If you look at my timeline, you will see I was livetweeting that evening."

But she could see where this was headed. She knew right-wing media and how it could stir up anger. Nina and her husband, Mike, had never been paranoid about security, but suddenly they felt they should buy a video camera for the front of the house. Mike sat at the island in their kitchen and opened his laptop to check the options as she looked over his shoulder. Their goal was to find a reasonably priced model they could get delivered quickly.

As they browsed, Samantha Vinograd, one of the senior DHS officials who'd conceived the board, texted Jankowicz asking to talk. The call that followed was not to check on how Jankowicz was doing on a difficult day, but rather to criticize her for tweeting without consulting her bosses first. (This account comes from Jankowicz. Vinograd declined to answer questions.) Vinograd said the "rogue" commentary undermined Secretary Mayorkas and the department's goals. Jankowicz was perplexed by the call and surprised at Vinograd's callousness. She said that she had simply tweeted about the creation of the board, a matter of public record and which had been authorized by her bosses, and then she had sought to counter mistruths about a tweet she'd made long before she came to the Department of Homeland Security on a subject that had nothing to do with DHS. "So what you're telling me is I can no longer tweet at all?"

Correct, Vinograd said.

Jankowicz began to cry. She'd heard nothing from anyone from DHS for the previous six hours and then got criticized for speaking up with the facts in response to an uproar that now forced her to buy a security camera.

Vinograd asked if she'd received a "direct threat." Not yet, Jankowicz said, but she said she knew that was inevitable. As she talked, Mike quickly scrawled a note advising her to admit she had screwed up. So Jankowicz obliged: "I'm sorry. I didn't realize that that was the guidance and it won't happen again."

Still, she knew the attacks were coming. Mike clicked "BUY" on one of the cameras he'd been hastily comparing. That night, he wedged the dining room chairs under the doorknobs of the front and back doors.

FALL 2021: THE IDEA

It was a simple idea: a group inside the big DHS bureaucracy to help officials coordinate their work on one of the most important problems of our time. That was the concept for the Disinformation Governance Board. Memos and interviews indicate it was born from officials at the top of DHS, somewhere in the policy shop, which of course was not known as the policy shop. (It's the Office of Strategy, Policy, and Plans, better known in emails as PLCY.)

The Department of Homeland Security needed this. The Disinformation Governance Board would help connect the twenty-two agencies that had progressively come under DHS's purview in the years since its founding in the wake of 9/11. The department was like a Frankenstein monster that included everything from customs and border protection to cybersecurity, from the Federal Emergency Management Agency to the Coast Guard and the Secret Service. DHS had been created in an emergency to fend off terrorist attacks, so it made sense at the time to bring together a bunch of disparate agencies. Now, to fend off the unrooted threat of weaponized mistruth, it made sense to create a new internal group to help them talk with one another. Disinformation touched all of the agencies—there were conspiracy theories about elections systems and border security and public health and disasters.

Those lies, big and small, could infect their work—or worse, become major crises that could put lives in danger.

But despite the seriousness of the threat, the Disinformation Governance Board had no real authority of its own. It was a working group; more meeting place for the sharing of expertise than Ministry of Truth, as had been bandied about online.

An early memo to Secretary Mayorkas from Vinograd and Rob Silvers, the head of PLCY, about the need for the Disinformation Governance Board included important caveats about protecting free speech and avoiding censorship. It said that the parent DHS "must ensure that its counter-disinformation efforts do not have the effect of chilling or suppressing free speech" and that DHS "should not attempt to be an all-purpose arbiter of truth in the public arena." The memo said DHS's role "should be limited to areas where there are clear, objective facts (i.e., medical evidence regarding COVID; factual information about elections administration and security . . .)."

Republicans would later get a copy of this memo—and publish it on the internet—but conveniently ignore those points about free speech and claim just the opposite, that the board was going to silence dissent. This not only became the running narrative about the board, but it also conveniently fit a theme of long-running Republican attacks on Democrats: They were too cozy with the tech companies and wanted to quash conservative voices.

And then there was the colossal DHS mistake: At some point in the fall or early winter, the group got its terrible name. The memos suggest the name sprouted from the policy discussions because "governance board model" was one of the options that officials presented to Mayorkas.

That name! Maybe it would be worse if they had given it a tongue-twisting collection of bland words that inadvertently got shortened to a giggle-inducing sophomoric acronym. But even that would not have provided the constant fuel for the critics as "Disinformation Governance Board." It sounded like it was straight from *1984*, an all-knowing agency run by Big Brother.

But it was too late. By the time Jankowicz came on in early 2022, the name was a done deal. When she received the call from Silvers to tell her she was being hired, he seemed to pause, as if he needed to look again to make sure he said the full name of the board correctly. *It was so bad that even its creator couldn't trust himself to remember it.*

But honestly, Jankowicz didn't give it much thought and assumed the pros at DHS would have a competent communications campaign to announce it. What mattered was the group's mission. She was excited to get to work helping DHS combat mis- and disinformation.

(A point of clarification: "Disinformation" is false content that is spread deliberately; "misinformation" is the umbrella term for false content that is spread knowingly or unknowingly.)

* * *

If only the Republicans had seen Jankowicz as the bird princess in the Hillsborough Township, New Jersey, Halloween parade when she was four or five, they would have known she would be a handful to deal with. She got annoyed with a boy in line and pecked him in the face with her beak. She was not to be messed with.

Her parents were small business owners—her mom ran a small temp agency and her dad had a stucco company. Business for both wavered in the late 1980s, so her mom ended up working in a FedEx call center while her dad worked in the paint department at Lowe's.

In high school Jankowicz joined the debate team and did Model UN and Model Congress. These activities were a preview of the passion for public service she would take with her to Bryn Mawr College, where she studied foreign affairs and the Russian language. She interned at the U.S. State Department and studied abroad in St. Petersburg, Russia, where she got interested in the issues surrounding democratization. She went on to earn a master's degree in Russian and Eastern European studies at Georgetown University, which put her on a path to be a foreign service officer at the State Department.

She loved the idea of working in diplomacy but didn't want the challenge of moving to a new country every few years, as the Foreign Service usually required. She'd met, fallen in love with, and gotten engaged to Mike along the way, and they didn't want that nomadic life. She was selected to be a Fulbright-Clinton Public Policy Fellow in 2016, advising the Ukrainian Ministry of Foreign Affairs on strategic communications, where she got experience with Russia's lies about Ukraine.

To understand Jankowicz and how she grew into an expert in foreign affairs, social media, and misinformation, just browse her Twitter account, @wiczipedia, over the years. The tweets offer a lively tour of all aspects of her life, professional, personal—and as a dog owner. When she started her account in 2012, her tweets reflected the earnestness of an ambitious Georgetown grad student with a joyous outlook on life.

"In awe of the amazing women in this room tonight," she posted at an event with Madeleine Albright and Samantha Power.

"Practicing my presentation in a Starbucks in Pittsburgh. People probably think I'm a nutt, talking to myself about Communism. Ah, academia."

"Just got back from hearing a talk by Zbigniew #Brzezinski and his Strategic Vision for the US. . . . #Brzezinski2016? :) I wish!"

"Interesting piece by George Packer that highlights the complexity of #Syria, puts the Kosovo comparison to rest."

"We just sent a few toys to kids in Puerto Rico! Such an easy way to pay it forward and spread joy. Hope you'll consider donating too!"

After she became a Fulbright-Clinton Fellow, she was sought out for TV and radio interviews to discuss Russian disinformation and Ukraine.

"Will be joining @JudyWoodruff this evening on @NewsHour to discuss what to expect when you're expecting more Russian election interference. . . . Huge pleasure to be on NPR today. . . . Pleasure to nerd out about #Ukraine with @brikeilarcnn . . . Thank you! I am indebted to the CNN hair and makeup team for making me look alive after a bachelorette weekend!" She also tweeted to promote her articles in *Wired* and *The Atlantic* and her book *How to Be a Woman Online* (she joked that her mom described it as "good and even funny here and there").

Twitter also was Jankowicz's political outlet, a place to grouse about everyone from Mitt Romney ("Romney: 'Expensive things hurt families.' You know what else hurts families, Mitt? DISEASE AND ILLNESS WITHOUT INSURANCE. #debates") to Trump ("Every time he uses the term fake news (esp when it's in all caps) a little piece of me dies.")

Twitter provides a glimpse into her love of pizza, her frustrations with public transit systems, and her fondness for Ben Folds. She revealed selected details about her personal life—lots about her dog, Jake, but little about her marriage to Mike, a software engineer who preferred to stay in the background (and did not want to be interviewed for this book). She did, however, tweet a lot about what she ate, read, sang, and listened to:

"Finally joined Pinterest. Goodbye productivity!"

"@AmericanAir. flight 1501 landed in MIA over 1 hr ago, still no bags, many waiting for connections. Expect better service from you guys!"

"My dad served in Vietnam. He was not killed in battle, but died decades later of Multiple Myeloma (bone marrow cancer) that he contracted from being exposed to Agent Orange during his service. #MemorialDay."

"So excited about the birth of a giant panda cub at the @NationalZoo. ! :)"

"@SaraBareilles. Reading your book. 'Red' is everything to me. From the Joni love affair to the study abroad stories. Thank you."

"Happy Birthday Dr. Seuss!"

* * *

Many college grads regard the prospect of a government job as drudgery, but Jankowicz was thrilled at the idea of a career in public service. Part of it was her roots: Her grandfather was an immigrant from Poland, and she felt an obligation to give something back to the country that welcomed him. Also, public service appealed to her nerdy side, the side that believed it was totally cool to be in Debate Club and Model UN and Model Congress. At heart, she was a policy wonk.

Her Fulbright experience in Ukraine in 2016–2017 inspired her even more. She was paid little—it probably ended up costing her more money than she earned— but she witnessed the effects of Russia's lies firsthand. She later wrote memos for the Biden presidential campaign about disinformation and possible strategies if Biden won. After he did, she sent additional ideas and feedback. She later regretted that those were so strong, believing her comments were a little too critical—but they apparently caught the eye of Rob Silvers, who was putting together the PLCY team at Homeland Security.

In 2020 she had published *How to Lose the Information War*, about how Russian disinformation was affecting five Eastern European nations. A *New Yorker* writer called it "a persuasive new book on disinformation as a geopolitical strategy." She was about to publish her second book, *How to be a Woman Online*, a guide for women who face online harassment.

There were no secrets about who Jankowicz was prior to her appointment. Tweets, articles, and interviews made it clear that she was a passionate Democrat who cared deeply about free speech but was concerned that many people were unprepared to sort out the facts in a complicated new media ecosystem. And she gave her vetters everything—her social media accounts and even a link to her Nextdoor account. Rob Schaul, an analyst at the Cybersecurity and Infrastructure Security Agency (CISA) in the Department of Homeland Security who knew her from the small community of misinformation experts and would become a good friend, was frankly a little surprised she was chosen. "Wow," he thought, "that's a spicy choice for a spice-adverse organization."

The process took a few months, but she finally received an offer in January 2022 and, after she passed her security clearance, started in March.

The job was not glamorous. Jankowicz's new office was in a complex formerly known as the Government Hospital for the Insane. Most cabinet departments were headquartered in the heart of Washington, often in grand buildings near the National Mall. But Homeland Security was based in Southeast Washington in a converted mental health complex famous as the longtime residence of John W. Hinckley Jr., who attempted to assassinate President Reagan.

Jankowicz, then eight and a half months pregnant, had to walk up a big hill from the parking garage to get to the building. She was sure her water would break right there, on her march to her office. The building was surreal. It was a maze just to get from one office to another (probably designed that way because of its former use). To get to a meeting, she often had to go down to the basement, switch elevators, and go back up. It was a lonely place because nearly everyone chose to work from home.

When Jankowicz first arrived in her office at the end of the COVID quarantine, it was a mess, with shredded paper scattered on the floor from whoever worked there during the Trump administration. It was an odd place to work because it was in a Sensitive Compartmented Information Facility, more frequently called a SCIF, a place designed to prevent electronic eavesdropping. SCIFs were fortified with thick concrete walls and special ventilation. Occupants had to abide by strict rules against bringing in cell phones and other devices. She couldn't even wear her Apple Watch.

Her office had a window, but it had a thick glaze so people could not see in, and, if she was looking out, she had difficulty knowing if it was sunny or raining. The office had a computer, but it took ten to fifteen minutes to connect to the internet. While she waited, all she could do was watch the office television, which she tuned to CNN for coverage of the Russian war against Ukraine.

SCIF rules could be absurd. Her job required lots of video meetings on Microsoft Teams, but her office computer didn't have audio, so she had to call in from her desk telephone. The connection was so bad it sounded like she was calling from the 1980s.

Still, as she met with her DHS colleagues in her first couple of months (mostly by video over Teams), Jankowicz was excited about the promise of her new job. She felt like she could have a real impact.

APRIL 28, 2022: THE PERFECT VILLAIN

Announcement day had been a disaster. Jankowicz ended the night in tears, shopping for a security camera to alert her about the stalkers she knew would be coming. When she awoke the next day, the attacks grew. How could her DHS colleagues be so clueless about this? They had blundered into this debacle by making the announcement in *Politico*, and now they seemed just as confused about how to respond to the mess they made.

The attacks continued on Twitter and now had spread to the Fox News Channel. "A *disinformation* board—think about that," said Kayleigh McEnany on the Fox show *Outnumbered*. "Do you want the government deciding what's disinformation or not?" A day had gone by, which should have given the DHS comms team plenty of time to regroup and push out its talking points, but the agency had said virtually nothing about what the board would do. That left the talking heads at Fox free to fabricate details and speculate wildly. Sean Hannity called Jankowicz "a far-left radical Democrat who believes her opinions are facts and your opinions are disinformation." Hannity then said the bigger scandal was "the existence, in a free country, of a government disinformation board. Our government does not get to decide what opinions are permissible. That is simply not the American way."

The Fox hosts didn't limit their comments to inaccurate claims about the board and Jankowicz's record. They made it personal. Tucker Carlson said she was an "illiterate fascist" while Hannity called her "a far-left lunatic." And it wasn't just Fox. She was a perfect villain for talk radio hosts, who just echoed the attack lines from Tucker and Hannity. Nearly all men, they attacked her politics and her intelligence. Mark

Levin, a radio host who drew an estimated 8 million listeners every month, said Jankowicz "sounds like a complete dimwit. . . . She is a certifiable idiot . . . she is a hardcore leftist Marxist." Jankowicz even made the cover of the *New York Post*, which depicted her in a cartoon version frowning and pointing, with the headline "BIG SISTER IS WATCHING YOU."

The false attacks fit long-running conservative themes that Democrats want to use the government to censor Americans, especially conservatives. Carlson declared: "Nina Jankowicz doesn't believe in the First Amendment!" Said Clay Travis, a sports journalist and talk show host with 1 million Twitter followers: "She is in charge of what's truth and fiction in America. Every time you think the Biden administration can't get more ridiculous, they do." (That tweet became the most widely seen about Jankowicz and the board, racking up 3.4 million views.)

Another false attack claimed she wanted to allow "editing" of other people's tweets. This distortion was made by a variety of Fox personalities from Jeanine Pirro ("Biden's new Disinformation Czar already thinks she's qualified to start editing your tweets") to Maria Bartiromo (Jankowicz "pitched the idea of allowing verified Twitter accounts to edit and add context to other tweets"). A chyron on Carlson's show said: "AWFUL NINA JANKOWICZ: I'M A TRUSTED & VERIFIED PERSON & I SHOULD EDIT YOUR TWEETS." (They were grossly mischaracterizing comments she made to Georgia librarians about a new Twitter program called Birdwatch. Her explanation had been generally accurate, but someone had posted a deceptively edited video of it that Fox used.)

Fox personalities criticized her for being a liberal, twisted her comments about a favorite bit of conservative lore, Hunter Biden's laptop, and derided her for working for the "globalist" Woodrow Wilson International Center for Scholars. They even insulted her singing.

Jankowicz had always loved to sing. In high school and college, she performed in musicals and recorded songs with a friend. After she got out of grad school, she continued in community theater as Audrey in

Little Shop of Horrors, Morticia in *The Addams Family*, and The Witch in *Into the Woods*. Videos of her singing were all over the internet. Once conservative trolls identified her as a villain, they dug them up and began using them in their attacks.

One attack centered on the Moaning Myrtles, a "wizard rock" duo that Jankowicz formed with a friend in high school and college. The songs were cheeky takes on Harry Potter such as "Prefects Are Hot," which had suggestive lyrics such as "Bathrooms are great for peep shows / Cedric Diggory's really hot without his clothes." That made them ideal for distortions by right-wing media organizations, which often pretended to be outraged by sexual topics. Breitbart writer Hannah Bleau Knudsen wrote as if she didn't get the jokes in "Prefects Are Hot" and was aghast at the raunchy allusions about the beloved children's book. Knudsen cherry-picked the most outrageous lyrics and characterized Jankowicz as "the radical left-winger" who "sang about dead child sex with fictional character Harry Potter."

Conservatives also dug up a video of Jankowicz's satirical performance of "My Simple Christmas Wish" in which she changed the lyrics from the original "What do I have to fake to be famous and powerful?" to "Who do I fuck to be famous and powerful?" It was a good punch line for the nation's capital—but easy to distort. The *New York Post* seemed to be outraged by her f-bomb-dropping, writing that "she once belted out a raunchy parody version of a Christmas song—changing the lyrics to ask who she needed to 'f–k' to be 'famous and powerful.'"

Critics on Twitter and Fox also belittled Jankowicz for a lighthearted TikTok video about disinformation that she posted in February 2021. Set to the Mary Poppins tune "Supercalifragilisticexpialidocious," she sang about the dangers of lies and the people who peddle them.

"Information laundering is really quite ferocious," she sang in her best Julie Andrews, emphasizing the *crisp diction*. "It's when a huckster takes some lies and makes them sound precocious / By saying them in Congress or a mainstream outlet, so disinformation's origins are slightly less atrocious . . ."

Then, a chorus of "It's how you hide a little lie—little lie. . . . It's how you hide a little lie—little lie. . . . It's how you hide a little lie—little lie. . . ."

The final verse: "When Rudy Giuliani shared bad intel from Ukraine / Or when TikTok influencers say COVID can't cause pain / They're laundering disinfo, and we really should take note. / And not support their lies with our wallet, voice, or vote."

The videos provided bonus material for Fox hosts and her many conservative critics. After lying about the powers and mission of the board, after distorting Jankowicz's role, after cherry-picking lines from her books and articles, after calling her stupid (or worse) . . . now they could insult her singing! And so they did, with fresh video clips. This went on for days with the videos replayed endlessly on Fox, talk radio, and Twitter and mentioned by Republicans in Congress.

"She's off-key in a really bad Julie Andrews impersonation, but it's off-key in more ways than one," Laura Ingraham said on Fox. "If we all didn't know that this was really happening, if we didn't just witness that, we'd think this was all some Orwellian spoof of what paranoid conservatives think the establishment on the left is planning. Part angry feminist, part frustrated karaoke singer, Jankowicz is the last person who should be trusted with distinguishing between fact and fiction."

Carlson, whose producers had reviewed Jankowicz's books and videos of her interviews, offered a few substantive critiques of her writing and interviews, noting comments she had made about disinformation and the need for regulation of social media platforms. But he cherry-picked the strongest comments and mixed them with gross exaggerations and falsehoods about the board and the Department of Homeland Security.

"Everyone involved in Joe Biden's new ministry of information is a buffoon," he said on his show. "They may be evil, but they're also ridiculous. Nina Jankowicz is the most ridiculous of all. So you read about her appointment in the *Washington Post* this morning, and you immediately thought of the NKVD [the interior ministry of the Soviet

Union], because, why wouldn't you? Yet even the NKVD, even at the height of Stalin's purges, never did karaoke—they were too dignified for that. But Nina Jankowicz happily does."

Actually, Fox viewers didn't need to *listen* to the shows—they could turn the sound off and get the gist from the artful chyron that pushed a steady stream of lies, distortions, and anti-Biden messages:

DEMS INCREASINGLY HOSTILE TO FREE SPEECH

TURLEY: DEMS CALLING FOR OUTRIGHT STATE CENSORSHIP

MEET YOUR NEW DISINFO OVERLORD: NINA JANKOWICZ

BIDEN'S BOTCHED DISINFORMATION CZAR ROLLOUT SLAMMED AS "UNSERIOUS"

OP-ED: DISINFO BOARD HEAD IS "PARTISAN HACK"

DHS SEC CLUELESS ABOUT HIS OWN DISINFORMATION CZAR

DISINFO CZAR'S "FIX" FOR TWITTER: EDITING PEOPLE'S TWEETS

THE LEFT'S FAR-REACHING CENSORSHIP CAMPAIGN

The irony: The Fox chyrons were more like *1984* than anything the bureaucrats at DHS had cooked up.

Another visual dig against Jankowicz—this one more subtle—was the choice of photos that were used on Fox and on partisan websites. Producers and editors managed to find the most unflattering pictures of her—frowning, scowling, or screengrabs of her Mary Poppins performance when they were discussing her professional work.

The discussion was more fact-based on *Potomac Watch*, a podcast hosted by writers from the *Wall Street Journal* editorial page. They noted the poor way that DHS announced the board and how there were many unanswered questions. "My concern," said Paul Gigot, the editor of the editorial page, "is that you're going to end up with this group being a kind of government version of PolitiFact, which is the media self-styled fact checker that looks at some statement by people and says, 'Aha, that's false,' or 'That's sort of true, or somewhat true,' or 'That's true.'"

* * *

White House Press Secretary Jen Psaki was caught by surprise when the furor about Jankowicz reached her podium the next day.

"Can you give us an idea of what this board is going to be doing, what their authority would look like?" a reporter called out.

"I really haven't dug into this exactly," Psaki said. "I mean, we, of course, support this effort, but let me see if I can get more specifics."

Another reporter pressed Psaki about Jankowicz: "There's been some criticism of the person who's been chosen to oversee this board. She had previously called the Hunter Biden laptop a 'Trump campaign product,' seeming to discredit its validity—or validity of reporting surrounding that. How can you assuage concerns of people who are looking at this person who's been appointed to this position and wondering if she's going to be able to accurately judge misinformation now that a lot of that reporting has been proven to be factual in some ways?"

Psaki demurred. "Well, I don't have any comments on the laptop. But what I can tell you is that it sounds like the objective of the board is to prevent disinformation and misinformation from traveling around the country in a range of communities. I'm not sure who opposes that effort, and I don't know who this individual is, so I have no comments on it specifically."

Inside DHS, there was no consensus about how to respond. Jankowicz, still angry at being told the first night that she couldn't speak out, argued for a multilayered strategy. She wanted to brief members and staff on Capitol Hill about the real powers and role of the board and release the charter, the legal document that made clear that the Disinformation Governance Board would not be a Ministry of Truth. She recalled saying, "Let me march my pregnant butt up to Capitol Hill and meet with these people because I'm far too charming for them to continue attacking me." She kept sending emails to the senior staff and the comms team with the message "we just have to do something." They scheduled a limited briefing for Hill staffers but canceled a separate press briefing at the last moment.

First, she had to go to a meeting at the White House, which produced a ridiculous moment she'll never forget. She was sitting in a high-level discussion with people at the National Security Council, a place where they seem to have a television in every office. The sound was off, but there she was on television!

As Mary Poppins.

The day didn't get any better. The Hill briefing was frustrating because she was told to give as little detail as possible. What kind of a briefing was that? The conversation got into ridiculous hypotheticals because they couldn't talk about real things. And so, as disinformation swirled about the board, Jankowicz was directed to say little to quell it. She wanted to scream. While DHS was dithering, her life was being ruined.

Schaul, then an analyst in the Cybersecurity and Infrastructure Security Agency at DHS, watched with alarm at the lack of response. He recalled later, "It could have been a nothing-burger, but they let it sit for—what?—three days before there was an official DHS response. And the official DHS response was to feed Jankowicz to the wolves."

Mayorkas, who had missed the opportunity to fully announce the board in his Capitol Hill appearance, went on two of the Sunday talk shows, CNN's *State of the Union* and *Fox News Sunday*, and made a belated effort to explain the board and respond to the critics. He is not a particularly compelling speaker on a good day, and as he robotically recited his talking points under the TV lights, he was only a little more enthusiastic than a high school senior reading his note cards during a social studies presentation.

"So, what it does," he said on CNN, "is it works to ensure that the way in which we address threats, the connectivity between threats and acts of violence are addressed without infringing on free speech, protecting civil rights and civil liberties, the right of privacy. And the board, this working group, internal working group, will draw from best practices and communicate those best practices to the operators, because the board does not have operational authority."

On Fox, Bret Baier asked Mayorkas about Jankowicz, mentioning her tweets and (of course) her remarks about Hunter Biden's laptop. "So do you really think that Jankowicz is anywhere near objective enough for this particular job?"

"Yes, I do," Mayorkas replied, "and by the way [she is] highly regarded as a subject matter expert, and I don't question her objectivity. There are people in the department who have a diverse range of views, and they're incredibly dedicated to mission. We're not the opinion police. She has testified before Congress a number of times, she's recognized as a tremendous authority, and we're very fortunate to have her." Watching him was miserable for Jankowicz. She spent the day getting made up for her maternity picture, and then after the photo session she returned home to watch the Secretary of Homeland Security trying to defend her on national television. It was awful.

The lies had stirred up tremendous anger toward her. As Jankowicz was headed to a friend's house to have pizza and unwind after a difficult week, she got a call from a security consultant she'd hired who had worked in the intelligence community. His message was alarming: She wasn't safe. She should consider moving to an Airbnb booked under someone else's name until this blew over. She discussed it with Mike, and they decided it wasn't practical to move. They had pets, and she was about to give birth. But they had the camera, and they continued to prop the chairs under the doorknobs.

On Monday, May 2, after five days of getting pummeled, DHS finally released a fact sheet about the board. It was headlined "DHS Internal Working Group Protects Free Speech and Other Fundamental Rights When Addressing Disinformation That Threatens the Security of the United States." In the cautious language of ashamed bureaucrats, it acknowledged that the rollout had gone poorly: "There has been confusion about the working group, its role, and its activities. The reaction to this working group has prompted DHS to assess what steps we should take to build the trust needed for the Department to be effective in this space." It emphasized that "the Department is deeply committed to doing all of its work in a way that protects Americans' freedom of speech, civil rights, civil liberties, and privacy."

Too little, too late. The outrage machine had already defined the board and Jankowicz: It was the Ministry of Truth, the censorship police, run by a lefty laptop denier who couldn't sing.

CHAPTER 2

A Taxonomy of Lying

For years, political reporters and fact-checkers were reluctant to say a politician lied. That was partly because the word packed a wallop, and lying was seen as a serious allegation. (Those were more innocent times.) Also, the journalists were trying to be consistent with the definition that a lie was "a false statement made with deliberate intent to deceive." How, they asked, could they know the politician's intent?

In the last twenty years, particularly in the age of Trump, many of us loosened up and accepted other, broader definitions for the word. *Merriam-Webster*'s definitions include "an untrue or inaccurate statement that may or may not be believed true by the speaker or writer." Even pre-Trump, when I created the Truth-O-Meter with my colleagues at PolitiFact, we made the lowest rating Pants on Fire. And every year, PolitiFact honors "The Lie of the Year" just as *Time* honors the Person of the Year.

For many journalists, the big turning point in using "lie" came in 2016, when the *New York Times* began using it for some of Trump's whoppers. The first was his repeated bogus claim that President Obama was born in Kenya. *Times* editor Dean Baquet told NPR that "to say that that was a 'falsehood' wouldn't have captured the duration of his claim [or] the outrageousness of his claim. I think to have called it just a falsehood would have put it in the category of, to be frank, 'usual political fare,' where politicians say, 'My tax plan will save a billion dollars,' but it's actually a half a billion and they're using the wrong analysis. This was something else. And I think we owed it to our readers to just call it out for what it was."

Today, there's still a range of opinions about using the word. Glenn Kessler, the *Washington Post* Fact Checker, uses it broadly to refer to Trump's "election lies" or "the big lie." FactCheck.org doesn't use it. But maybe we've been too cautious. A 2018 study by researcher Paul Mena found a disconnect between journalists (68 percent of whom opposed the use of the word) and the public (20 percent opposed).

I was a holdout for many years. Even after the *Times* broke the barrier, I stuck to using "falsehood" and "false claim." But I reconsidered as I realized the magnitude of the problem, and concluded that, in most cases, the politician knows they are lying. Also, I realized that in the real world people don't draw such stark lines about the definitions. They know politicians lie. They may not like it, but they are very aware of it.

In this book, I'm using "lie" and "lying" broadly to refer to both the overall phenomenon *and* individual falsehoods when I believe the person making the false charge knew it was false. Purists might quibble with that. But I believe that retreating to the semantic safety of the past cloaks the serious problem of lying that is threatening our political discourse (and that is the reason I wrote this book).

Another clarification about my terminology: A broken promise is not a lie. Although they are sometimes referred to that way, a broken promise is a separate political act and deserves its own category. At PolitiFact, we created a feature called the Obameter to track President Obama's promises, an unprecedented undertaking that initially followed 508 things he vowed to do during the campaign, everything from "Provide a path to citizenship for undocumented immigrants" to "Fund proposals to help fish and game survive climate change." The Obameter inspired promise tracking by fact-checkers in other nations and prompted us to create more than a dozen meters that have tracked the promises of mayors and governors around the United States. Together, these efforts contribute to a unique form of journalism that goes beyond fact-checking in holding politicians accountable.

* * *

A TAXONOMY OF LYING

After talking with dozens of politicians, candidates, and political operatives for this book, I've realized that lies come in many shapes and flavors. They vary in severity, type, and technique. In this chapter, I've put together a short taxonomy to sort them out.

SEVERITY

Some lies are serious. Others, not so much. I think of them on a continuum, with innocent lies at one end and more serious ones at the other.

"Under-the-lights" mistakes: At PolitiFact, we used this phrase to indicate any minor error that was clearly accidental, a slip of the tongue, like one said under the glare of TV lights. Politicians sometimes confuse the names of states or fumble a statistic. That doesn't make a mistake into a lie.

White lies: These are the small, innocent falsehoods that lubricate our politics—the praises and boasts and innocent commitments that won't be kept. They were summed up best by Robert Bauer, the White House counsel to President Obama, who told me in an interview, "To be a politician, you have to periodically, maybe systematically and hopefully skillfully and with some retention of a moral sense, deceive people." Bauer then pretended to be one and declared, "I'm standing next to Bill Adair, who is one of the finest journalists of his generation." (I was deeply offended that Bauer would use me in his example of lying, particularly because I consider him one of the finest political attorneys of his generation.) He then explained, "Some politicians are really good at it, and I admire them enormously, and I don't think they're liars. Other politicians are liars because they're bad politicians or they're corrupt politicians. But I don't think you can separate politics from deception at all."

Misdemeanor lies: These are lies that often use numbers and claims about broad topics to mislead voters: *Inflation has been down since I became president. We're closing the achievement gap in our classrooms.* They are more nerdy than malicious. They don't target anyone in particular but still make sweeping false claims about a group or trend.

Felony lies: Stark and serious, they move the needle and are more likely to have consequences. Felony lies are often targeted at someone, such as the attacks on Nina Jankowicz. They stoke prejudice or threaten a key element in our democratic system, such as the integrity of voting. They are our big lies that take us to war. As political scientist Brendan Nyhan put it to me, "There's a difference between politicians lying to cover up some misdeed and lying to try to overturn democracy."

TYPES OF LIES

Lies about accomplishments: Elected officials love to brag about what they've done in office. But they often stretch the truth . . . a lot. Trump did this to ridiculous extremes, lying about the impact of the border wall (no, it didn't drive down crime in El Paso), the size of his tax cut (no, it wasn't the largest in history), and his health care policy (no, it didn't "save" pre-existing conditions), among many other topics. Other politicians make false claims by cherry-picking the most favorable time period.

Self-defense lies: When a politician is accused of a crime or implicated in a scandal, lying is often their first line of defense. *I did not have sexual relations with that woman, Miss Lewinsky. . . . I did not email any* *classified material to anyone*. . . . Sometimes they will try a trick we could call leveraging a lie, when they find a small flaw in an otherwise true allegation and then use that to discount the entire allegation. That was Bill Clinton's strategy with Lewinsky, when he narrowly defined sexual relations to not include oral sex. Others have used a similar approach in response to a devastating investigative report by a news organization. The politician will simply decry it as "a false report" without saying what's false and what's true. Eric Jotkoff, a Democratic strategist, sums this one up as "you get caught with your hand in the cookie jar . . . and you lie."

Lies attacking opponents: These are the staple of modern campaigns, the wild exaggerations made by candidates and the political parties. They are leveled by both parties and are distinguished by a unique art form—campaign ads and internet videos in which producers find the most unflattering photos available. (A consultant I know once bragged that she was particularly skilled at finding awful photos of opponents.)

Lies about policy and issues: This broad category includes a wide range of falsehoods on everything from abortion to immigration to crime. They are the bulk of political lies, the fast food of the American discourse. The Lie of the Year, PolitiFact's choice of the most significant falsehood, is typically about policy. Some of the honorees: the claims that Obamacare included "death panels" (2009); that Obamacare was "a government takeover of health care" (2010); "If you like your health care plan, you'll be able to keep your health care plan" (2013); and the denial and downplay of the coronavirus (2020).

HOW THEY LIE

Political liars have a variety of tricks in their playbook that can be quite effective at fooling their target audience. Here's a look at some of their more common techniques. (Some lies use more than one.)

Cherry-picking: This is my favorite technique because it can sometimes be quite obvious—yet they do it anyway. The liar simply chooses the most favorable time period or condition for their claim while ignoring the larger reality that tells a different story. They tell about one quarter but ignore the other three. It's wonderfully deceptive.

Repetition: There's an old saying that if you repeat a lie often enough, it becomes the truth. Many U.S. politicians follow this advice, repeating their falsehoods despite much debunking. That was most famously the case with the lie that Trump won the 2020 election, but it's also the case with many talking points from the political parties. Kessler, the *Washington Post* Fact Checker, calls them "zombie claims" because, like zombies, they will not die.

Up is down: Tim Miller, a former communications director for Republican campaigns, used this phrase to describe bald-faced lies, when facts clearly prove a claim is wrong. He also referred to these as "Trumpian lies," citing the former president's insistence that his inauguration crowd was the largest ever, despite photo evidence to the contrary.

Exaggeration: Some of the simplest lies are just bigger and bolder than reality. Most probably are considered half-truths, but the big ones qualify as lies.

Prediction: These are lies that look ahead and exploit uncertainty. An example from the 1970s: conservative activist Phyllis Schlafly's warnings about the Equal Rights Amendment, which fizzled in 1982 after it failed to be ratified by enough states. Schlafly's extreme warnings about the amendment surely played a role. She had predicted that passage would "absolutely and positively make women subject to the draft," "abolish a woman's right to child support and alimony," and deprive American women of many "fundamental special privileges" such as the right "(1) NOT to take a job, (2) to keep her baby, and (3) to be supported by her husband."

Fear: The most effective lies strike a chord with the recipient, and the ones that invoke fear are especially potent. When my research assistants analyzed hundreds of lies, they found a large portion of them tried to invoke fear—of economic loss, physical harm, or damage to property. Both parties use this technique. Democrats try to scare senior citizens with false claims that Republicans are going to take away their Medicare and Social Security. Republicans use scary claims of immigration and crime.

CHAPTER 3

The Lying Hall of Fame

In my Lying in Politics course at Duke University, I taught the history of political mendacity by having students nominate people and groups for a Lying Hall of Fame. I collaborated with journalists and political scientists to come up with a broad group of nominees and then assigned students to write a paper and make a presentation about why their nominee deserved a spot. Some nominees didn't make the cut. (Hillary Clinton, for example, didn't lie enough by volume or magnitude.) The list, like my research, leans more to recent times and provides a revealing stroll through the history of lying.

THE INSTITUTIONS

BIG TOBACCO

In the 1930s and '40s, tobacco companies used images of smiling doctors to trick people about cigarettes. "20,679 physicians say 'Luckies are less irritating,'" said one magazine ad that featured a grinning doctor holding a pack of Lucky Strikes. Another said, "More doctors smoke Camels than any other cigarette." The surveys mentioned in the ads were bogus because doctors had been given free cartons of cigarettes to encourage favorable responses. That paved the way for decades of lying as the companies tried to counteract mounting evidence that their product was deadly.

Big Tobacco earns a spot in the Hall of Fame for decades of lies about a product that has killed tens of millions of people. In the early 1950s, as independent researchers discovered a link between smoking and lung cancer, the companies worked with the PR firm Hill & Knowlton to discredit the findings. "We should create a committee with 'research' in the title so that the public recognize the existence of weighty scientific views which hold there is no proof that cigarette smoking is a cause of lung cancer," Hill & Knowlton wrote in a 1953 memo to tobacco executives. They did— the Tobacco Industry Research Committee, which was staffed by twenty-three PR employees.

The following year, the companies published "A Frank Statement to Cigarette Smokers," an ad that disputed the growing scientific research: "For more than 300 years tobacco has given solace, relaxation and enjoyment to mankind. At one time or another during those years critics have held it responsible for practically every disease of the human body. One by one these charges have been abandoned for lack of evidence."

As emerging science provided more proof that smoking was harmful, Big Tobacco tried to raise doubts by funding its own favorable studies and promoting them through its front group, then called the Council for Tobacco Research. It claimed that the legitimate studies were flawed, that the link between smoking and lung cancer was "incomplete," and that the increase in lung cancer had been exaggerated because of "overdiagnosis." The approach established a model that would be used by the oil and food industries when their products came under attack.

Then, a turning point. In 1994, the tobacco company CEOs testified before a congressional committee. Henry Waxman, then the chairman of the committee, told me he remembers their testimony vividly because, one by one, the CEOs kept lying by claiming that their products were not addictive. Waxman said he knew those denials were untrue. "So what our hearings, the court system and investigative journalism uncovered was probably the longest-running and most deadly disinformation campaign in our history."

Today, after thousands of company documents have been made public because of court settlements, we know the vast extent of the industry's mendacity. The companies falsely denied that they manipulated nicotine to make their products more addictive, they falsely claimed cigarettes did not cause disease, and they denied that secondhand smoke was dangerous. "People lied before [tobacco executives did] and people have lied after them," Waxman told me, "but I think the tobacco industry has to be given a special place in the history of liars."

EXXON

Call it the bank-shot lie. Exxon mastered the art of surrogate lying, paying millions of dollars to think tanks and influencers to spread doubts and falsehoods about climate change.

The giant energy company actually was an early and serious player in climate research. As early as the mid-1970s, Exxon knew that fossil fuels were accelerating climate change. The company's scientists alerted the Exxon leaders that the problem was serious. Harold Weinberg, the director of the company's Research & Engineering's Technology Feasibility Center, wrote to another executive: "This may be the kind of opportunity that we are looking for, to have Exxon technology, management and leadership resources put into the context of a project aimed at benefiting mankind." But rather than embrace bold action, the company opted for deflection and denial to protect its core business.

Exxon learned from the masterful work of Big Tobacco and threw up a smokescreen of doubt. The company and its allies didn't always need to lie. They could just raise questions about the mounting scientific evidence that carbon dioxide and other greenhouse gases were causing the planet to grow warmer. A famous 1998 strategy memo from the American Petroleum Institute proposed that the company and its partners focus their PR effort on "uncertainties in climate science." The strategy, like the one used by tobacco companies, was to create doubt about the science.

To spread doubt, they spread the wealth, paying millions to counter the growing narrative that fossil fuels were causing climate change. Exxon (later called ExxonMobil) helped create the Global Climate Science Team, which coordinated the effort to raise questions about climate science. By paying a wide range of think tanks and advocates, they created the impression that the doubts were more genuine and widespread, which gave many elected officials political cover to dodge the issue and avoid action.

Kert Davies, who has tracked and exposed Exxon's techniques for Greenpeace and now does so for the Center for Climate Integrity, says the company had an opportunity fifty years ago to be responsible but instead chose tactics that have had terrible results for the planet. "They had people on staff who said this could be catastrophic for a sizable portion of the world's population," he told me. But "they went on about their business selling oil and enabling various actors who would deny the whole thing."

RUPERT MURDOCH

When David Folkenflik thinks of Rupert Murdoch's reputation in the world of lying, he remembers a big, bold headline in 1989 in the British tabloid *The Sun* after ninety-seven soccer fans were crushed to death when they crowded into pens in a stadium. The story had a number of falsehoods that alleged the fans of the Liverpool soccer team were to blame. The article became quite controversial and prompted the anger of the victims' families, in part because of its screaming headline: "The Truth."

Folkenflik, the author of *Murdoch's World: The Last of the Old Media Empires*, says the headline was a stark example of how a Murdoch paper would distort the facts to get a good story. "That's not public service; that's a financial transaction," Folkenflik told me.

Murdoch, whom communications professor Robert McChesney called "unquestionably the single most important media figure of our times," created an unparalleled global empire that still helps spread political lying today. Murdoch began by following the lead of his father and launching or buying newspapers in Australia, eventually owning two-thirds of the country's papers by the early 1980s. He then moved to Britain and bought the *News of the World*, *The Sun*, *The Times*, and the *Sunday Times*.

He then came to the United States and bought the *New York Post* and the *Wall Street Journal*. Folkenflik, who is NPR's media reporter, notes that in all three countries Murdoch owns a paper that gives him respectability (*The Australian*, the *Wall Street Journal,* and *The Times* of London) and tabloids that give him outlets for his mischief (*The Sun*, the *New York Post*, the *Daily Telegraph* in Australia). Newspapers are just part of his empire. In the United States, the main platform for Murdoch's political agenda has become the Fox News Channel.

An in-depth examination by the *New York Times* said his empire "has given him influence over world affairs in a way few private citizens ever have, granting the Murdoch family enormous sway over not just the United States, but English-speaking countries around the world." *Times* reporters Jonathan Mahler and Jim Rutenberg noted that his outlets have helped "politicize the very notion of truth."

Murdoch earns a spot in the Hall of Fame not just for his tabloids and the culture they have fostered but also for the huge number of falsehoods spread by the Fox News Channel. As the Jankowicz episode shows, Fox acts like a daily talking-point factory for the political right—regardless of whether those talking points are true. (When the network launched, he played down the idea of it being a conservative voice, probably because of the difficulty he was having getting access to cable systems in liberal cities.)

Ultimately, "News Channel" is a misnomer because Fox has relatively few reporters who actually cover news. The network's daily schedule is dominated by opinion programs, such as Sean Hannity and Laura

Ingraham's shows, which are megaphones for lies. Fox's hosts have dreadful records from PolitiFact—more than 60 percent Mostly False or worse for Hannity and more than 90 percent for Ingraham.

To call Murdoch conservative is too simple, Folkenflik said. He usually just wants whatever is best for his company, News Corp, even if that means flirting with Democrats or, in Britain, leaders of the Labour Party. That was apparent in the Dominion Voting Systems case, which revealed that he was aware of the lies on Fox but failed to stop them because of the perception that the network's audience believed them and wanted to keep hearing them. He allowed the lies because they were good for business.

At one point Murdoch sent an email to a Fox executive while watching a news conference in which Rudy Giuliani was unleashing a stream of falsehoods about the election. "Watching Giuliani!" was the subject line. "Really crazy stuff. And damaging," Murdoch wrote. But he didn't stop the lies.

ROGER AILES

Roger Ailes was the perfect person to build the Fox News Channel for Murdoch. Ailes had played many roles at that point in his career. He'd been a TV producer—not in news, but on the entertainment side for a variety program called *The Mike Douglas Show*. He'd consulted for President Nixon in a role that that recognized the rise of television as a factor in campaigning and governing.

Ailes's consulting had aided a wide range of Republicans, from Ronald Reagan and George H. W. Bush to Mitch McConnell and Al D'Amato. Ed Rollins, who had been Reagan's campaign manager, called Ailes "the premier guy in the business. He was our Michelangelo." He kept his hand in television, producing entertainment talk shows and New York theater. "Ailes was never a news man, he never reported a story," said Folkenflik, who chronicled his rise and fall for NPR. "He was a showman. He was a partisan. He was a brawler. And he had contempt for people who would carefully try to tease out facts and ambiguity. That wasn't his shtick."

Ailes ran CNBC, the business news channel, and launched a new NBC cable channel called America's Talking. That channel had a mix of talk shows that included a morning program hosted by Steve Doocy, a former TV features reporter who would go on to fame at Fox, an advice show hosted by writer E. Jean Carroll, who would later win a defamation and sexual abuse lawsuit against Donald Trump, and a show hosted by Ailes himself. When NBC executives decided to scrap America's Talking and convert it into MSNBC, an unusual partnership with Microsoft, he jumped at the chance to run Murdoch's new network.

At last, Ailes got a chance to build the network he'd always wanted: an alternative voice to the liberal bias he'd always despised, a place where he could showcase Republicans and their ideas. When it launched, Ailes and Murdoch planted the seeds of their lie that their network (which was full of conservative bias) would somehow be objective. Murdoch told a New York news conference that they would label analysis and opinion to distinguish it from news, and that the network would be "fair and balanced" in reporting. That slogan, which came to define Fox, emerged on Day 1—and it worked. A study by political scientist Jonathan S. Morris found that people who believe the media is biased were more likely to rely on Fox News as their primary source of news.

Fox became such a powerhouse that it not only shaped Republican talking points; it won votes for the party (which was precisely what Ailes wanted). A 2007 study of voting in more than nine thousand towns by economists Stefano DellaVigna and Ethan Kaplan found that Republicans gained 0.4 to 0.7 percentage points in towns that carried Fox—enough to tip a close race. The study also showed the network boosted Republican turnout and the party's share in Senate races.

Ailes, who was ultimately brought down because he used his power to sexually harass women who worked for him, is one of the worst villains in the Lying Hall of Fame. He was a brilliant pioneer of political image-making who understood how to blend politics and entertainment into effective propaganda. But he used deceit and what Folkenflik calls "a conveyer belt of bullshit from morning to night" to build his audience.

Jankowicz and Dominion are just two recent targets of Fox lies. Others include Smartmatic, an election technology company that was targeted with ridiculous claims like Dominion, and Seth Rich, an employee of the Democratic National Committee, whose random murder became the subject of many conspiracy theories pushed by Fox hosts until his family sued the network.

Ailes deserves a spot in the Hall of Fame because he not only constructed a network that was built on a lie of balanced coverage, but he also hired a roster of hosts who made Fox a megaphone for misinformation.

THE FOX & FRIENDS COUCH

The curvy couch from *Fox & Friends* is the only piece of living room furniture to warrant a spot in the Hall of Fame because it is such a brilliantly conceived launching pad for lies. Every morning, the Friends—Steve Doocy, Ainsley Earhardt, and Brian Kilmeade—sit on the white cushion and serve a few spoonfuls of deceit with the morning coffee.

The couch is the centerpiece of a show that sets the agenda for the daily discourse on Fox and by the nation's conservative elites. In *How to Watch Television: Media Criticism in Practice*, media scholar Jeffrey P. Jones wrote that "the show is designed to thrust the viewer in the world of common-sense groupthink, complete with all the rumours, smears, innuendo, fear-mongering, thinly veiled ad hominem attacks, and lack of rational discourse they can muster."

The Friends are masterful at this. Sometimes they slip in a Republican talking point that fact-checkers have rated False or Four Pinocchios (such as the well-debunked line that Joe Biden plans to hire eighty-seven thousand new IRS agents). Or they'll deceive using less obvious tactics. They will talk about "unanswered questions," call attention to the documents that Republicans just haven't been able to get from Democrats, or toss in some innuendo about the villain of the day.

The Friends aren't fact-checked often, but when they are, they typically earn False and Pants on Fire ratings. Sometimes they welcome a guest to the curvy couch, nearly always a Republican, someone who won't upset the homogeneity. In these situations, the couch transforms from a falsehood launching pad into a pitching machine that tosses only softballs. (The Friends are careful not to ask tough questions or fact-check their guests.)

There is a sly incongruity here. The couch seems like an unlikely place for political propaganda because it invokes a cozy living room vibe. But that's the whole idea: to cloak the messages in the chitchat of happy people on a bright morning. Folkenflik noted that the couch doesn't appear to be very comfy, that the Friends sit stiffly at the front of the couch. Maybe they need more pillows.

FACEBOOK

The staff investigators for the House committee on the January 6 attacks had stock questions they asked the people who stormed the Capitol, basics like hometown, education, occupation, and what social media platforms they used. *Twitter? Instagram? Reddit? Gab? Parler?* For the most part, the investigators found that the people who stormed the Capitol didn't connect in the dark corners of the web or even in the friendly confines of a conservative app. They met on Facebook.

Twenty years after it was launched in a Harvard dorm room as a way for college students to connect, Facebook has grown into a tremendous way for people to spread political lies and make friends with others who do. It is a wonderful incubator for misinformation, a place where falsehoods can sprout and spread. Facebook's groups and Feed are the perfect vessels for short posts full of lies. Instead of thoughtful discussion, they are echo chambers fueling anger and distrust.

In *The Chaos Machine*, Max Fisher's meticulous analysis of the many ways social media is harming our discourse, Stanford researcher Renée DiResta said Facebook provides lies to people who want them: "There's this conspiracy-correlation effect in which the platform recognizes that somebody who's interested in conspiracy A is typically likely to be interested in conspiracy B, and pops it up to them." Facebook also has been a frighteningly powerful tool to spread hate speech and misinformation in Sri Lanka and Myanmar, where lies have led to violence and deaths. Said Yanghee Lee, a United Nations investigator studying the cause of the genocide in Myanmar, "I'm afraid that Facebook has now turned into a beast."

After the 2016 U.S. election, there was an awakening about Facebook's role in spreading misinformation. Journalists and researchers discovered that people had used the platform to share fake articles, especially ones that appeared to benefit the Trump campaign. Although research later found those stories were not sufficient to tip the election, Facebook was widely criticized and soon after launched a partnership with fact-checkers (including PolitiFact) to reduce the spread of false content. The fact-checkers are paid to research questionable posts. If they are found to be false, Facebook will label them and reduce their spread.

That program is effective with the relatively small number of falsehoods that fact-checkers identify, but it is a small effort in comparison with the giant flood of misinformation on the platform every day. And, by design, it does not fact-check politicians. (Facebook says it wants to respect the democratic process and does not want to inhibit free speech.)

Facebook earns a spot in the Hall because it helps lies grow at an unprecedented scale. The platform makes it easy for liars and scoundrels to connect with one another and spread their nonsense without friction.

TUCKER CARLSON

The former Fox host has contributed a lot to the art of lying. He co-founded the *Daily Caller*, an early breeding ground for misinformation.

He brought conspiracy theories about race and the January 6 attack into the mainstream. But maybe his greatest accomplishment is that he mastered the art of lying without lying.

He is an artful liar, able to make false claims in ways that often elude fact-checkers. Sure, he has the kind of dreadful record you would expect (more than 70 percent False or Pants on Fire from PolitiFact), but his real skill is the ability to make subtle claims. My research assistant Nicole Kagan analyzed five episodes of his Fox show, *Tucker Carlson Tonight*, and identified the sly ways he uses rhetorical questions to plant the seed for a falsehood in his viewers' minds without directly telling a lie. ("Really? A shot that gives young people heart inflammation will help protect them from COVID?" he asked in his sly takedown of the vaccine. "That's safe and effective?")

Kagan also showed how Carlson uses over-the-top exaggeration and sarcasm to belittle his enemies and make false points ("The media and politicians, the people in charge, have talked about January 6th every day since it happened for twenty-six months."). Many of his lies strike a chord with his older, white audience because they invoke fear—of immigrants, of government bungling about COVID-19, and of election fraud.

I first became aware of Carlson's importance in misinformation when I was the editor of PolitiFact and our reporters began seeing a pattern in false claims from Republicans and conservatives in social media. They originated with the *Daily Caller*. After he started hosting his Fox show in 2016, I saw he was a wily liar, a troll who knows how to use sometimes-ridiculous lies to irk his enemies.

Indeed, he lies so prolifically that Fox's lawyers used that as their defense when the network was sued for defamation by former *Playboy* model Karen McDougal. She claimed that Carlson defamed her when he said she had extorted Donald Trump in exchange for her silence about their alleged affair.

Fox's lawyers contended that the "general tenor" of Carlson's show was that he was not "stating actual facts" about the topics he discusses and is exaggerating and making "non-literal commentary." They wrote in a brief that given Carlson's reputation, any reasonable viewer "arrives with an appropriate amount of skepticism" about the statements he makes. U.S. District Court Judge Mary Kay Vyskocil (a Trump appointee) agreed and dismissed the case.

Carlson has earned a spot in the Hall of Fame because he is a prolific liar, he has been shameless about using fear in his lies, and he even persuaded a federal judge that lying is just part of his shtick.

TALK RADIO

The journalists and academics who analyze the media often forget about conservative talk radio. That's understandable because it's not popular in the spaces where lefty pundits and college professors typically hang out. It's found in the dashboards of millions of cars and trucks, in thousands of small and medium-sized towns.

They should listen to it more. Talk radio is a powerful force that spreads and echoes the conservative talking points of the day—including lots of lies. Its audience is huge but difficult to calculate. The best numbers come from a website called Talkers that estimates the listeners for the top hosts. For June 2023, for example, the top five shows (Sean Hannity, Dave Ramsey, Clay Travis/Buck Sexton, Glenn Beck, and Dan Bongino) totaled 56.5 million cumulative listeners each week.

Those listeners are typically heavy consumers who tune in during long commutes, hearing the same talking points over and over, said Dan Shelley, former news director of a news-talk station in Milwaukee who now heads the Radio Television Digital News Association. They get addicted to the conservative voices. "You hear something that you like because it reinforces your worldview, and you can't get enough of it," said Shelley.

Talk radio is especially effective because the medium is so personal. The best talk show hosts develop an intimate connection with their listeners. "You're close to the hosts," Katie Thornton, the host and producer of the podcast *The Divided Dial*, said in an interview with NPR.

"They're in your kitchen with you while you cook. They're in your car on your commute. But they're also just really good at talking off the cuff, at sort of taking a germ of truth and a germ of a critique that many people sort of across the political spectrum might have and really turning it to their perspective, offering the sole solution."

Thornton's podcast, part of the public media show *On the Media*, exposed how talk radio hosts spread falsehoods about topics such as the 2020 election, COVID vaccines, and the Great Replacement theory. Her findings are supported by fact-checkers, who have found talk radio and podcast hosts often spread misinformation. For example, PolitiFact rated nearly two-thirds of Rush Limbaugh's claims False or Pants on Fire. Joe Rogan, whose Spotify podcast had an audience of more than 10 million in 2023, has often been criticized for repeating or supporting lies about vaccines, COVID, and other topics. I've found similar patterns analyzing the "Ministry of Truth" lies about Nina Jankowicz. They were repeated often by many talk show hosts.

Talk radio, which is dominated by conservative voices (liberal shows and networks have never caught on), will soon need a rebrand. The shows are no longer just available on the radio. The most successful hosts, such as Rogan, stream on the web, sometimes with video, and have huge audiences for their podcasts.

"The big national marquee conservative talk hosts are very good at digital," said Shelley. "They understood early and correctly that digital amplifies their message. And instead of being on the air for three hours a day, somebody could consume their content 24/7/365."

THE POLITICIANS

LYNDON JOHNSON

Long before Lyndon Johnson became president, he had a reputation for lying. In college, he was known as "Bullshit Johnson" because he was the biggest liar on campus, someone who "seemed almost unable to tell unvarnished truth about even the most innocuous subject," wrote Robert Caro in the *The Path to Power*, the first volume in his epic biography of the Texas politician. Robert F. Kennedy said Johnson "just lies continually about everything . . . he lies even when he doesn't have to lie."

As president, Johnson lied about the Vietnam War so much that it spawned a phrase—"the credibility gap." The first big deception involved two destroyers that reported they had been fired on by North Vietnamese forces in the Gulf of Tonkin. Johnson used those incidents to justify a major escalation of the war, even though the second one did not occur. Although historians have not been able to nail down exactly when he knew the truth about the second attack, they agree that he used the incidents to quickly obtain approval to escalate the U.S. presence even though there was much uncertainty about what happened. Three days after the second attack, Congress passed the Gulf of Tonkin Resolution giving Johnson authority "to take all necessary measures to repel any armed attack against the forces of the United States and to prevent further aggression."

"The consequences were enormous," Julian Zelizer, a historian at Princeton University, told me in an interview. Johnson's deceptions created momentum that led to "so many people dying in Vietnam." The number of troops grew from 184,000 in 1965 to more than 500,000 in late 1967. The vast majority of U.S. military deaths occurred after the U.S. escalation.

Americans grew suspicious, then tired, of his lies, which soured the nation on his leadership and marked a turning point for trust in the presidency. "I do think he was part of a generation that was still wedded to norms," said Zelizer. "Generally you either had to be somewhat honest, you could hide things, but it wasn't an era where just openly saying things that were untrue all the time was either seen as acceptable or politically tolerable. That was a generation where if you were lying, you'd better cover it up, you'd better hide it, you better do it carefully." Eric Alterman, author of *Lying in State*, a book about presidential lies, wrote that "Johnson's lies had poisoned not only his presidency and his war but American political life itself."

RICHARD NIXON

John A. Farrell, author of an acclaimed biography of Richard Nixon, says the thirty-seventh president's parents were competing forces in teaching him about right and wrong. Nixon's mother, a progressive, was saintly and always tried to bring out the best in her son. His father was haunted by bitterness, conspiracy theories, and anti-Semitism. He told his son to do whatever he needed to get ahead. "His father was the little devil sitting on one shoulder," Farrell told me, "and on the other shoulder was his mother, the angel with the heart telling him, 'No, be good, Richard, be good.'"

Too often, he took his father's advice. Nixon lied big and lied small, seeking to gain every advantage he could. He lied in his House and Senate campaigns and earned the nickname Tricky Dick. In *Richard Nixon: The Shaping of His Character*, Fawn Brodie wrote that "Nixon lied to gain love, to shore up his grandiose fantasies, to bolster his ever-wavering sense of identity. He lied in attack, hoping to win. . . . And always he lied, and this most aggressively, to deny that he lied. . . . Finally, he enjoyed lying."

Nixon was caught in his own trap by tapes from a secret White House recording system that revealed his fakery. "You listen to the tapes," said Farrell, "and over and over again, he's trying out these lying scenarios on his staff, sure amongst themselves and to himself that nobody will ever be able to listen to the tapes or get any of them to have to testify on Capitol Hill and reveal the depth of the lying. And so, especially in Watergate, he's just terribly, terribly brazen in his lying."

His up-is-down Watergate lie: when he falsely claimed that his White House counsel John Dean had conducted an investigation and found nothing. Nixon then declared "categorically . . . that no one in the White House staff, no one in this Administration, presently employed, was involved in this very bizarre incident."

Farrell said the American people were more bothered by the lies than the break-in itself, and they led to his downfall and eventual resignation.

Nixon grudgingly acknowledged his lying in his interview with David Frost in 1977 but still maintained he was a victim of his enemies. "I brought myself down," he told Frost. "I gave 'em a sword. And they stuck it and they twisted it with relish."

NEWT GINGRICH

One of Newt Gingrich's biggest lies was actually an illusion. It was a trick by the Georgia representative and other Republicans of giving speeches to an empty House chamber, which came to be known as "camscam." They would deliver passionate nighttime attacks on Democrats while the C-SPAN cameras were zoomed in and prohibited from pulling back or panning the chamber to reveal the members were alone. Viewers were left with the impression that Democrats were not responding to the attacks.

In May 1984, things came to a head when House Speaker Thomas P. "Tip" O'Neill got so fed up that he left the rostrum and went down to a lectern on the floor to criticize Gingrich for attacking Democratic House members. "You deliberately stood in that well before an empty House and challenged these people, and challenged their patriotism, and it is the lowest thing that I've ever seen in my 32 years in Congress."

Zelizer, author of *Burning Down the House*, which documents how the Georgia Republican transformed the Republican Party, said Gingrich then shrewdly used O'Neill's attacks to stir up controversy and get publicity. Gingrich understood—in the days before the internet and partisan media—that conflict created the opportunity to get news coverage.

"He understood what he was saying was theater. It wasn't fact," Zelizer told me in an interview. In Gingrich's view, "manipulating the truth was totally legitimate as an act of partisan politics." With his bare-knuckled approach to the Democrats, Gingrich set the mold for today's say-anything Republicans. He transformed the culture of the party to make attacks and lying acceptable.

In an *Atlantic* article titled "The Man Who Broke Politics," journalist McKay Coppins wrote that "few figures in modern history have done more than Gingrich to lay the groundwork for Trump's rise. During his two decades in Congress, he pioneered a style of partisan combat—replete with name-calling, conspiracy theories, and strategic obstructionism—that poisoned America's political culture and plunged Washington into permanent dysfunction. Gingrich's career can perhaps be best understood as a grand exercise in devolution—an effort to strip American politics of the civilizing traits it had developed over time and return it to its most primal essence."

BILL CLINTON

When Bob Kerrey said Bill Clinton was "an unusually good liar," he said it with admiration. But Kerrey, a Democrat who represented Nebraska in the Senate from 1989 to 2001, does not believe Clinton deserves to be in the Hall of Fame, nor was he referring to the lie Clinton made about having sex with intern Monica Lewinsky. No, Kerrey made the remark in 1994, several years before Clinton's epic lie about Lewinsky. Kerrey told me a reporter had asked him, "Why do you guys all lie?"

> And I said, "Look, the only human beings who aren't lying are the guys on the street corner saying the world is going to come to an end. That's how we get through life. We're all a little delusional. . . ." So I said, "Some of us are good eggs, some of us are not. Take Bill Clinton, for example, he's an unusually good liar, unusually good." I meant it as a compliment. The president did not [take it that way], I think.

Kerrey says he was referring to Clinton's general skills as a prevaricator, which have been celebrated and condemned. When he ran against Clinton for the Democratic presidential nomination in 1992, Kerrey got so frustrated that he said, "Clinton is just so full of shit!" One of his aides replied, "Yeah, but it's pretty good shit."

When Clinton was governor of Arkansas, he was dubbed "Slick Willie" by Paul Greenberg, then the editorial page editor of the *Pine Bluff Commercial*. Greenberg told the *Washington Post* he meant the nickname to identify "a particular subspecies of lying. It's a very lawyerly, sophisticated, elastic lie. In my opinion, the old-fashioned lie would be a step up." Mike McCurry, Clinton's White House press secretary, said his former boss "had that ability to kind of wind his way politically through a lot of treacherous political waters. And he's navigated pretty well."

Clinton is, of course, most famous for the on-camera, finger-wagging claim when he said, "I did not have sexual relations with that woman, Miss Lewinsky." At that time, the self-defense lie about his relationship with the former White House intern was probably the boldest falsehood uttered by a president. (He was impeached for lying under oath about the encounter, as well as obstruction of justice.) McCurry reminded me that during the debate over the lie, Clinton made the excuse that it was not a lie because they had oral sex but not intercourse. "In Clinton's mind, no, it was not a lie. I mean, he was truthfully reacting to a definition of sex that he had been given." But McCurry said most people, such as his wife, would reject that narrow approach. "If you ask Mrs. McCurry, was that sexual relations? I think she would have a different definition."

Kerrey, who admired Clinton's lying skills and also got frustrated by them, told me over breakfast that he doesn't believe they warrant Hall of Fame status. He says Clinton's lies, even about Lewinsky, are small by comparison with the internet-fueled whoppers today that are spread by people who "get all their news through the fillings in their teeth." He says, "The nature of today's lies is different than what Bill Clinton was doing trying to talk his way out of an affair with a White House aide."

I covered Clinton's impeachment as a reporter in Congress and heard all the explanations. But with apologies to the former senator from

Nebraska, Clinton's false claim about Lewinsky and his long reputation for bending the truth make him a clear choice for the Hall for the Fame.

DONALD TRUMP

In 2011, Chuck Todd invited me on his MSNBC show, *The Daily Rundown*, to discuss a lie by Donald Trump that Barack Obama was born in Kenya. Trump had added his voice to the "birthers," the fringe movement that included a dentist and a longtime conspiracy theorist trying to raise doubts about whether Obama was eligible to be president. As I walked into the studio and stepped up to the set, Todd was talking on his cell phone. "Yes, Donald . . . yes, Donald. . . . Look, Donald, I have to go. Thanks, bye." Todd turned to me. "Man, Donald Trump really hates you."

"He hates PolitiFact?"

"No," Todd said. "He hates *you*."

"How can he hate me? He doesn't even know me."

"Well, he just told me all the reasons I shouldn't have you on the show. He's been researching you."

Trump or one of his aides had noticed the promos for my appearance and then Trump had called to personally undermine my credibility to sabotage the segment and rattle Todd. The strategy didn't work and he asked questions as planned, and I explained why Trump and the other birthers had no evidence to back up their ridiculous claims.

The episode is just one illustration of how far the nation's most prolific and damaging liar will go to protect his lies. In volume (the *Washington Post* counted 30,573 false or misleading claims in his presidency), severity (his lies about the 2020 election threatened the framework of our democracy), and sheer silliness (he made Press Secretary Sean Spicer claim the 2017 inauguration crowd was the largest ever), Trump is unmatched.

He pretends to ignore fact-checkers (but will shamelessly quote them when it suits him) and repeats some falsehoods hundreds of times.

(Glenn Kessler, the *Washington Post* Fact Checker, created "the Bottomless Pinocchio" rating for these.)

He not only has a dreadful record himself; he normalized lying in the Republican Party. Members of Congress and a frightening number of state and local officials have adopted his disdain for the truth, parroting his false talking points, repeating (and sometimes believing) the Big Lie that he won the 2020 election.

Tony Schwartz, who co-authored the best-selling *The Art of the Deal* with Trump, told Jane Mayer of *The New Yorker* that "lying is second nature to him. More than anyone else I have ever met, Trump has the ability to convince himself that whatever he is saying at any given moment is true, or sort of true, or at least ought to be true."

From that moment on Chuck Todd's show through the January 6 insurrection and Trump's long-running lies about the 2020 election, he has baffled me. How could he lack a moral compass? To answer that, I called Dr. Lance Dodes, a psychiatrist who wrote a chapter in *The Dangerous Case of Donald Trump*, a collection of speculative essays by mental health professionals. I asked Dodes about Trump's internal justification for all of his lying.

"The idea that it would be justified suggests that he has a need to justify," Dodes said. "In other words, you and I each have a conscience and would want to make ourselves feel okay about doing whatever we do with how we justify that to ourselves. It doesn't apply to Donald Trump because he lacks a conscience."

Dodes said that Trump lives (and lies) for himself, in everything he does. He is like a predator who exists to feed his own needs and nothing else. He doesn't care about democracy or other people. Dodes said his lack of a conscience is "part of being a sociopath or a psychopath. That's one big part of what makes him different from other human beings."

CHAPTER 4

Consumed by Lies

I learned about Eric Barber from a classic Washington document dump.

In the final days before Republicans took control of the House of Representatives in early 2023, the Democrats who controlled the January 6 committee released hundreds of transcripts, emails, and reports. Because Republicans planned to abolish the committee when they took over, the Democrats gave the documents to the U.S. Government Publishing Office, which posted them on a little-noticed website.

Scattered throughout the site were more than a dozen interviews with people who had invaded the Capitol or otherwise been involved in the insurrection. It took me some time to decipher the messy system for storing the transcripts—it was like the Democrats had tossed the transcripts in a closet as they were rushing to vacate an apartment—but I eventually identified the ones for the January 6 attackers. Individually and collectively, the interviews told a detailed story about the attackers' backgrounds, education, occupations, sources of political information, and what motivated them to come to Washington to join Trump's protest. The investigators were methodical and asked similar questions of each person.

As I compiled quotes of the attackers, two patterns emerged. One involved the social media that the insurrectionists used to connect with one another and get their political news. The investigators asked them if they relied on widely used platforms such as Facebook, Twitter, Reddit, and Instagram, and also asked about smaller apps and sites that were used by conservatives and the far right such as 4Chan, Gab, Truth Social (founded by Donald Trump), and Parler. But the transcripts revealed the smaller conservative sites were not popular with the people who stormed the Capitol. When the investigators asked about social media, they heard one answer over and over.

Facebook.

The investigators found a similar pattern when they asked about news sources. The January 6 attackers had some variety in the sites they used to keep up with politics—a few occasionally looked at the mainstream media and a couple of them said they even checked out the much-derided CNN—but there was one source that nearly every one mentioned.

Fox News.

* * *

I decided to feature five of the attackers in a lesson in my class. They included a cabinetmaker who recorded a Facebook video about his adventures, the owner of a charter bus company who drove people to Washington, and a business development manager with a logistics company. The most interesting character was Barber, who had been a city council member in Parkersburg, West Virginia. He wore a combat helmet into the Capitol, which indicated he had come expecting violence. His answers to the committee investigators seemed thoughtful, introspective, and sometimes quite funny.

Barber, who was forty-two at the time of the Capitol attack but looked five or ten years younger, had short, dark brown hair with some gray on his temples. He sometimes had a beard with a few days of stubble, but when he donned a suit, he looked like he could be the next representative from West Virginia's First Congressional District.

As I dug into his life story, I found a sad tale. His parents abandoned him, leaving him to his grandmother and then the foster care system.

He got expelled from high school and was sent to prison from ages twenty to twenty-four after he was convicted of breaking and entering and petit larceny. He often mentioned his time "in Supermax" and said it taught him to be a fighter and gave him "a yard mentality." His philosophy was "if you aren't willing to fight and engage, the people will bully you." But he also emphasized that he was baptized in prison and came "from a strong Christian upbringing."

While in prison Barber earned his GED and took vocational training, and he has bounced around in a variety of jobs since then. He was a heating and cooling technician until he lost his job because of his involvement in the Capitol attack. He then found a job related to his longtime love of stock cars, working in a racing shop. "I never made more than $20,000 a year," he told the investigators.

He decided to run for City Council in 2016 after he bought a $12,000 house in a foreclosure sale and was appalled at the poor state of the neighborhood. He assessed the field of opponents the same way he would if he were racing. With two people running as Republicans, he decided to file as a Democrat. He said he had been a lifelong independent and he was doing it "just for fun, just for the life experience of being a candidate." But he connected with voters as a regular guy who lived in the poor part of town. Wendy Tuck, a Parkersburg social worker and fellow Democrat, described Barber as "very thoughtful, high energy. He's a little bit wound up sometimes, but he felt like the kind of guy that was going to roll up their sleeves and get to work. And I thought, this neighborhood needs guys like that." He won by six votes.

Barber had a turbulent four years on the council. He initially joined fellow Democrats in backing an ordinance that would protect people from discrimination based on sexual orientation or gender identity. But when a Christian group opposed the measure and threatened him with a recall, he got scared and voted against it. "I just took the politician's road," Barber told filmmaker Christopher Jones for a short documentary produced by The Intercept. "I went with what I thought was the best play." His switch angered Democrats, who felt he had betrayed them. He then left the party, claiming he opposed the local chairman's "anti-Christian rhetoric" and the party's "liberal activism and agitation."

About that time, he got into a tussle with police after he allegedly yelled obscenities at a neighbor who had summoned medical help. He was charged with disorderly conduct and obstruction. That prompted the local newspaper, the *Parkersburg News and Sentinel*, to dig into his past and uncover his lengthy criminal history, which included his time in prison as well as guilty pleas for DUI, possession/delivery of a controlled substance, and fleeing on foot. Still, Mayor Tom Joyce was optimistic about his colleague. "I think Mr. Barber has a lot of potential. He's an intelligent young person, but it's obvious he's made some poor decisions."

At council meetings, on Facebook, and every chance they got, Democrats blasted him for deserting them. They were literally in his face, because his seat was directly in front of the podium where people could address the council. They sent him hate messages and, he claimed, even tried to get him fired from his job. The attacks made him bitter and pushed him more to the right. His prison yard mentality came out.

His party shift wasn't difficult because his views had always been center-right. He says he had "a strong faith background," he liked Reagan, Bush 41 and 43, conservative judges, and nationalism. He hadn't been a Trump guy—he opposed the border wall and was bothered when Trump said bad things about John McCain. But now Barber found himself joining the culture war that Trump had stirred up. He started to talk like Trump, an angry, ass-kicking populist. "By the end of my city council term, I was recognized as one of the hardest-core conservatives around," he said.

He liked his new identity and his growing legion of followers. "The more the hard left hated me, the more I searched out the warm embrace and hug of conservatism," he told The Intercept. His shift also translated into "likes," the ego-boosting thumbs-ups on the social media platform: He might get three if he published a post about a neighborhood housing program, but if he said something about opposing abortion or something positive about Trump, the reaction was off the charts. Facebook was his information source, his way to connect with his followers, and the force that radicalized him.

Seeing his new life through the prism of Facebook warped how he thought about people and politics. "Within 12 to 18 months I'm convinced we're in a cultural war for the soul of our country. And it just fed into what I was already kind of predisposed to believe," he told the January 6 investigators. The more he consumed the right-wing posts, the angrier and more convinced he became that if his side didn't win, "it's going to be over for America."

By the end of his term in 2020, "even other Republicans considered me a radical." His persona and philosophy, he said, "was all born on social media."

* * *

Facebook's algorithm had fed Barber a tasty offering of conservative news sources, especially clips from Fox News. He recalls a steady diet of forty-second nuggets of Sean Hannity, Tucker Carlson, and Laura Ingraham. That's where he learned about antifa, which the Fox clips portrayed as a violent left-wing group running rampant in America, setting fire to churches and courthouses.

That narrative about antifa continued through 2020 and early 2021 as conservatives blamed members of the group for violence and alleged that they disguised themselves as Trump supporters to stage the attack on the Capitol. Antifa was a perfect villain . . . even though the facts didn't support the hype.

In truth, antifa (short for "anti-fascism") was more a movement than a group, a loosely knit collection of people who opposed authoritarian, homophobic, racist, and xenophobic positions of far-right organizations. The number of people in the movement was estimated to be quite small, but the lack of a centralized organization and the constant drumbeat of misinformation from conservative news sources created the false impression that local antifa groups were larger than they really were. Fox, in particular, offered a drumbeat of coverage that suggested antifa was a serious threat to the nation.

Experts who studied the movement said there was little evidence to back up the conservative fearmongering. There were occasional flare-ups, but not the widespread violence that Fox and other conservative media portrayed. "These groups are rarely militant or violent," Stanislav Vysotsky, author of *American Antifa: The Tactics, Culture, and Practice of Militant Antifascism*," wrote in an essay for The Conversation. "Most of them engage in commonly accepted forms of political activism." The *New York Times* documented how people and groups ranging from talk radio hosts to congressional candidates to a chamber of commerce had spread false rumors about antifa attacks in forty-one cities. When I watched a sampling of the Fox coverage, it was clear the producers cherry-picked a few video clips and put them on heavy rotation to make it appear that antifa was a big and scary group.

Barber was persuaded. The way he described his impressions to the investigators, antifa and Black Lives Matter were filled with violent rioters who were marauding through cities big and small. He also blamed a local Black Lives Matter organizer for personal attacks against him that included threatening messages to his mother when she was dying of cancer. He wanted revenge.

Facebook and Fox also were his sources for information on the 2020 election, where he received Trump's "Stop the Steal" falsehoods. Trump had shrewdly laid the foundation for this with months of suggestions that the election was going to be rigged. That tapped into the long suspicion by many Republicans that Democrats had conspired to encourage unregistered people to vote multiple times.

Barber told committee investigators he was convinced that the election had been stolen from Trump and rattled off a variety of false talking points that had made the rounds on Fox and other conservative media: anomalies with voter registration, improbably high turnout, election officials' refusal to conduct audits, and legal challenges dismissed simply because appellants lacked standing. His detailed descriptions of those claims reveal how steeped he was in the election lies. This wasn't just a passing muse about the outcome. He had seen and heard them repeatedly and was primed to act on them. So when he saw a Facebook ad for Trump's January 6 rally on the Ellipse in Washington, he immediately decided to come.

* * *

Barber had grand expectations for the rally and its aftermath. He saw it advertised on Facebook along with Trump's promise that it "will be wild." He envisioned the National Mall filled with a sea of people like it was for Martin Luther King Jr.'s "I Have a Dream" speech. He felt a personal obligation to go since Trump had asked. He felt great loyalty to the president, the leader of his new political party, the man who had done so much to inspire him. "If this is the only thing he is going to ask of me," Barber thought, "I'll do it." He also liked Trump's promise that it would be wild, which appealed to his thrill-seeking side.

He was excited to do Facebook Live videos from the rally. Although Barber had lost reelection by ten points, he still had a substantial following on social media and wanted to show his GOP fans what he was doing. He'd accepted his loss (even though he suspected shenanigans with some of the votes), but he was heartened that Republican leaders kept telling him he had a bright future and could run for another office. He planned to remind them of his passion with some live video from Trump's rally.

When the investigators asked what he expected on January 6, Barber said he did not envision the massive crowd storming the Capitol, but he did expect things to get rough on the streets of Washington. After the rally he figured the older people would get back on buses and depart, leaving behind the scrappier Trump supporters like himself who would "get a chance to fight antifa rioters that had been plaguing D.C." He said he pictured it "like a *Gangs of New York* scene with the Dead

Rabbits versus the natives, except it was going to be the conservatives versus the militant progressives." That scene in the Martin Scorsese film is incredibly violent, with men pummeling one another with clubs and slashing and stabbing one another with meat cleavers and knives. By the end, the snowy ground is covered with blood and dead bodies.

"I was absolutely convinced that we were just going to fight antifa," Barber said.

On January 6, he departed early for Washington, parked his car, and walked to the Ellipse, the area south of the White House where Trump was holding the "Stop the Steal" rally. He got a spot in the front row on the side of the stage, close enough that he was able to livestream video of Trump getting out of his limo.

The rally felt patriotic. People waved American flags and everyone seemed to be in a good mood. Donald Trump Jr. was his usual animated self, but Barber found the other speeches disappointing. Rudy Giuliani talked about the constitutionality of the Electoral Count Act of 1887 and crooked Dominion voting machines and crooked ballots. But Barber had never been much of a Rudy fan, and his remarks fell flat. And President Trump, the reason Barber was standing here in the cold, was dull. He repeated the same talking points that Barber had heard over and over.

Boring.

Barber had come for action—he brought a combat helmet!—and this was a snooze. Trump droned on about how he rebuilt the military and helped the VA and how Mike Pence could do the right thing. For Barber, this was a rerun. About halfway through the rally, he decided to go back to his car. His phone needed to be charged and he wanted a full battery so he could get photos and do a livestream on Facebook from the Capitol.

He loved Facebook. Since he'd lost the election, it gave Barber a welcome ego boost, a reminder that he was still appreciated. At the rally, he had 100 to 150 people back home watching his Facebook Lives. The likes and shares nourished his soul.

While Barber was back at his car, Trump continued to rattle off false claims ("In Detroit, turnout was 139% of registered voters") and tried to fire up the crowd. "And we fight. We fight like hell. And if you don't fight like hell, you're not going to have a country anymore," he told the crowd. "We're going to walk down Pennsylvania Avenue . . . I love Pennsylvania Avenue . . . and we're going to the Capitol."

When Barber rejoined the group and walked down Pennsylvania, a guy told him that Alex Jones, the conspiracy theorist who owned InfoWars, was going to have a rally later at Freedom Plaza. Barber thought Jones was a nut, but maybe that event would be the opening act to the battle with antifa that he was hoping for. As he got closer to the Capitol, he saw the gallows that had been erected on the west front of the building. He felt a distinct mood shift. He could see it in everyone's faces. The happy, patriotic crowd had turned angry, chanting slogans such as "Hang Mike Pence!"

He made his way to the Capitol and walked up to a broken window and looked in. There was a cop inside with his hands in his pockets. He wasn't stopping people who climbed through the window, so when Barber got waved in by a guy he believed was an Oath Keeper, he decided to go in.

The hallways were loud and crowded. Capitol Police would temporarily block the rioters, prompting them to holler and scream, but then the police would give up and everyone would break loose and continue marauding through the hallways and offices of the historic building. Barber was in awe of the place—the grandeur and the statues and the paintings. But he was frustrated because he couldn't get good Wi-Fi or a cell signal to transmit video. He took a lot of selfies that didn't require a connection. He'd post them later.

He made his way through the building toward the House side and heard more chants of "Stop the Steal!" and "Hang Mike Pence!" As he got into Statuary Hall, which was circled with thirty-five statues of famous Americans ranging from Amelia Earhart to Barry Goldwater, he realized it had become a riot. While he was in Statuary Hall, he stopped at a stand where members of a C-SPAN crew had abandoned their equipment—computers, tablets, even their camera. His phone battery had just died, so he rummaged around until he found a charger and stuck it in his pocket. He walked away.

At one choke point he got caught in a crowd and found he had an advantage: his helmet. He asked someone, "They're giving us the building?" He then smacked his helmet, emboldened to wade into the crowd, and plunged forward. He got close to the Speaker's Lobby, an ornate room adjacent to the floor of the House where Ashli Babbitt was trying to break through a doorway. As she tried to climb through a broken door, a Capitol Police officer shot her and she fell backward. Police took control of the area and told the crowd, which included Barber, to leave the building.

He walked back to his car and drove home. He was on the road and out of D.C. by 6:00 p.m. He did not get to battle antifa.

Eager to tell people about his involvement at the Capitol, he talked to the *Parkersburg News and Sentinel* and a local TV station, WTAP, and shared photos with them. He lied to the newspaper and said he did not enter the Capitol. He said he thought the riot went too far. The newspaper quoted him saying, "I don't think it should have been done, but I understand why people are angry. That was . . . little better than what antifa does. And then Trump Nation failed when they were supposed to abide by a set of principles that does not include riotous behavior." His short segment on WTAP focused on how the Capitol Police failed to prevent the riot. "I think at any point, the Capitol Police could've stopped what was happening, but they just didn't."

In the week following the attack on the Capitol, the FBI got seven tips that Barber had, in fact, been inside the building. Someone even sent a photo taken inside the Capitol and helpfully circled Barber, who was wearing his green combat helmet. He was charged with Entering and Remaining in a Restricted Building; Disorderly and Disruptive Conduct in a Restricted Building, and Parading, Demonstrating, or

Picketing in a Capitol Building, as well as a separate theft charge for stealing the phone charger.

He later pleaded guilty to one count of Parading, Demonstrating, or Picketing in a Capitol building and theft. He was sentenced to forty-five days in jail and twenty-four months of probation and had to pay $500 restitution to the Architect of the Capitol (as his share of the damage to the building) and $52.95 to C-SPAN for the charger.

At his sentencing, Barber and his attorney told the judge that he had expressed remorse from the day it happened. But District Court Judge Christopher Cooper still gave him a scolding.

"It's troubling that you still seem to have a mindset of 'There's a bully out there. I need to prime for the fight.' You did not go for self-defense, but you went with the helmet, ready to punch somebody or affirmatively engage in violence," Cooper said. "You clearly recognize the dangerousness of the situation and the potential for violence when you went in through a broken window and obviously saw what was going on around you and heard the alarm. You also went in private parts of the building, which I think is a distinguishing factor, not just the Rotunda or Statuary Hall that would have been open to the public."

Cooper got personal. "You're too old and you're too accomplished and you're too smart to be getting involved in nonsense like this, okay? You can say anything you want. This is not about the First Amendment. You are free to express your views and to support any political candidate or positions or issues that you want. I encourage that, but enough of this nonsense. Okay?"

The scolding didn't work. After the sentencing, Barber not only seemed remorseless; he seemed angry toward Judge Cooper, an appointee of President Barack Obama.

"A stolen phone charger is nothing compared to a stolen election," he told the *Parkersburg News and Sentinel*. "Any crimes I committed Jan. 6 pale in comparison to the lifelong criminal enterprise Nancy Pelosi has engaged in during her decades in Congress."

He said he would not have received a jail sentence if the judge had been a Trump appointee. "Unfortunately, I had [an] Obama appointee, and as a result I'll have to do six weeks in a minimum security facility as a political prisoner."

* * *

Why did Barber fall for the lies about the 2020 election? Why did he drive three hundred miles to attend a rally about those lies and to fight a largely imaginary enemy?

He says Facebook was the biggest factor. Although he briefly mentioned other sites such as YouTube and Breitbart, he made it clear in his interview with the committee investigators that Facebook was his news source and his fan base. After he switched parties, it became a place where he found friends, reassurance, and support. When he posted something Trumpy, he got dozens of likes—a lot more than when he'd been a Democrat.

In March 2022, more than a year after the attack on the Capitol, he sat in his grandmother's house in Davisville, West Virginia, and spoke with investigators through a video system called Webex. He noted that he was a father of two daughters—one then eighteen months old and the other eight years old—and he reflected on the state of politics and the national discourse. Although he did not retreat from the election lies (he still believed that Trump won), he blamed Facebook for being the force that radicalized him and millions of others.

"I don't know how you put the social media genie back in the bottle, and I know there's no legal way to limit speech." But he said it "caused the riot and caused all of the divisiveness, all of the cultural turmoil that we've experienced as a nation. It's social media. But I honestly believe social media is going to destroy America."

He mused about how things could have turned out differently. "If I didn't have Facebook, psychologically, I would have done a lot better, and I probably would have never been as motivated to engage in some of the behavior I did."

* * *

The investigators who interviewed Barber were members of the Red Team, a unit on the January 6 committee that was focused on the people who invaded the Capitol, their backgrounds and motivations. The team questioned more than twenty rioters and others who took part in the attack and came away with an in-depth assessment about why they fell for the election lies.

Marcus Childress, one of the Red Team investigators, found the job fascinating and, at times, depressing. He was an attorney who had been a federal prosecutor and assistant staff judge advocate in the Air Force who had handled a variety of felony cases ranging from assaults to bank fraud. His most interesting case had involved the Outcast motorcycle gang. Most biker gangs had all white members, but the members of Outcast, like Childress, were Black. Childress became an expert on the group's culture—its hierarchy, terminology and how it communicated with members.

When he started doing interviews for the January 6 committee, he found parallels between the rioters and biker gangs. Both were quick to believe in conspiracies and were fueled by fears of threats to their community that didn't really exist. Both also lacked skepticism about things they read on social media. The hours that Childress spent talking with the biker gang members made him a better interviewer with the rioters. He tried not to be judgmental or cynical. He knew that everybody had different values and motivations. He asked questions without being confrontational. He was there to learn.

During the two-hour interview, Childress found he liked Barber, who didn't seem as angry as the other guys the Red Team had questioned. Barber was jovial and charismatic. He seemed like he was genuinely struggling to understand how he'd been manipulated by what he'd read and heard. "The entire interview, I felt like he was actually just getting stuff off his chest and thinking through it," Childress told me.

That was especially true for Barber's comments about how he got addicted to the adulation he received on Facebook and how the skewed news feed affected him. "I thought he was being incredibly truthful and reflective about his desire for being liked on social media," Childress said, "and I actually admired how he was even able to come to terms that he was almost being fake about [it]. He was one hundred percent saying he was being fake." Nearly all the rioters continued to believe the Big Lie that Trump won, but Barber had been so thoughtful and reflective that Childress thought he "might be able to snap out of it."

But alas, it appears that Barber didn't. Although he discussed how he was pushed to extremes by Facebook, his comments indicate he still believes there were many "anomalies" in the election. Childress said that only one of the twenty-plus rioters he interviewed has renounced the election lies. The rest still believe the election was stolen by President Biden. "It shows why, at times, I left the committee feeling helpless about the 2024 election, and why that election gives me so much anxiety," Childress told me. "It's sad and makes me really nervous for the next election."

Childress worries because the lies came from the top, from the president and senators and other elected officials.

"This was a glimpse of what can happen if you have politicians knowingly spreading lies. The members knew this was a lie, but they were still willing to go on Fox News and peddle these talking points," he said. "I truly believe that if certain members of Congress and certain presidential candidates just rebutted these conspiracy theories with the platforms they had, we would not be having these discussions. But instead, many of our leaders allow the conspiracy theories to flame on, and sometimes they pour gasoline on them in a way that is just superdangerous."

* * *

The forces affecting Barber were bigger than Facebook, Fox News, or a conservative echo chamber. Social media and conservative news organizations fed him the lies, but he was primed to fall for them. When you overlay his profile and news sources with academic research on why people fall for misinformation, it becomes clear why he and millions of others got caught up by the election falsehoods (and many other false beliefs). Here are some of the big reasons why he and so many others have fallen for the lies that Donald Trump won the 2020 election:

1. **Lack of skepticism**: Barber, like all of us, was conditioned by evolution to trust that incoming information is true, a theory developed by University of Alabama professor Timothy Levine. As writer Malcolm Gladwell summed it up, "Our preferred position is to believe that the world is telling us the truth." This usually is a helpful posture: It makes us right most of the time. But it also makes us susceptible to occasional deceit.

2. **"Overconfident" consumers fall for bogus news:** Individuals who overestimate their ability to discern between credible and false headlines are more likely to engage with inaccurate news sources. A study of more than eight thousand people found the overconfident group, which is more likely to be male and Republican, is more likely to visit false news sites, like and share misleading content (especially if it aligns with their political beliefs), and fail assessments about current events.

3. **A "home team" mentality:** As Barber became more conservative, he believed lies that supported his political party, a phenomenon known as directionally motivated reasoning. It says people are more susceptible to falsehoods when they are consistent with their group's positions or identity. "Maintaining a sense of comfort with who you are is more comfortable than confronting an uncomfortable truth," said Jon Roozenbeek, a postdoctoral researcher at the University of Cambridge who studies misinformation. This love for the home team is so strong that in one study of COVID-19 policies, participants disproportionately credited their party for achievements and blamed their opponents for negative outcomes.

4. **The Network of Lies:** Fox, the network that Barber relied on for his election information, carries far more falsehoods than other networks. This was especially true about the election, when the network hosted many Trump aides and allies who made false claims about voter fraud and turnout. (This was documented in the Dominion lawsuit against Fox.) But it's also been true for many years, as proven by countless fact-checks on Fox personalities and network comparisons by PolitiFact. (John Lee, a member of my research team, took phrases that Barber used in his interview about anomalies/irregularities with voter registration or difficulties with mail-in ballots and found frequent matches with similar phrases mentioned on Fox.)

5. **Repetition, Repetition, Repetition:** The legendary claim that a lie, once repeated, becomes the truth has . . . some truth to it, according to researchers. It's a phenomenon known as the "illusory truth effect," a concept that repetition can persuade someone to believe a falsehood. A 2023 study published in *Public Opinion Quarterly* found Republicans were more vulnerable to Trump's repeated lies than Democrats. This applied in Barber's case because he likely saw and heard the same election lies repeatedly—to the point where he could regurgitate them to the committee investigators more than a year later.

* * *

I messaged Barber through Facebook in August 2023 to see if I could interview him at his home in Davisville. Facebook had deleted his original account, which had his political posts and his videos from January 6. But he had a new one that was all about his kids and stock car racing. He had told the committee investigators, "I don't follow any type of conservative craziness" on the new account.

I exchanged messages with him for two days and tried to persuade him to do an interview. He was reluctant because he said other journalists had not treated him well, but he floated the possibility of a conversation in Washington (he said a federal judge was going to revisit his "illegal" sentence) and then sent me a photo of his legs and feet up in a chair in Washington, with the laces missing from his shoes. He apparently was still angry that the District of Columbia jail had not returned them. He also referred to himself as a "J6 defender," an indication that he hadn't changed his opinion about the election.

The second day of our conversation, he sent me photographs of his stock cars, which lacked the usual decals of sponsors. He wrote: "When I build something I have to pay for the materials. . . . As you can see, I don't have sponsorship or anything like that." It was clear he was asking me to pay him to do an interview, something that is generally not ethical in journalism, so I tried to diffuse the tension by joking that I wanted his car to say: "Read the liberal media!"

He then said that others involved in January 6 were paid for interviews and he indicated that if I did, he would "open up lawyer stuff and my discovery . . . plus the pictures I haven't released. And I give very good quotes and soundbites. I was the go-to guy on council because the media always got really great quotes from me."

He later said he would charge me $1,000 "for the interview and quotes" and $500 for photos that had never been seen before. Or instead of paying *him*, I could make a $2,000 donation to Toys for Tots in Parkersburg. I replied that either way, I couldn't pay because it's not ethical for journalists to pay for interviews. He said I'd have to rely on the many comments he had made elsewhere. (He eventually had lengthy conversations with me on Facebook Messenger.)

* * *

Eric Barber is a case study in why political lying is a grave problem facing our nation. He not only was fooled by the president's election lies; he became so obsessed with them that he could still recite them more than a year later. Politically and personally adrift, Barber found comfort in Facebook, which rewarded him for becoming more radical with positive feedback in the form of more friends and likes. It became a vicious cycle: Facebook then served him more lies and clips from Fox that reinforced the lies that made him even more radical.

Barber is an extreme case. He went to Washington hoping for a violent confrontation with antifa and ended up joining the marauders at the Capitol. There are tens of millions of other people who were fooled about the election but did not raid the Capitol or seek violence. They all are victims of a twisted ecosystem that incentivizes lying by our politicians, who trick their followers into believing the falsehoods and then fool them into donating money.

In the pre-internet, pre-cable days, elected officials were criticized for "playing to the cameras" to get more news coverage. (When I covered Congress, we had a joke in the press gallery that the most dangerous place in the Capitol was if you got between Sen. Chuck Schumer and a TV camera.) But today, politicians are not so focused on getting on *the news* (the mainstream media), but in getting on partisan cable channels and generating content for their social media feeds and fundraising emails. That has changed their calculations about what they say because, for those platforms, they don't need to worry about sticking to the truth. They have the freedom to lie with little scrutiny.

Brendan Nyhan, a political scientist at Dartmouth College who studies misinformation, said one big lesson of Barber and the millions of other people who fell for the election lies is that the falsehoods were pushed from the top by our political leaders. "Political elites are taking advantage of people," Nyhan said. "They're misleading them, they're abusing their power and the trust that people have in them, and that's problematic and even dangerous in a democracy."

* * *

After his guilty plea, Barber's Facebook page became a photo gallery of his racing and his trips with his daughters and their mother. But I found two posts that showed he still had some political interest. One was a July 2022 Breitbart article about Ron DeSantis that quoted the Florida governor saying, "You gotta be ready for battle. So put on the full armor of God. Take a stand against the Left's schemes."

The other was a September 2022 photograph of Barber holding a microphone at an unidentified meeting. His post read: "It's been almost two years since I've made a political speech. The amount of support and encouragement I received tonight was both humbling and uplifting at the same time. It felt great to be surrounded by so many good conservatives and patriots. While I'm not ready to fully re-enter the political arena . . . I'll always be present on the cultural battlefield."

CHAPTER 5

Catching the Liars

The 1988 presidential campaign between Vice President George H. W. Bush and Massachusetts governor Michael Dukakis brought a storm of TV ads that were filled with exaggerations and lies. After the election, *Washington Post* columnist David Broder began what he called a "crank crusade" to persuade fellow reporters to fact-check ads in future campaigns. Broder, one of the nation's most respected political writers, said it was time for journalists to start calling out the liars.

That sounded good, but it wasn't in the journalists' DNA. Political reporters were afraid they would be called biased if they became fact-checkers. Kathleen Hall Jamieson, an influential scholar who studied political ads and their impact, said reporters often told her that calling out falsehoods was not their responsibility—that was up to the competing campaign. Reporters found comfort in the "he said–she said" approach and resisted her suggestions that they become more assertive.

Broder was relentless with his crusade. In column after column he called attention to the problem of false ads and said it was time for reporters to fact-check them the same way they checked any claim by a candidate. He said reporters should demand that candidates be personally available to answer questions about every mailing and TV ad. "No ducking and hiding behind campaign managers or other intermediaries," he wrote in a 1990 column. He said journalists should be blunt. "We ought not to be squeamish about saying in plain language when we catch a candidate lying, exaggerating or distorting the facts."

(A quick clarification on the definition of fact-checking: It is often confused with the process that magazine editors use to verify the accuracy of articles before publication. That process, which has the same name, has been around since the 1920s, according to *Deciding What's True: The Rise of Political Fact-Checking in American Journalism* by Lucas Graves. Broder was calling for a new type of journalism that also came to be known as fact-checking. I think of the two this way: Magazine fact-checking is part of the editorial process to ensure accuracy; political fact-checking is a genre of journalism that holds politicians accountable for what they say and produce.)

Before Broder's call to action, there had been scattered attempts to fact-check speeches and ads. The *Post* and other news organizations had published occasional checks of commercials and debates; Richard Threlkeld at ABC News had won acclaim in 1988 for a segment that debunked claims in an ad from Vice President Bush that attacked Dukakis. But it took Broder, whose columns were syndicated in three hundred newspapers, to get the nation's editors and TV producers to launch "ad watch" features across the country. "David Broder really made the difference," Jamieson told me.

A typical ad watch story by the *Atlanta Journal-Constitution* in 1992 called out Democrat Wyche Fowler for distorting the facts in an attack ad against Republican Paul Coverdell. The ad claimed that Coverdell's mismanagement of the Peace Corps led to two investigations. The newspaper provided a smart analysis that showed how Fowler was twisting the details.

The early reviews of the new features were positive. Readers and viewers said they liked the new scrutiny that campaign ads were receiving. But after an early surge of growth, the movement sagged. A study examining the practice from 1992 to 1996 found ad watch stories dropped by 68 percent on television and radio and by 20 percent in print. Studies by Jamieson raised questions about the effectiveness of the ad watches on TV news programs. Viewers sometimes ended up believing the ad even more after seeing the fact-check.

Another problem: Many of the fact-checks became wishy-washy. This was especially true for the newspaper ad watches. Instead of providing clear conclusions about whether claims were true or false, many political writers resorted to the familiar on-the-one-hand, on-the-other-hand approach, or just wrote an analysis of the strategy behind the ad. Political reporters were still afraid to call out a politician for a false ad because they did not want to upset a candidate or aide they might want as a source for a future story. As the national movement declined, local fact-checking was spotty. Many states and media markets had little or none. But a few, such as Miami and Minneapolis, had aggressive fact-checkers.

In 2003, the national movement got a boost from an unlikely place. Jamieson, then at the University of Pennsylvania, decided to get into the fact-checking business. She hired Brooks Jackson, a veteran CNN political reporter who had been released by the network, to launch an organization at her university. They called it FactCheck.org.

Jamieson said she didn't have a grand vision for the organization other than to give Jackson a job so he would keep calling out falsehoods, which he had done for years with his sharp-tongued segments at CNN. He launched FactCheck.org with a note to readers that said: "I can think of no better job for a journalist than holding politicians accountable for getting the facts right, regardless of their party or political philosophy." The site's articles, with headlines such as "Gephardt Ad Quotes Dean out of Context" and "Bush a Military 'Deserter'? Calm Down, Michael," reflected his deep knowledge of Washington and his curmudgeonly personality. The site got an early boost when Vice President Dick Cheney mentioned it in a debate, prompting such heavy traffic that the site's server crashed.

* * *

I was impressed by FactCheck.org, but I felt it needed a rating system that would capture an article's conclusion in one or two words. I also wanted scorecards that would tally those ratings for each politician to show how they compared with one another. I told my bosses at the *St. Petersburg Times* that we should start our own fact-checking website with a Truth-O-Meter.

In the summer of 2007, I traveled from Washington, D.C., to St. Petersburg, Florida, to make my final pitch to editors of the *Times* to start PolitiFact. I brought a poster board to the meeting that showed a mock-up of the site I wanted to build with some prototype fact-checks I had written. The poster, which used our working title, "The Political Referee," wasn't the kind of professional mock-up you might expect for a serious business venture. I used a glue stick to attach the prototypes to the board and drew arrows with a Sharpie to show how each web page would link to another. It looked like a poster board from a middle-school science fair. Still, when I explained the various elements, everyone understood how the website would work.

I wasn't the first to use the name Truth-O-Meter for a device that would assess someone's honesty. For years, writers had used that name as a magical tool that could be used in politics and elsewhere. But it became the central identity of PolitiFact and a perfect way to summarize our research.

We gave the Truth-O-Meter six ratings—True, Mostly True, Half True, Barely True (later changed to Mostly False), and False, plus a lighthearted rating of Pants on Fire, which used an animated GIF showing the meter in flames. We planned to use Pants on Fire for frivolous remarks like Joe Biden's claim that "President Bush is brain-dead." But the rating became so popular that we ended up using it for more serious claims that we deemed ridiculously false. Pants on Fire now accounts for about 16 percent of all PolitiFact ratings.

Another unusual feature of our approach: True ratings. Some of our competitors, including FactCheck.org, primarily publish articles only when they identify an exaggeration or falsehood. They rarely say something is true. But I felt that gave a distorted view that politicians were always lying. So we decided that PolitiFact would check any claim that we believed people were curious about, even if the claim turned out to be true. (About 5 percent earn True ratings.)

There wasn't much mystery about the outcome of the meeting when I flew to St. Pete. Neil Brown, the newspaper's executive editor, had made it clear that he supported the idea. But it was still an opportunity for senior editors to speak up about concerns they might have. Starting a national fact-checking site was a gutsy move for the *Times*, an independently owned regional newspaper, and I figured there might be a few editors who were uncomfortable with the idea.

About a dozen senior editors filed into the third-floor conference room. Brown gave everyone a chance to say what they thought of the idea and whether they believed we should move ahead. Everyone was supportive, with one particularly revealing comment. When he came to Adam Smith, the *Times*'s political editor, I got a reminder about the sensitivity of fact-checking. "I think it's a great idea, and I think we should do it," Smith said, "and I want nothing to do with it." He didn't elaborate, but he didn't have to.

Smith was a well-regarded political writer because he got scoops from people in both parties. But if he began calling politicians liars, his sources might dry up. I understood his position and didn't quibble. Journalists' instinct for self-preservation, which resulted from the drumbeat of complaints from conservatives about liberal bias, enabled Republicans to get away with a culture of lying that ultimately created the great disparity between the parties that we have today. (I'll discuss that in detail later in the book.)

I knew that I was venturing into a disruptive new form of journalism, and the reaction would be mixed. I knew that on some days I would make both parties mad. But I was hopeful that the balance of work would ultimately satisfy them.

We launched PolitiFact in August 2007 and got a friendly greeting from Jackson, who emailed thousands of FactCheck.org subscribers that he welcomed another organization in the new field. "So far we like what we've seen. The writing is crisp and clear, sources are clearly cited with hyperlinks where appropriate, and the Web site is nicely organized," he wrote. His collegiality set the tone for a long, friendly relationship in a field that could have been much more competitive. The *Washington Post* Fact Checker, then Michael Dobbs, launched a few weeks later with a rating system of one to four Pinocchios to indicate the severity of the falsehood.

When I saw the initial fact-checks that had been written by our small staff at the *St. Petersburg Times* and some recruits from our sister publication *Congressional Quarterly*, I was amazed at the broad scope of our work. We had a Half True for Mitt Romney's claim that President Clinton had dismantled the military after the end of the Cold War; a False rating for a viral chain email that claimed Barack Obama refused to say the Pledge of Allegiance; and a Mostly True for a claim by Sen. John Edwards that Hillary Clinton had accepted money from Washington lobbyists. I also realized the power of the Truth-O-Meter. It wasn't just effective on presidential candidates. It would work on members of Congress, governors, even mayors.

The campaigns were perplexed by the rise of fact-checking. Barack Obama's, a trailblazer in using the internet in many ways, was stuck in the past with the other campaigns when it came to adapting to our new journalism. As misinformation swirled about Obama's birth and his patriotism, the campaign failed to recognize that we could help debunk the falsehoods. The campaign assigned a junior staffer to deal with us, and he bristled when we requested documents such as the candidate's birth certificate. Hillary Clinton's campaign also seemed surprised by our frequent requests for backup materials for her factual claims.

The arrival of PolitiFact and the *Washington Post* Fact Checker in addition to FactCheck.org created a critical mass at an ideal time. The internet was just becoming a source of political information for a significant share of Americans. The iPhone launched that year, and Facebook was up to 50 million users. Misinformation was beginning to spread through chain emails, a phenomenon I would later call "the Uncle Bob problem," to describe a well-meaning but out-of-touch relative who would forward an email of conspiracy theories to everyone in his contact list.

In 2009, PolitiFact was awarded the Pulitzer Prize for National Reporting. Honoring a website that had a rating called Pants on Fire was a big step for the sometimes-stodgy Pulitzer Board. But the board recognized that our work was old-fashioned accountability journalism packaged in a modern format. Walking up the steps to the Columbia University library to attend the Pulitzer luncheon with colleagues from the *Times* who helped create the site, I got choked up at the thought that fact-checking had won journalism's highest honor.

CHAPTER 6

The Ministry of Truth, Part 2

MAY 10, 2022: WHERE WERE THE FRIENDLIES?

Republicans smelled blood. Only two weeks had passed since the Disinformation Governance Board had been introduced, but its survival was in doubt. They kept up the pressure to kill the board and moved to cash in on their new villain.

In the week after the *Politico* announcement, about 70 percent of all one-hour segments on Fox mentioned either Jankowicz or the board (frequently just calling it "the Ministry of Truth"), according to an analysis from Advance Democracy, Inc. (ADI). Those ninety-three Fox segments were collectively seen by about 144 million households, according to Nielsen estimates.

The conservative outrage machine was so good at this! Everyone had learned their lines—they seemed to do it by simply watching and listening to the other actors—and then repeated them on Fox and talk radio and Twitter and Facebook. Talk radio listeners heard hosts such as Ben Shapiro repeat the same lines that Fox viewers were getting every night: "Executive Director Nina Jankowicz once described Hunter Biden's laptop as a 'Trump campaign product' . . . this is an actual tape of her singing about disinformation to Mary Poppins. So we've got theater kids running disinformation departments inside the Department of Homeland Security. The Ministry of Truth is here."

In that first week, Jankowicz was mentioned in 141,986 tweets—with more than a third also mentioning "ministry of truth" or "minister of truth," according to the ADI analysis. They peaked on April 29, two days after the announcement, with more than 44,000 that day alone. More than twenty-seven hundred Facebook posts mentioned her from people and organizations such as Fox News host Sean Hannity, former Rep. Tulsi Gabbard, Breitbart News, and Brent Bozell, the conservative media critic.

The attacks got personal. Brian Kilmeade on Fox:

> By the way, she's eight months pregnant. If you're going to take over a brand new bureau, shouldn't you not need maternity leave the first few weeks in? Just sayin."

The Republicans leading the attacks mostly came from the far right of the party—Reps. Lauren Boebert and Jim Jordan, and Sens. Josh Hawley and Tom Cotton. They were joined by Kevin McCarthy, the party leader who would later become the Speaker of the House (only to be ousted after nine months in office).

Their language was angry and, at times, warlike. On Twitter, Boebert likened the board to something from Mao or Stalin and suggested its elimination was "the hill to die on." ADI's analysts noticed a violent stirring in the far-right social media platforms such as Patriots.win and Gab. On a Gab post of that Boebert tweet, a commenter replied wishing for assassins to take out the "guv'm't bastards." A Gab post that included a Tucker Carlson segment about Jankowicz prompted anti-Semitic comments and musings about killing her and Mayorkas. (They were wrong about her religion. Jankowicz is not Jewish.) On Patriots.win, someone posted a video of Carlson's coverage of Jankowicz. Comments on the post read: " Well when those Nazi ſucks knock on the door. They should be greeted with Mr. 12 Gauge Slugs."

Someone sent her a photo of an empty egg carton, insinuating that she had no eggs left. She got hundreds of Facebook messages a day—some using the "minister of truth" talking points and others that were just vulgar. One said: "You and your fucking family should be sent to Russia to be killed." Someone on Twitter wrote: "I don't support doxxing by any means, but someone should definitely take a shit on Jankowicz' doorstep every single day for the rest of her pathetic life." One man sent Jankowicz a message telling her she was "Biden's cum dumster." Another sent her a Facebook message every day that said "Cunt" over and over.

Jankowicz tried to make sense of the terrible attacks. She understood that she was the ideal target for the Republicans and their boosters on Fox and elsewhere. She was a Hillary-supporting feminist and a graduate of an all-women's college. She fought against disinformation and, best of all, she sang, which gave them video that they could ridicule and play endlessly on television and radio. But this is what the lies had created: hatred, anti-Semitism, and threats of violence. Jankowicz was hurt, worried, and baffled. Who were these people? What sort of person could have so much hate and be so harmful to another human being? And how could the Republicans foster this with their angry rhetoric?

* * *

McCarthy, then the party leader in the House, introduced a bill to eliminate the board, and others chimed in with their support. Some of the most ridiculous lies and distortions came from Boebert, the Colorado Republican known for embracing QAnon, heckling the president, and making anti-Muslim remarks. On May 10, she spoke on the House floor beside a big poster of Jankowicz that quoted her saying, "Who do I need to f**k to be famous and powerful?" (The poster, of course, failed to point out that quote was from a satirical cabaret performance.)

"The American people will not have their speech monitored by corrupt, career professional politicians who lie day in and day out.

And now the DHS, a militarized department, has established a new Disinformation Governance Board, or more accurately known as the department of propaganda. DHS was created to stop terrorism. Now it is being used to terrorize the American people," Boebert said.

"And who did Mayorkas hire to run this Orwellian ministry of truth? This lady, Nina Jankowicz. Mayorkas calls her an expert on disinformation, probably because she tells lies all the dang time. *Nina* [Boebert, her voice dripping with disdain, half shouted her name] said that President Trump would embolden ISIS. Well, he defeated it! *Nina* said the Hunter Biden laptop from hell was a Trump campaign product. *Nina* said that concerned parents who wanted a say in their children's education were pushing disinformation, and *Nina* said Big Tech should censor the Wuhan lab leak theory because it was, you guessed it, disinformation.

"*Nina* doesn't seem to have a good relationship with truth and will surely use this board to silence Americans. *Nina* is no public servant. How is that, you say? Don't take it from me. Here are her words," Boebert said, gesturing to the f-bomb quote on the poster.

"Are these the words of a public servant?" she asked without noting *THE WORDS WERE SATIRE AND FROM A SONG.* "What do I need to do to— Well, Madam Speaker, I will let you read the rest of that. This doesn't sound like someone who should be monitoring Americans' speech. The Democratic Party has truly lost their minds, from intimidating judges at their homes, burning down pregnancy centers, and vandalizing churches, to calling moms and dads domestic terrorists, and now creating this department to censor free speech because extremists are scared of, what, Elon Musk?"

The next day, Boebert joined McCarthy and other Republicans at a news conference in the House Press Gallery to promote the bill to eliminate the board. They mentioned all the talking points: *Ministry of Truth . . . Democrats controlling free speech . . . the Hunter Biden laptop . . . colluding with Big Tech.* "I wouldn't trust Biden and his incompetent misfits to take care of one of my goats," Boebert said, "and I certainly don't trust them to be the arbiters of truth."

Rep. Steve Scalise asked, "What is it that Joe Biden has against people expressing their views if it goes against his far-left, Soviet-style radical ideology? That's really what this is about—it's been about government control from the beginning. They want to control what people say; they want to control what people think; they want to control the people's ability to enjoy their own freedoms."

Meanwhile, some Republicans moved swiftly to monetize their ridicule of Jankowicz. Sen. Josh Hawley of Missouri sent a fundraising pitch that said: "The head of Biden's ominously named *Disinformation Governance Board* has already gained quite a reputation for posting cringe-worthy Tik-Tok videos, peddling left-wing conspiracies and being dead-wrong about claims of Russian disinformation. This is the kind of person hand-picked to censor conservative voices and push left-wing propoganda [*sic*]." It urged supporters to "chip in today and help us get off to a strong start in May!"

Rep. Mike Johnson of Louisiana, who would later succeed McCarthy as Speaker of the House, warned in a fundraising email of his own that "Republicans WILL BE HER FIRST TARGET.... Rush in a donation if you disapprove of this radical attack on freedom."

* * *

In Washington, politics is a team sport. You're red or blue. This shows up not just in obvious places like congressional committee assignments but also in the think tanks and advocacy groups that fuel the political discourse. Many of the groups align closely with one party.

These groups are the "friendlies" that provide reinforcement for each party so Washington doesn't appear to be as bitterly partisan as it really is. Journalists often fall for this deceit, referring to the groups as nonpartisan, which, though technically true, ignores the reality that they nearly always side with one party. This creates parity in a typical Washington battle and in typical Washington political coverage. In the fights over tax policy and immigration and health care and countless other issues, there are groups on each side that provide ammunition to the partisan warriors. They provide talking points and witnesses for congressional testimony and guests for C-SPAN and authors for op-eds.

But the battle over the Disinformation Governance Board was lopsided from the start. As Republicans unleashed their heavy artillery of lies, repeated by their boosters on Fox and talk radio and in conservative groups, Democrats and their supporters said virtually nothing. There were no counterpoints to the Republican lies. Jankowicz wanted to know: Where were the friendlies?

It appears they were scared away by a combination of incompetence by the Department of Homeland Security and wariness about the department's history on civil liberties. Other than the one briefing for Capitol Hill staffers a few days into the controversy that Jankowicz says was not well organized, there was not the kind of repetitive, coordinated effort that was needed to respond to the massive Republican disinformation effort. In a town where talking points drive the daily discourse, the sluggish, bumbling response by DHS officials gave Democrats and their allies few good lines to use. It looked like the Biden administration didn't believe in the board.

The other factor: apprehension about DHS, a department created by President George W. Bush that had a questionable history in the eyes of the civil liberties and free-speech groups that might have spoken up for Jankowicz. Combine that with the terrible name and the no-details announcement, and left-leaning groups such as the ACLU and the Knight First Amendment Institute not only took a pass, they added their voices to the criticism from the conservatives.

"DHS hasn't adequately explained the need for or scope of its eerily named Disinformation Governance Board," the ACLU tweeted on May 5, *after* Mayorkas had explained himself on the Sunday shows. "We're skeptical of the government arbitrating truth and falsity. How concerned we should be depends on the function and authority of this position."

The Knight Institute, the Electronic Frontier Foundation, and Protect Democracy wrote a letter to Mayorkas saying they appreciated the board's mission but were wary because of the poor way DHS announced the new effort. "The Department has a history of flouting the Constitution in flagrant ways. It is one of the least politically accountable agencies in our federal government, and it has often violated individuals' civil liberties," the groups wrote. They urged DHS to either reconsider the board or clarify what it was going to do and not do.

Now Jankowicz sank to her lowest point. She felt helpless. She had sent her colleagues several options for communications strategies, but they continued to dither. Maybe it was time to go rogue, to violate their gag order and simply start talking with reporters about what the damn board was going to do. Her bosses would probably fire her, but at least she'd get to tell the truth. Or maybe she should just quit. She'd put up with so much misery in just two weeks: the brutal attacks online and the smears about her work and reputation . . . all because of lies from the Republicans. And the reason for those lies? Her bosses had bungled the rollout of the board and given it the worst name ever.

Jankowicz knew how rough-and-tumble the internet could be. After all, she was the author of *How to be a Woman Online: Surviving Abuse and Harassment, and How to Fight Back*. ("To be a woman online is an inherently dangerous act," she wrote. "The attacks we endure are meant to silence us. They are meant to encourage us to stay home in 'traditional' women's roles and not engage in politics, journalism, activism, academia or public life more broadly.") But now that she was in the crosshairs of these terrible people, enduring the most horrible attacks right before she was going to give birth, she felt vulnerable. She had hired a private security investigator to monitor the dark web, where he found even scarier things, like people posting "you will be held accountable" and that she would be sent to Russia or China and killed.

Rob Silvers called. He was the head of PLCY, one of the DHS officials who had pushed the idea for the board, and the one person in the whole department who had shown even an inkling of humanity about all the pain she'd been going through. He'd been calling regularly to see how she was doing. (This account comes from Jankowicz. Silvers did not respond to invitations for an interview.)

"I'm going to have to go rogue if we don't do something," she told him.

"I can't condone that," he said.

She broke into tears. She'd had enough. She was fine with dealing with the bullshit from strangers who harassed her, but now it was different. A member of Congress had slandered her on the floor of the House of Representatives.

Silvers was sympathetic and said he'd been recommending the department let her speak. But somewhere between PLCY and the White House, someone, or a group of someones, was not allowing that, which had slow-rolled the whole response. Was it Secretary Mayorkas? White House Chief of Staff Ron Klain? The roadblock was a mystery.

In the meantime, Jankowicz was a few weeks from delivering her baby and under tremendous stress. Her blood pressure was up, which was worrying her doctors and her family. Everyone was telling her not to stress out. *Sure! Easy! Thanks for the advice!*

* * *

In the increasingly desperate effort to save the board, Jankowicz said DHS officials considered two big moves: rewriting the charter, the internal document that created the board, and giving it a new name. The idea was to get past the "Ministry of Truth" criticisms and give the board a fresh start.

Names were tossed around, none particularly good. She recalled they had words such as "coordination" and "council" and "working group." She workshopped them with her team and came back to DHS leaders with the consensus: "I think they're all bad. No matter what we do, it doesn't matter. Changing the name is not going to undo the damage that's been done by these conspiracists."

Likewise, rewriting the charter would do nothing to appease the critics, who had not seen the original charter. If they had, they would have seen that it emphasized protecting free speech—and just ignored it anyway. For the Republicans, this was about scoring points, not having a serious discussion about policy.

MAY 14, 2022: THE PAUSE

After a three-week barrage of lies, DHS officials were ready to surrender. Silvers and another DHS official, Jen Daskal, called Jankowicz to give her the news and discuss her future. They said it looked like Mayorkas was going to kill the board but that she could keep working as a policy adviser.

Jankowicz pondered her options. She considered taking the new position but had an important request: She wanted to talk freely about the board and defend herself and respond to the lies. Would they let her do that?

No, they said.

She couldn't tolerate that. She knew the attacks would continue, people would still think the board was in power, and the Republicans would keep attacking her. She decided to resign. They came back a couple of days later saying that Mayorkas had decided to just "pause" the board and let an advisory council conduct a review. The board might come back to life. But still, she couldn't speak.

Sitting on her back porch in Arlington, grappling with the worst heartburn of her pregnancy, she considered the offer. But she concluded that nothing had changed. She needed the freedom to speak. She was still going to resign. In her letter to Mayorkas, she included a subtle dig: "I wish the Department conviction as it continues its vital work in responding to disinformation that affects the homeland." Of course, the department had shown little conviction in standing up for her in the past three weeks.

The department announced the pause and Jankowicz's resignation on May 18. In a statement to news organizations, DHS groused that the board had been "grossly and intentionally mischaracterized: it was never about censorship or policing speech in any manner." DHS also made a late and feeble effort to defend Jankowicz, saying she had been subjected to "unjustified and vile personal attacks and physical threats."

Now that she was free, Jankowicz gave her first on-the-record comments to reporters. She told the Associated Press, "We need to have a grown-up conversation about how to deal with threats to our national security, and that's not what happened here. I'm not going to be silenced."

Republicans and their boosters cheered the news. They had stopped the board and taken down Jankowicz. Boebert tweeted: "When we put pressure on this administration, they fold like a house of cards. The so-called Disinformation Governance Board is done. Hopefully Nina figures out another way to get famous. Watch out for that!"

Benny Johnson, a conservative influencer with 1.9 million followers on Facebook, posted a video in which he bopped to the Kool & the Gang song "Celebration." "We have done it, yes indeed," he said as the music played in the background. "Nina Jankowicz, Misinformation Mary Poppins, is done for. . . . That's right, Mary Poppins is *bye bye, see ya! Sayonara!* She is finished and the Joe Biden Ministry of Truth is done for. . . . And we're dancing! And we're dancing! You know why? Because this person can no longer censor your Facebook posts . . . this person can no longer censor your Facebook feed. . . . We are chalking up wins for the good guys left and right."

JULY 2022: "FAMILY MEN"

Jankowicz was gone and the board was paused, but the Republicans weren't done. A "whistleblower" emerged, presumably someone inside the Department of Homeland Security who provided them with "disclosures" that could actually reveal the Disinformation Governance

Board to be the Ministry of Truth that the Republicans knew it really was (but had never actually proved).

Whistleblowers have a storied history in Washington. From Daniel Ellsberg, the leaker of the Pentagon Papers, to Edward Snowden, whose documents revealed the inner workings of the National Security Agency, they have provided important revelations about the government. But in this case, the whistleblower—who was never publicly identified—produced little more than ordinary memos and a routine meeting preview. But that didn't deter the Republicans from making it sound like the revelation of a far-reaching conspiracy.

On June 7, 2022, Sens. Charles Grassley and Josh Hawley sent a letter to Mayorkas saying that information obtained "through protected whistleblower disclosures raises serious concerns" about the recently paused board and its role in the department's counter-disinformation efforts. In dramatic language, the letter accused Mayorkas of misleading a Senate committee about the board, which was really going to determine what was "disinformation" (in quotes, a sign of the Republicans' continuing cynicism that it was a real thing).

The letter, like many coming from Capitol Hill, was intended more for the media and partisan audiences than for the actual addressee. It was a five-page exercise in cherry-picking, but it contained nothing explosive or even significant. Besides the original memos and charter, its flimsy evidence included a calendar preview for Silvers of a meeting with two Twitter executives in which they planned to discuss how DHS could help the tech company combat mis- and disinformation. Overall, the letter just plucked a few choice lines from the emails and the charter, tossed in some hype describing Jankowicz as "a known trafficker of foreign disinformation and liberal conspiracy theories," and mixed them together in a suggestive stew.

Grassley and Hawley concluded by asking Mayorkas to answer questions and provide documents to show whether DHS was truly in cahoots with Twitter, Facebook, and TikTok. Among them: whether DHS had requested they remove or "censor, flag or add context to" any posts believed to be disinformation; whether DHS sought to suspend or ban accounts believed to be promoting disinformation; and to provide documents about the creation of the Disinformation Governance Board and the selection of Jankowicz.

* * *

"They're profiting by ruining my life," Jankowicz said.

She was sitting across from me at a picnic table at Northside Social, a coffeehouse in Arlington, Virginia. She still had her sense of humor about the ordeal, but after three months of attacks, she had reached a breaking point. She was out of a job—one she chose to quit rather than be muzzled—and her career and reputation were forever tarnished.

Hawley, Ron Paul, and at least a few others had been raising money using lies about her and the board, and she'd been enduring a continuing onslaught of online harassment. She wrote a letter to Hawley and Grassley asking for compassion. "I write to you in my personal capacity as a new mother and an American citizen concerned with the state of political discourse in the United States," she began.

Her letter recounted the facts—the "aggressive, sexualized, vulgar, and threatening messages" she'd received, the overwhelming majority based on distortions of what she and the board were going to do. She was surprised by Grassley's involvement because he had invited her to testify before the Senate Judiciary Committee in the previous few years. Hawley, she wrote, had taken a few things from her past and distorted them in ugly ways, ignoring her commitment to the First Amendment and falsely portraying her "as a rabid idealogue" rather than the serious nonpartisan scholar that she was.

> As a result of this warped narrative, tens of thousands of my fellow Americans, by the most conservative estimate, so strongly believe I am a threat to their freedom that they took time to defame, harass, stalk, and threaten me.

> The last trimester of my pregnancy, the birth of my first child, and the first weeks of his life—a time that should have been joyful and as calm as possible—were and continue to be marked by stress, fear, and concern for my growing family's safety. As family men, I hope you can empathize with how difficult this experience has been.

She said she didn't object to them carrying out their duty in conducting oversight of DHS and investigating whistleblower claims, but she asked them to condemn the attacks against her and stop promoting the false narratives. "As Senators, you have the power to set a different tone and example. I hope you will do so."

She emailed it and posted the letter on Twitter and got a tweet back from Hawley within ninety minutes. He was not persuaded by her account of the harassment, nor was he interested in changing his tone.

"The Biden Admin lied about their censorship board for months," he said in his tweet. "Only when a patriotic whistleblower came forward with documents did we learn the truth. Now Nina Jankowicz is trying to shut down questions based on whistleblower revelations. She should come & testify. Under oath."

CHAPTER 7

Why They Lie (and the Tale of Mike Pence)

In December 2002, a new family moved in four doors down from our home in Arlington, Virginia. They were quick to decorate their new house for Christmas, and within a few weeks their kids and ours—they had three about the same age as our three—were playing together. My wife, Katherine, and I soon met the parents: Mike and Karen Pence.

The Pences transformed the character of our street. Arlington, an inner suburb of Washington, D.C., had always been a great place to raise kids, but many of us were overly cautious about letting our children wander in the neighborhood. We scheduled play dates and walked them to soccer practice—just to be safe. We were a little paranoid about what might happen to them if they got out of our sight.

The Pence kids—Audrey, Charlotte, and Michael—were from a small town in Indiana and didn't share our urban worries. Their attitude was that everybody was friendly and inviting, so they just banged on our doors when they wanted to play. Suddenly 28th Street was alive with the sounds of our children shouting and having fun. You'd see packs of kids running from house to house and playing hide-and-seek and Four Square and street hockey and basketball. The Pences put a basketball hoop in the street and left a ball so anybody could play.

Politically, they chose hostile turf. Mike was a new House member from Indiana and a conservative Republican, and Karen seemed to share his views. Our street was otherwise pretty much all Democrats. Most worked in government or in jobs that depended on the government—the sort of people that Mike supposedly disliked as a loyal Reaganite. But politics didn't matter when you were chatting while doing yard work or standing around at the block party.

Mike and Karen became two of our closest friends. They often sat with us on our front porch, discussing the challenges of parenthood and home ownership and our favorite TV shows (they loved *Modern Family*, which struck me as unusual because Mike was opposed to gay marriage and the show was one of the first to feature a gay couple). Mike and I were both big movie fans, and we'd quote films back and forth to each other, such as *Ghostbusters*, *Airplane!*, and *Animal House*. We didn't talk much about our jobs, which was the nature of parent conversations in the Washington suburbs. Your family life mattered more than your work.

I didn't cover Capitol Hill much in those days, but I kept an eye on Mike as he rose through the ranks of the House Republicans. He became the chairman of the Republican Study Committee, the main conservative caucus in the House, and established himself as an affable voice on the right, where many members were more focused on anger and aggressive tactics. His slogans were "I'm a Christian, a conservative, and a Republican, in that order" and "I'm a conservative, but I'm not angry about it." He tried to get noticed. He partnered with Democrats on a media shield law that would protect journalists from being forced to reveal their sources in federal courts. He was the lead House sponsor on an immigration bill with Kay Bailey Hutchison that tried to provide a compromise to allow migrants into the United States, before that concept became radioactive for members of his party. I once rode to work with him before his meeting with President George W. Bush to strategize about that bill. (It never passed.)

As he became more prominent on Capitol Hill, Mike got more news coverage and began saying things I found dubious. (By this time, I had founded PolitiFact, so I established a rule to recuse myself from any fact-checks on him.) He joined other Republicans in making extreme claims that suggested President Obama's economic stimulus bill was filled with waste. PolitiFact awarded him a False that the bill had $30 million to protect mice in San Francisco, but a True that it had $25 million for off-road ATV trails. He ended 2009 with a mixed record—three True ratings, two False, and a few in the middle. All would fit my definition of misdemeanors. I looked at his record with amusement, figuring it was a typical start for an ambitious new party leader. He was using bold lines to get quoted by the news media, and in a couple of cases, he went too far.

(I learned later, in researching this book, that many of his questionable claims had escaped scrutiny by fact-checkers over the years. In 2015, investigative journalist Andrew Kaczynski, then of BuzzFeed, dug up some old posts from a 2000 campaign in which Mike said "global warming is a myth" and "Despite the hysteria from the political class and the media, smoking doesn't kill. In fact, 2 out of every 3 smokers do not die from a smoking related illness and 9 out of ten smokers do not contract lung cancer." He seemed to imply that it was acceptable that one out of three smokers died.)

Our families stayed close. We played football, went sledding, and watched the Super Bowl together. Mike taught my kids how to play penny poker. When the Pences went away, my daughter took care of their dog, Maverick, and cats, Oreo and Pickle. When I spoke with Mike, politics rarely got discussed. If we talked about work, it was most likely to be Capitol Hill gossip about a journalist, like, "Did you hear that so-and-so is moving to CNN?"

I knew a lot of politicians, some who were a bit stiff or even phony, and some who were more genuine. Mike was definitely one of the genuine ones, at least back then. He and Karen chose to live with their family in the Washington area so they could be together more nights a week. That was politically risky because the optics were not as good as living in their congressional district in Indiana. Mike mowed his own lawn and drove an SUV. When a neighbor was dying of cancer, Mike visited him nightly, sitting by his bedside for long periods of time and comforting him until he died.

Mike showed his ambition. He got elected the chairman of the House Republican Conference, the No. 4 spot in the party leadership. That brought more attention to his increasingly outlandish claims. In 2010 and 2011, he earned all Falses and Mostly Falses from PolitiFact. Most were for regurgitating inaccurate Republican talking points. For example, he earned False ratings for revisionist history on taxes and an overly hopeful claim about a Republican plan for Medicare.

Then, he decided he wanted something bigger. In 2011, after a decade in Congress, Mike decided he wanted to be an executive instead of facing the constant frustrations of being a legislator. He flirted with running for president but ultimately decided to run for governor of Indiana. He and Karen told people in our neighborhood that they would be selling their house and moving back to the place they still called home.

Katherine and I hosted the neighborhood farewell party in our backyard. I gave a toast. "Mike and Karen are going back to Indiana because they want to live in public housing," I said, referring to the governor's mansion. "But I think they'll be back in our area sometime soon. They'd like to live in public housing here in Washington." Everyone laughed and toasted our departing friends. Katherine and I gave them a framed photo of the street sign outside our house and told them they would always be our neighbors. Mike got choked up.

* * *

Mike is famous for "Confessions of a Negative Campaigner," a 1991 essay he published in Indiana newspapers in which he vaguely apologized for personal attacks he made in his unsuccessful congressional campaigns in 1988 and 1990. He tried to practice what he preached in his 2012 campaign for governor. *The Atlantic*'s McKay Coppins reported that in the final days when the race was neck and neck, Mike resisted a recommendation from his advisers to attack his opponent, John Gregg.

Mike squeaked by to win with less than 50 percent of the vote and became a pretty typical Republican governor. He signed bills to cut taxes and chip away at abortion rights and got tangled in a couple of significant controversies. One involved a state-run news service he wanted to start that was going to provide struggling media organizations with ready-to-publish articles about state government. But critics said his "JustIN" service was just a front for taxpayer-funded state propaganda and he ended up scrapping the plan.

His biggest controversy involved a bill that was called the Religious Freedom Restoration Act. Though it was framed as a way to protect people's rights to practice their religion, the LGBTQ community said it was really just a sneaky way to discriminate against people because of their sexual orientation. Mike made a clumsy attempt to defend it on *This Week with George Stephanopoulos*, six times ducking the question of whether the bill discriminated against gay people. Facing a huge backlash from corporations and trade associations, he and the other Republicans backed down and approved another bill to protect against discrimination.

His reputation for stretching the truth continued to grow. A fact-check by the Associated Press caught him exaggerating his accomplishments with education, tax cuts, and unemployment ("some of the victories Pence is claiming aren't quite as shiny as the governor makes them out to be"). PolitiFact gave him a Half True for his defense—that Barack Obama voted for an identical bill to the Religious Freedom Restoration Act and that sexual orientation didn't have anything to do with the law.

Our families stayed in touch. When Karen was back in our neighborhood, she stopped by to hang out on our porch and gave us a jar of honey made by bees at the governor's mansion. Another day, when I was out of town, Mike and Karen dropped by in an SUV driven by

Indiana state troopers and took Katherine to dinner at our favorite neighborhood sandwich joint. Katherine said Mike acted weird. He was aloof and seemed caught up in the trappings of being governor. He waited for a state trooper to open his door like he was some kind of royalty. Katherine considers that a turning point for Mike: when he stopped being the guy who mowed his own lawn and who sat with a neighbor while he was dying of cancer, and became an out-of-touch politician. For me, his turning point was still to come. He was about to join forces with the greatest liar of all time.

* * *

The courtship between Mike and Donald Trump was quick and perfunctory. It was more arranged marriage than love affair. Trump needed Mike to shore up the Christian right; Mike needed Trump because of his own ambition to someday become president. They met a few times and Trump made the announcement on Twitter. Suddenly Mike, who was unknown to nine out of ten voters according to a CBS News poll, was paired with his polar opposite. Mike was gentle; Trump was ferocious. Mike read history; Trump watched television. Mike was a student of policy; Trump was a student of himself. But they pretended to like each other, and Mike had to live with one of Trump's biggest traits: lying.

In the summer that he became Trump's running mate, PolitiFact and FactCheck.org called out Mike for big exaggerations and falsehoods about Hillary Clinton's email server, her actions on the attack on Benghazi, and the poverty rate under President Obama. The falsehoods piled up at the vice-presidential debate, when he faced scrutiny from an expanded group of checkers that included the *New York Times* and the Associated Press. He did poorly. For this book, my student researchers put his fact-checks and those of Democratic nominee Tim Kaine on a chart and color-coded them from green to red, true to false. The Kaine side had nine claims colored red, but mostly yellows and greens. Mike's side had thirteen reds.

After he and Trump were elected, Mike's slide into mendacity continued. He wasn't fact-checked often, but when he was, he typically earned low ratings for parroting false Republican talking points:

President Donald Trump's proposal to allow Americans to buy health insurance across state lines would make it the same as "the way you buy car insurance" today.

False.

"Along the southern border of the U.S.," the government apprehends "seven individuals a day who are either known or suspected terrorists."

Pants on Fire.

"The reality of voter fraud is undeniable. . . . In my own state of Indiana in 2012, there was a Democrat super PAC that was involved in our elections, that literally, there was a group of people that were prosecuted for falsifying ballots."

Four Pinocchios.

When COVID-19 struck, Trump appointed him the chair of the administration's Coronavirus Task Force. Mike got further tangled in Trump's lies—and added his own. To help spread the administration's unrealistic optimism about the disease, Mike published an op-ed in the *Wall Street Journal* headlined "There Isn't a Coronavirus 'Second Wave.'" It claimed "we are winning the fight against the invisible enemy" and that people shouldn't be fooled by the media's scary stories. "We've slowed the spread, we've cared for the most vulnerable, we've saved lives, and we've created a solid foundation for whatever challenges we may face in the future. That's a cause for celebration, not the media's fear mongering."

Critics said he was cherry-picking positive stats to paint a rosy picture. "Nowhere does he acknowledge that nearly 120,000 people have died in the United States in just over four months," Glenn Kessler, the *Washington Post* Fact Checker, noted on Twitter. A week and a half later, Mike continued to downplay the severity of the disease at a briefing for reporters but got called out by fact-checkers for his exaggerations and falsehoods. The headline in the *New York Times* read: "As Cases Surge, Pence Misleads on Coronavirus Pandemic."

As the reelection campaign gathered steam, Mike went full Trump. He spewed false talking points on fracking, the stockpile of medical supplies, abortion, tariffs, and health care. His debate against Kamala Harris provided fresh scrutiny from an expanded group of fact-checkers. Once again, my research team compared the two candidates using a color-coded chart. Harris had three false claims. Mike had twelve.

Of course, Mike ultimately stood up to Trump when it mattered most. He did not block the certification of Joe Biden's victory in the 2020 election. Some of my friends wanted me to congratulate Mike for being heroic. Yes, it was great that he stood up to the biggest lie (and saved our democracy). But he could have shown this courage much earlier. And he lost his backbone quickly. In fact, two months after he certified the election, he wrote an op-ed for the conservative Heritage Foundation that kowtowed to the election deniers, stating: "After an election marked by significant voting irregularities and numerous instances of officials setting aside state election law, I share the concerns of millions of Americans about the integrity of the 2020 election." When he has been asked about what he did, he's been wishy-washy and careful about offending Trump voters who continue to reject the truth.

* * *

Journalists rarely ask politicians why they lie. I find that surprising, given the magnitude of lying these days. Journalists aren't usually bashful about asking tough questions. But in researching this book, I discovered we rarely ask directly about it. I suspect that's because we expect lying politicians will simply deny they do it, sending the conversation down a rabbit hole. There's also the reluctance about using the word "lie." Many journalists aren't sure they have the goods to prove it and are reluctant to confront someone about doing it.

I made the question a standard part of most interviews for this book: Why do politicians lie? What's the payoff? In the split second when they consider whether to utter something they know isn't true, what is their calculation? I posed those questions to current and former members of Congress, political operatives, local officials, congressional staffers, current and former White House aides, and campaign consultants. I came away with a range of answers that provide a fascinating picture of the motivations of the nation's many political liars.

Few would admit to lying themselves. That was partly a function of the people who agreed to talk with me. Many members of Congress declined to be interviewed. Press secretaries also declined, although they typically did not specify a reason or just didn't reply to my requests. Politicians who consented to an interview usually claimed they never lied. I had the most success with former Republicans who left the party at least in part because of Trump's many lies. Freed from their allegiance to the GOP—and often no longer in politics—these former Republicans offered some of the most candid answers and anecdotes about the motivations of the liars.

In Mike's case, as with many elected officials, his lying seemed to be a product of political ambition. Olivia Troye, who worked as a homeland security adviser in the vice president's office from 2018 to 2020, told me that she saw two Mikes. As a boss, he was caring and compassionate and wanted the facts. But he always seemed to have an eye on the Oval Office, both to please Trump and, someday, to be there himself. "It was like watching Jekyll and Hyde sometimes," she said in an interview. In meetings, she found him deeply engaged and concerned about details. He was attentive and asked smart questions. But he would compromise all of that when he was asked to parrot the Trump administration's talking points. That was especially noticeable on COVID-19, her main issue during the last six months in his office.

"At the beginning of the COVID pandemic was probably the most honest I saw Mike Pence ever be, in the entire tenure of topics that I was working on," she said, noting that she persuaded him not to refer to it as "the China virus," a phrase that Trump used. She thinks the *Journal* op-ed marked a turning point when he came under pressure from the White House and then echoed their talking points about the news media and cherry-picked the data on cases.

A 2018 profile of Mike in *The Atlantic* quoted his fraternity brother saying that even in college, everyone knew he wanted to be president. Others in Indiana, his home state, felt he had sold out while serving as Trump's No. 2. Scott Pelath, the Democratic minority leader in the Indiana House of Representatives, told *The Atlantic* he was saddened to see Mike relinquish his soul to Trump: "Ambition got the best of him."

Looking back, Troye still struggles to reconcile the two faces of Mike. She said there is a "genuineness to him. But I think that he's also a political animal. . . . He's power hungry. And I think he really wants to be president, so that anybody around him can feel that. I think that is his lifelong dream. And I think he'll do anything he has to do to get there."

Mike is not unique, of course. I believe the justification for lying can be reduced to something like a point system. Every day, politicians try to score points with key constituencies—not just voters but also party leaders, influencers, and key people in the media. A decision to lie is a simple math equation: *I am likely to score enough points with this lie that it will outweigh any consequences it might have from voters/donors/the media.*

"They gain political favor or, ultimately, they gain election," said Mike McCurry, former White House press secretary under President Clinton. "They get a political reward for that." Former Sen. Bob Kerrey put it more simply to me: "It's human nature to want to get a standing ovation."

Several politicians and operatives I interviewed said lies are intended more for the base, the party activists who want a high-calorie, low-nutrition jolt to reassure them about their commitment. "There is a base to play to, a narrative to uphold or reinforce," said Cal Cunningham, a Democrat who ran unsuccessfully for the U.S. Senate in North Carolina in 2020. "There is an advantage that comes from willfully misstating the truth that is judged to be greater than the disadvantage that may come from telling the truth. I think there's a lot of calculus in it." Jim Kolbe, a former Republican member of Congress from Arizona, put it terms that were almost sexual. A lie, he said, "arouses and stimulates their base."

Lies are easy ammunition to attack political opponents. Damon Circosta, a Democrat who served as chair of the North Carolina State Board of Elections from 2019 to 2023, said lies are used in political attacks "to take points off the board for the other candidates."

In the old days, "if someone would say something outlandish, they would be shamed," Dr. Anthony Fauci, the former head of infectious diseases at the National Institutes of Health, told me in an interview. Attitudes have changed. "There is no shame in lying now. There is no shame in developing your own 'alternative facts'—untruth, conspiracy, lies have become normalized."

Fauci said he was a victim of lies by Republican politicians who portrayed him as a villain for his response during the pandemic. Sen. Rand Paul, a Republican from Kentucky, repeatedly attacked Fauci for supporting a government-funded laboratory research that Paul claimed led to a leak of the virus. At a hearing, Paul accused Fauci, one of the nation's top public health professionals, of "trying to obscure responsibility for four million people dying around the world from a pandemic." Fauci, baffled that the senator would make such a charge, told me his reaction was, "Like, what the fuck?"

Fauci said the lawmakers lied to discredit him and then cash in. Sen. Roger Marshall, a Republican from Kansas, claimed that Fauci would not give people access to his financial statement when, in fact, he filed the disclosures every year and they were available to anyone who requested them. Still, Republican politicians would accuse Fauci of lying, call for his dismissal, and use his face on their fundraising mailings. He brought one of the mailings to a congressional hearing to show how members were cashing in on their lies. He told me, "It said 'Fire Fauci' and then on the bottom, 'Donate even $10, $20, $50, $100, $200.' So there wasn't any ambiguity."

* * *

As I mentioned in the introduction, one of the first lies I encountered was the "death tax," two words that fooled people about the estate tax, which at the time affected less than 2 percent of the people who died. Kessler said converting complex policies into simple phrases is a shrewd tactic. "The more complex a subject is, the more susceptible it is to politicians lying about it," he told me. "How many people really understand the intricacies of the federal budget or the intricacies of health care policy? So particularly if you're trying to sell it or you're trying to put it in an ad . . . you can get away with it."

At the local level, lying can mean promising to solve huge problems that politicians know they really can't solve, said Jillian Johnson, a former member of the City Council in Durham, North Carolina. A case in point: gun violence, a complex societal problem that has defied many solutions. She said some Durham officials have misled residents to believe that they can have a serious impact with ShotSpotter, a technology that detects gunshots and quickly dispatches police to the scene. It's a lie, she told me, "to make people think that you're going to solve the problem even when there's no way you could ever solve that problem."

Several people I interviewed mentioned the role the partisan media plays in fostering more lying. Jackson, a Democratic member of Congress from Charlotte, North Carolina, said the outlets expect politicians to repeat falsehoods as the price of admission. The benefit for politicians "is access to an echo chamber where certain lies are treated as fact. And if you're not willing to treat certain lies as fact, then you simply won't be invited to address the echo chamber," Jackson told me. If you don't play there, "you just won't exist to those people. So you won't have their votes, you won't have their money, you won't have their applause, and you won't have their recognition."

Jackson, whose district was eliminated for the 2024 election when North Carolina Republicans redrew congressional maps, said some House members are more interested in playing to the cameras than in telling the truth. They are just auditioning, "Here's what you can expect if you have me on your show tonight."

Tim Miller, a former Republican operative who left the party in 2020 and wrote *Why We Did It*, a book about how the party went gaga for Trump, said gerrymandered districts create an environment for representatives to lie. "Most of the voters in your district are getting their information from Fox, conservative talk radio . . . maybe from Facebook and conservative outlets, maybe they still read their local newspaper, but probably not. And so you just have this whole bubble of protection around your lies in a way that wouldn't have been true before, fifteen years ago."

Neil Newhouse, a Republican pollster, blamed the decline in local news coverage. "There's no local reporters following these races," he said. "All of these local bureaus have been just wiped out, and so there's nobody following this shit on a day-to-day basis and keeping people accountable."

Politicians also lie to defend themselves. Some of history's most famous lies fall into this category, from Nixon's claims about Watergate to Bill Clinton's falsehood about Monica Lewinsky. "Nixon lied about Watergate in what he saw as self-preservation. And he lied because he saw it as pursuit of a bigger good, which was his own reelection," Anita Dunn, a senior adviser to President Biden, told me in an interview. But Nixon did not lie about the EPA, poverty, or other policy matters. He lied "because he got caught doing something . . . which, you know, is kind of human behavior, right?"

Lying is a last resort, said Eric Jotkoff, a communications adviser to many Democratic campaigns. "When you have no defense, no truthful defense, you have no alibi, you make one up."

Lying to the media is a strange art, Miller told me. If you are hired to do it for Trump, you have to defend what Miller describes as the "up-is-down lie," a preposterous claim like that the inauguration crowd was the biggest ever or the bogus claims that Trump won the election. It takes "a certain kind of demented person to do that and to be able to go to sleep at night and to keep their lies straight." But then there's the job of defending the slick lying that the Clintons practice, which he described as "artful wordsmithing." A spokesman for one of them might want to go to confession more often, "but it's kind of easy to do Clinton lies."

* * *

Politicians have long used lies to stoke divisions about race. One of the most insidious was the birther lie about Barack Obama, which was a racist dog whistle. At PolitiFact, we encountered several versions: that Obama was born in Kenya, that he was Muslim, that he attended an Indonesian "madrassa," and that his birth certificate was a fake, among others. Some related falsehoods said he didn't say the Pledge of Allegiance and that "he turns his back to the flag and slouches." The lies began in 2004, picked up momentum with chain emails when he was seeking the Democratic nomination in late 2007 and early 2008, and then regained momentum from Trump in 2011.

The cornerstone of the conspiracy theory was the suggestion that Obama's Hawaiian birth certificate, a computer-generated "short form" of data entered when he was born in 1961, was somehow a fake because he was really born in Kenya. Never mind that there was an undisputed birth announcement in Honolulu newspapers ("Mr. and Mrs. Barack H. Obama, 6085 Kalanianaole Hwy., son, Aug. 4.").

Robert Bauer, White House counsel under Obama, said the birther movement tapped into a belief held by some Americans that Obama didn't belong in the nation's highest office. They believed "he doesn't represent American values. He doesn't have American interests at heart. He's just not one of us. And what the hell is he doing there?"

Obama advisers were reluctant to give the claims any credibility by responding to them too prominently. Instead, they left the debunking to a junior aide who spent a fair amount of energy discouraging news organizations from covering the bogus claims. But in the meantime, the falsehood was spreading through chain emails and social media, taking root with many conservatives.

Valerie Jarrett, one of Obama's closest advisers, wrote in her memoir, *Finding My Voice: My Journey to the West Wing and the Path Forward*, that the campaign took too long to respond:

> What we learned over time was that just because a baseless rumor wasn't in *The Washington Post* didn't mean a lot of people weren't hearing it, over and over again. Repetition without pushback led many people to believe the absurdities. Because this was the first presidential campaign that had to contend with the growing use of social media, we were unprepared for the convincing power of lies spread in new ways. It took us a long time, too long, to realize that by not calling out these lies and nipping them in the bud, we allowed them to gain traction.

Despite thorough debunking by fact-checkers and, somewhat belatedly, by the Obama campaign, the lie was still being discussed in conservative media when Obama took office in January 2009. Michael Steele, who became chairman of the Republican National Committee at about the same time, told my Duke students that in his first month on the job the RNC staff gave him a draft of a speech that promoted birtherism and the lie that Obama was a Muslim. Sitting at his desk, he read the speech, and then looked up at the staff, dumbfounded that they would write something so racist. He looked back down at the speech and then back up at the staff.

"You guys know I'm Black, right?" he recalled asking them. "I can't go out and say this. First off, we know this is not true. I'm not going to say this about Barack Obama. Second of all, I'm not going to talk about a Black man the way you guys are."

The narrative was set, Steele said. "The expectation for me coming in the job was, you will continue that narrative, without any thought to the fact that, as a Black man, I had to go back to a Black neighborhood and explain to my neighbors why I just said Barack Obama was not a U.S. citizen, let alone all the other stuff they wanted."

Looking back, Bauer seethes, particularly when he recalls the final White House briefing when he provided the press corps with copies of the long-form birth certificate. He's not furious at Trump, whom Bauer expected to make irresponsible lies, but at the journalists who kept discussing the birther lie as if it were a real controversy. They took Trump seriously, gave him lots of coverage, and elevated the whole thing into an unwarranted political dispute between a distinguished president and a buffoon. "In that particular episode, I think that they played a particularly unhealthy role in elevating a lie, and putting the administration or the president on the defensive on a matter that should not have occupied thirty seconds of our time," he told me in an interview. "I don't recall a single serious question that was asked of me in the press briefing room."

CHAPTER 8

Orca and the Teacher Who Wouldn't Lie

In this chapter, we meet two Republicans who wrestled with the implications of lies. The first, Tim Miller, a spokesman for the 2012 Romney presidential campaign, found himself telling lies to reporters on Election Day. In the second story, which was reported and written by my research assistant and veteran journalist Sara Israelsen-Hartley, Arizona State Senator Paul Boyer casts the deciding vote about whether to support the Big Lie, a vote that could lead to the arrests of his fellow Republicans on the local board of supervisors.

* * *

Tim Miller is one of only a handful of people I interviewed who was courageous enough to acknowledge he lied. His story from Election Day 2012, when he was a Republican National Committee staffer assigned to the Romney presidential campaign, provides a glimpse into another reason for lying: to protect a candidate from embarrassment. It is a tale of a campaign in panic mode.

The backstory: Republican strategists not only wanted to win that year, they were eager to show their technical and internet prowess after getting clobbered by the Obama campaign in 2008. The Obama campaign's mastery of social media and its sophisticated use of databases had been so dazzling that the Obama nerds had been heralded as whiz kids who would give Democrats an edge in future elections. The Republicans wanted to show they could write code too.

The Romney software developers put a lot of resources into their get-out-the-vote effort, a complicated undertaking in every campaign that tracks whether their likely supporters have gone to the polls. For years, this Election Day effort had relied to some extent on computerized voter lists, but the software developers at the Romney campaign wanted to bring it within a single application that could be accessed from anyone's smartphone. Volunteers at the polls in key states would enter the names of people who had voted, enabling the campaign to quickly identify those who had not. The goal was to create a single program that could provide up-to-the-second data about how Romney was doing and where volunteers were needed to make calls and drive people to the polls.

The engineers named the program Orca, a dig at the Obama campaign's much-hyped voter effort, which was named Narwhal. (Orcas eat narwhals.) The Romney team developed the software quickly and did not leave sufficient time for user training or for a full dry run. The day before the election, the campaign announced it with lots of confidence.

Spokeswoman Gail Gitcho told PBS that Orca would be so good that "at 5 o'clock when the exit polls come out, we won't pay attention to that. We will have had much more scientific information just based on the political operation we have set up." Romney himself made a video boasting about the program for campaign workers. "You'll be the key link in providing critical, real-time information to me and to the staff so that we can ensure that every last supporter makes it to the polls," he said. "With state-of-the-art technology and an extremely dedicated group of volunteers, our campaign will have an unprecedented advantage on Election Day."

The next morning, Orca struggled. Volunteers couldn't log in; the backup system failed. When volunteers finally started entering data, the system got overwhelmed and crashed. Some volunteers were told to record everything on paper and enter the data when Orca came back to life. It never did.

Word trickled out that Orca was in trouble. Political reporters began calling the campaign to ask if the much-hyped killer whale had failed. Miller, a Republican National Committee communications staffer based in Washington, had come to the campaign's Boston war room to help with Election Day duties. Throughout the day he did live interviews with local TV stations and chatted with national political reporters. He had always been technically savvy and comfortable with stats, so he ended up fielding a lot of the calls about the rumors that the app was having trouble.

Politico reporter Steve Friess pursued the tips and found plenty of evidence the app was in trouble. On Twitter and elsewhere, Romney supporters groused that they couldn't log in, that it lost data, or that it simply crashed. But he quoted Miller saying, "Orca is running. We're getting data here in real time. The reports were false. It's been running all day."

That was a lie. Orca was a disaster. "It totally didn't work," Miller told me in an interview for this book. "The thing went belly-up. We had no data." But campaign officials had decided they couldn't tell the truth, at least not yet. It was Election Day, and they didn't want the media to know the embarrassing news that their much-ballyhooed get-out-the-vote effort was a failure. So he spent much of the day "lying to reporters . . . saying 'data' when we know nothing. I didn't want it to get out."

At the time, he justified the lie by saying it was a short-term thing and the truth would get out eventually. He recalls one time pulling up random numbers that he found on Twitter about a precinct in Colorado, saying something like, "It's all these great signs for Mitt and Mitt's going to win!" Finally, he'd had enough. He told his boss, "It's fucking over. I can't bring myself to do that one more time."

* * *

Paul Boyer's office was more like a history professor's sanctum than a politician's war room. A plaster bust of Pericles, the fifth-century B.C. Athenian politician and general, stared piercingly from the front corner. Behind his chair was a large American flag, flanked by a print of Raphael's *School of Athens*, with a line of toga-wearing academicians crowding the long marble steps.

For ten years, Boyer juggled his elected job as an Arizona state legislator with his day job as a teacher of Humane Letters and Latin in junior and senior high school. In the mornings he taught teenagers to digest the mind-stretching works of Greek and Roman philosophers. In the afternoons he wrangled bills and budgets—six years as a representative, four years as a senator.

Boyer had the standard résumé of a lifelong Republican. Eighty-hour work weeks as a student intern on the 2004 Bush-Cheney presidential campaign in Arizona and New Mexico; an after-college stint in Washington, D.C., in the pro-Israel organization AIPAC; then back to Arizona for jobs in government communications and public relations before his first run for office in 2012. As a representative and later a senator for a suburban Phoenix district, he established himself as a solid conservative. He chaired the House Education Committee and fought for better health protections for firefighters and first responders. He is most proud of his bill that increased the state's statute of limitations, allowing victims of childhood sex abuse more time to confront their abusers in court. Boyer voted for Trump in 2020. He believes in school choice and balks at abortion.

Yet Boyer's political influences were unique.

Although he admired contemporaries like Sen. Ben Sasse (who has a doctorate in history) and former Sen. Jon Kyl, his real heroes were Cicero and Socrates. He talked about the two ancient minds as if he had had lunch with them last week. Boyer's love of history shaped how he saw the political world and his role in it. For him, the proceedings in the wood-paneled Arizona Senate chambers were merely echoes of what began in the dusty Greek agora, where philosophers and politicians first grappled with questions about the good, the true, and the beautiful.

He frequently sought guidance from Plato's *Republic*, or Cicero's *On Duties*, a collection of letters from a father to his son about how to live an upright life. Boyer kept his own dog-eared copy on his Senate floor desk. It reminded him that as an elected official—let alone a husband, father, and devout Christian—his first duty was to the truth. Not just to the words spoken but also, as Cicero cautioned, to the intent behind them.

After reciting this adage, Boyer sighed. "We don't have enough of that."

* * *

About 11:00 a.m. on February 8, 2021, Democratic State Senator Sean Bowie popped his head into Boyer's office to gauge where Boyer stood on the day's bills.

They were the odd couple of the Arizona Legislature, a Republican and Democrat, intellectual and political friends who provided support for each other when their parties were often at war. The pair's close and unusual friendship had begun two years earlier when Bowie had refused to accept a favorable legislative deal that would have sunk Boyer's statute of limitations bill.

"The fact that he was willing to stick with me on such an important issue, we began to build a level of trust that I don't have with any other members down here," Boyer said.

From that point on, the two tall, slender brown-haired politicians found themselves stopping by each other's offices almost daily to talk about upcoming bills.

A Carnegie Mellon public policy graduate, Bowie appreciated Boyer's philosophical approach to governance, while Boyer appreciated Bowie's keen eye for policy flaws. After hearing Bowie's thoughts, Boyer would often vote "no" on his own Republican colleagues' bills. Together, the bipartisan colleagues killed dozens of bills.

On this day, the focus was SR 1005, a bill that was fueled by the Big Lie that Donald Trump won the 2020 election. At seventeen lines, the bill's brevity belied its raw political purpose. It was a power grab for Trump.

The bill gave the legislature power to hold the Maricopa County Board of Supervisors in contempt—and even call for supervisors' arrests—for failing to turn over voting information demanded by a legislative subpoena. Even though Biden had already been sworn in, Republican leaders in Arizona kept parroting the "stolen election" lies coming from Trump, and believed an audit conducted by the Cyber Ninjas would prove them right. (The Florida-based company was later revealed to be funded by Trump partisan groups, through a lawsuit filed by the *Arizona Republic* asking for records of the audit, and would eventually shut down.)

Yet the county Board of Supervisors was waiting for a judge to rule on the legality of handing over sealed voting records and kept asking for more time.

That Monday morning as Bowie entered, Boyer was at his desk looking over the day's legislative calendars. "I'm going to vote 'no,'" Boyer told him.

That startled Bowie, who immediately realized this decision would make headlines.

All sixteen Republican senators had already agreed to sponsor or co-sponsor the bill—including Boyer, who said he supported it on the advice of a longtime staffer he trusted. But that didn't mean he was locked into voting for it later. And the more Boyer thought about it, the more conflicted he had become. He spent the weekend of February 6 and 7 at a ministry retreat outside Ensenada, Mexico. But instead of enjoying the beautiful Rancho El Refugio with its dusty brown and red landscapes, Boyer was going through file folders of upcoming bills, reading early in the morning and late into the night. He couldn't stop thinking about SR 1005, a momentous bill with huge implications—all to defend a lie.

Not one to talk politics outside the office (not even with his wife), Boyer kept his struggle to himself, excusing himself during Friday's dinner to take a work call. He ate street tacos and drank a Coke in the parking lot while talking to the chief of staff for the Senate Democrats, who asked him to vote "no" on the bill.

By the time Boyer arrived back in Phoenix late Sunday afternoon, his mind was made up.

"I've thought about this bill all weekend," he said, looking up from prepared notes during his speech on the Senate floor Monday morning. He told the legislators he still hoped they could reach an amicable, bipartisan solution. "My 'no' vote today will give the board time to resolve itself on how to legally proceed with providing these public records for independent sunshine and scrutiny, while also providing 100% protection for the private nature of an individual's vote. This is Arizona. We know how to walk and chew gum at the same time."

Without him, the Republicans lost. The bill failed in a 15-15 stalemate. There would be no arrests of the five-member Board of Supervisors—four of whom were also Republicans. The bogus Republican narrative about a stolen election now had a very visible dissenting Republican voice.

News of Boyer's vote hit social media and newscasts almost immediately. And suddenly he became the scapegoat for everything wrong with America.

Trump supporters posted Boyer's personal cell phone number, home address, and private email on local Gab and Telegram pages. Messages flooded in—and didn't stop for the next two years. By the evening of February 8, he had nine thousand text messages and twenty thousand emails. He lost track of the number of voicemail messages.

Most were nasty and threatening. "I usually begin with a greeting however you deserve none," came one email. "Jesus is watching and if you think for a minute that you and your family are 'safe' from this JUST WAIT!" The writer concluded: "You will go down in history as a traitor! Sincerely, An American a true American."

Trump tweeted that Boyer was a RINO and "nothing but trouble" (a moniker Boyer happily used in his Twitter profile for a while.)

"Every person is watching all over the country," another man wrote. "You blocking what the people requested goes against the constitution and WE THE PEOPLE. If you do not get back on board you will be tried for TREASON and the sentence is Hanging. No threat just truth."

Boyer set up an auto-reply that laid out a timeline and facts but occasionally couldn't help himself from replying personally. When a woman wrote: "You will not be accepted into the Gates of Heaven. Your actions have literally placed you in the pits of Hell when your time on this Earth has ended. You can be a murderer and still get to Heaven, but your black evil soul will never be saved by Jesus," Boyer wrote back asking for the scriptural references.

That conversation spanned a few heated emails before Boyer closed by writing: "I believe God will honor me for not lying to my constituents about charges of fraud based upon ignorance of Arizona election law and protocols."

* * *

Over time, Boyer grew accustomed to the threats. But that first night they were terrifying. As texts began pouring in, Boyer rushed home to gather toothbrushes, extra clothes, and diapers. He and his wife and young son would sleep somewhere else that night. Maybe for several nights.

It was a long night. He was anxious but focused as he read his email and text messages. The Maricopa County Sheriff's officers told him to keep an eye out for legitimate, specific, and first-person threats. Things like: "I am coming to your home tonight to kill you and your family." (After screening hundreds of emails, Boyer said it was strange to find himself excited about identifying potentially real threats.) He forwarded several and got a new number.

Boyer and his family didn't return home until they had a 24/7 security detail. Once home, Boyer immediately fixed his half-broken backyard gate and ordered internal security doors.

A few months later, Boyer went into the Arizona Capitol and noticed his desk was missing. A junior Republican's desk stood in his old spot—second row on the right, flanking the aisle.

Looking around, he soon found his desk—back row, left side. With the Democrats. The Republican leadership's message was less than subtle: *You're not one of us anymore.* He also became the only Republican member of the Senate who no longer received group text messages from Senate President Karen Fann. (Not a huge loss, he said. He hated group texts anyway.)

In December 2021, Boyer was named one of six Arizonans of the year by the *Arizona Republic.* All key figures in fighting the election lie, they were honored for "their integrity under fire, their backbone to stand against the high-pressure tactics of a president of the United States and for their unwillingness to yield to high authority in the state Legislature that had so obviously lost its bearings."

Across conventions, TV screens, and legislative chambers, Boyer saw more and more politicians locked in showdowns like Rock 'Em Sock 'Em Robots. Driven to win at all costs, they would say whatever it took. He couldn't even escape it at church. Parishioners saddled up next to him in the pews, wanting to argue about the 2020 election and push fringe theories of fraud. They wanted to fight and rehash the lies. Boyer wanted the truth. And the truth was Maricopa County ran a sound election. Donald Trump lost Arizona and the overall election. And Boyer was not going to lie about either one of those facts.

Eventually it became too much. Boyer needed a break from the legislature and believed he could make a difference as mayor. In 2024, following what he said were many, many requests, he ran for mayor of Glendale, a Phoenix suburb. Defending a political position against ideological attacks is one thing, but when truth becomes totally malleable and something to be ignored, that's a different battle.

As with most things, he found a parallel between his own experience and that of his historical hero. Around 406 BC, Socrates refused to go along with an illegal decision of the Athenian Council despite threats of arrest and potential violence.

"I made up my mind that I would run the risk," Socrates said, "having law and justice with me, rather than take part in your injustice because I feared imprisonment and death."

Boyer has read this dozens of times, in a variety of translations. His favorite is a more modern take: "Death is something I couldn't care less about, but that my whole concern is not to do anything unjust or impious."

The ancient echoes are unmistakable.

"You've got this historical example of a guy who valued the truth so much he was willing to risk his life over it," Boyer said, "not just in word, but in deed. And so, that, for me, is something I carry with me."

CHAPTER 9

Patterns of Lying

When I lied to Brian from Michigan on C-SPAN, I had a pretty good idea of the real score. I knew Brian was right that Republicans had a worse record than Democrats. But how lopsided was it? Although PolitiFact kept individual report cards back then, we didn't keep an overall tally by party. Today, because major fact-checking organizations enter their work into a database called ClaimReview, we have an easy way to add up everyone's fact-checks and see the score. Fact-checks have become data.

I wasn't alone in dodging the which-party-lies-more question. Glenn Kessler, the *Washington Post* Fact Checker, had long used a line like mine to duck the pesky Brians. The line had once been largely true for Kessler, but he had noticed that Republicans had gradually earned more four-Pinocchio ratings, his equivalent of Pants on Fire, since he began writing the Fact Checker column in 2011. A longtime *Post* reporter with extensive credentials, he had covered the White House, Congress, the State Department, airline safety, and Wall Street before he became well-known as the Fact Checker. In his first couple of years, he found there was roughly a partisan balance to the falsehoods. Then, the balance changed.

"I would always be asked that question when I gave a speech," Kessler told me in 2022. "I would always sidestep it like, 'Oh . . . they're both equal.' You can't say that anymore." He now says the fact that Republicans lie more "is a problem . . . it's a real problem."

Kessler cites two factors in the GOP's decline. An early one was Newt Gingrich, who Kessler found had lied boldly beginning with his rise in the 1990s and stoked the party's distrust of facts and experts. But the bigger problem was the ascendence of Trump and his impact on elected officials throughout the party. "Trump legitimized lying," Kessler told me. "It's not really about policies anymore; it's about power. And Trump showed you could be president and not have real policies, only be consumed with power, and you could lie with impunity and not be punished by your supporters for it." Kessler said the new generation of Republicans—Lauren Boebert, Marjorie Taylor Greene, and Josh Hawley, among others—mimicked Trump's behavior, making preposterous claims that were catnip for the right-wing media and the MAGA audience.

So Kessler and I had noticed that Republicans lied more. But did the data from our sites back that up? To find out, my research team analyzed fact-checks from PolitiFact and the *Post*.

We began with thousands of PolitiFact checks. We removed groups and nonpoliticians that get checked, such as bloggers, conspiracy theorists, and assorted Facebook members whose claims had spread misinformation. We also removed Donald Trump, because we wanted to assess the GOP without his outsized impact on the data. Once we removed Trump and the nonpoliticians and sorted people by party, we ended with 1,284 Democratic claims and 1,099 Republican claims for January 2016 through June 2021.

It's important to note that our data has limitations. Although the ClaimReview database provides a new and creative way to analyze political falsehoods, it is a product of journalists, not social scientists. The articles were created for readers based on the daily decisions of editors and reporters about what is newsworthy and relevant to check. It is not a random sample. Still, it has been used by other academic researchers because it's the best data available for analyzing the accuracy of politicians' claims.

Our hunch about the partisan divide was right. For PolitiFact, the results confirmed our hypothesis regardless of whether my team combined the claims into a "false-ish" category (those rated Mostly False, False, and Pants on Fire) or we looked at those ratings individually. For Democrats, false-ish ratings accounted for 31.3 percent of all the claims; for Republicans, the share was significantly higher—55.9 percent.

When my team examined the data by rating, the divide was even more stark. Pants on Fire claims accounted for three times as many of the Republican claims (7.0 percent) than the Democratic claims (2.3 percent). And Republicans had twice as many rated False.

Others have analyzed the work of PolitiFact and seen similar patterns. Researchers at George Mason University examined 100 PolitiFact fact-checks in 2013 and found Republican claims were rated False three times as often as Democratic claims. Eric Ostermeier, a University of Minnesota research fellow, analyzed 511 checks in 2010–2011 and found a similar ratio—76 percent of the 98 statements that were rated False or Pants on Fire were from Republicans. (The authors of both studies suggested that the pattern was a function of selection bias, which I address later in this chapter.)

How about Kessler? He uses a scale of one to four Pinocchios to assess the accuracy of a claim. The Geppetto Checkmark is awarded for statements that are "unexpectedly true," One Pinocchio is comparable to PolitiFact's Mostly True, Two Pinocchios is similar to Half True, Three Pinocchios is Mostly False, and Four Pinocchios is roughly the same as False/Pants on Fire. (An important note on his scale: He primarily checks statements that fall at the false end of the spectrum, so politicians from both parties rarely earn Geppetto Checkmarks or One Pinocchio.) According to our tally of 456 claims in 2016–2021 (which also removed Trump), about 75 percent of Republican claims earned Three or Four Pinocchios, compared with 59.1 percent of Democratic claims. And because he had kept his own tally for his early years, our data confirmed his belief that the Republicans' record had deteriorated. In 2011, Republicans were slightly worse than Democrats, but they had declined sharply by the period we studied, which ended in 2021.

Overall, the PolitiFact and *Washington Post* data was clear: Republicans lied more—and they lied worse.

Why are they such big liars? I posed that question to a broad group of people in politics: elected officials, journalists, campaign operatives, and current and former members of Congress. Several are former Republicans who left the party because of Trump, so they brought special insights about GOP behavior.

Miller, who worked as a communications director for Jeb Bush, Mitt Romney, and other GOP candidates before he left the party because of Trump, said there are sharp differences in the parties' cultures that affect the accuracy of the messages. "The type of person that's drawn to Republican political campaigns is much more nihilistic, much more of a person that just wants to win at all costs, does not care that deeply about the issues. And the type of person drawn to Democratic campaigns is almost, sometimes to a fault, earnest."

Matthew Dowd, a former media consultant who worked for Democrats and Republicans (including President George W. Bush), mentioned the same cultural difference. He said that Democrats feel a deep responsibility to get the facts correct while many Republicans often don't care. Democrats "take on shame way too fast, and Republicans have none," said Dowd, who has advised politicians ranging from Sen. Lloyd Bentsen, a Texas Democrat, to California governor Arnold Schwarzenegger, a Republican. "Depending upon the outlet that's confronting them, they'll take it [lying] as a badge of honor." Chris Quinn, the editor of Cleveland.com who established a policy against publishing comments of falsehood-spewing candidates, put it more bluntly: "The Democrats care that you call them a liar. The Republicans don't."

Trump has cemented the culture of lying and the party's elected officials don't want to challenge him, said Steele, the former chairman of the Republican National Committee. "A lot of that's driven by the fact that they know what the consequences are, but they are too afraid to say or do anything about it," he told my students in February 2021. "I think the party has spiraled itself into a hole."

Former senator Gary Hart said he didn't believe there was an imbalance until Trump came along. He prompted other Republicans "to repeat his untruths at every opportunity. This is a major deviation from most of American history and very damaging to public confidence in and trust in government."

At the state level, this pressure has driven many election officials to go along with Republican lies about the vote in 2020, said Michigan secretary of state Jocelyn Benson, a Democrat. "That's the root of it, that they're fearful of what could happen to them politically if they speak out," she said.

Al Franken, the former Democratic senator from Minnesota, told me that lying has been part of the Republican ethos since the early 1990s. "Gingrich used it, and they haven't stopped," he said over breakfast one morning in New York. "And it's just gotten worse and worse because of these outlets, because of Fox, and then because of social media.... They all do it now."

The stark cultural difference hinders Democrats. Valerie Jarrett, a longtime aide to President Obama, told me Democrats fret about small stuff while Republicans just lie: "Democrats often try to be accurate and give long explanations. Republicans, on the other hand, opt for repeating the pithy sound bite without being concerned with it being accurate."

Several people I interviewed said Republicans believe lying is justified because they see victory as part of an epic struggle. Denver Riggleman, a former Republican member of Congress from Virginia, told me, "If you believe you're in an existential battle for the souls of Americans, if you believe that millions of people are making bad decisions based on globalists, the deep state, or you believe that somehow a secular America is overwhelming the basic underpinnings of our Constitution... When you start to sort of add all that together, why is lying so bad?"

Riggleman said he saw plenty of lying from Democrats during his one term in Congress, but that "on the right, there's a different energy, there's a different power there. Because in some respects, they do believe this is a battle [of] good and evil."

There also is an air of desperation that motivates Republicans to lie, some Democrats said. As their base shrinks—a core of older white conservatives gradually being overtaken by younger nonwhite voters—GOP leaders have turned to the politics of grievance to fire up their faithful. "If you're the party that basically has to rely on white, conservative, mostly male support, then your whole political infrastructure is evaporating around you," said Mike McCurry, the White House press secretary for President Clinton. "So you've got to fight against that or find ways to counter that. And so what you have to do is invent these narratives that will actually keep your people aroused."

Stuart Stevens, a longtime Republican consultant, watched that happen in slow motion over the last few decades. He finally left his consulting firm and wrote a book called *It Was All a Lie* because he felt GOP leaders abandoned their principles. "When the reality doesn't meet with your political necessity, you lie," he said. "Lying is basically trying to change the rules of the game. It's a form of cheating, and no one ever tries to change the rules of a game they're winning."

Party leaders had an opportunity to recognize and adapt to the changing demographics. But they decided to use a narrow, cynical strategy that used race and fear. "There was another course to take, which was to adapt and change and do what it takes to earn the trust of the majority of the country—and the Republican Party has failed to do that. So it has to lie," Stevens said. "If you are trying to motivate people on fear . . . you have to scare white people. You have to invent caravans of people who are coming. . . . You have to invent Mexican rapists at the door."

The GOP is misleading its voters, said David Jolly, a Republican member of Congress from Florida in 2014 to 2017 who later left the party. "They're suggesting that in these cultural fights for greater justice on issues of race or economy or economic disparity, that somehow, if greater equality is brought to America at large, it's a zero-sum equation; [one group's gains] must take from people who currently have it," Jolly told my students. He said a more truthful approach is to explain that equal justice "doesn't take from somebody else to provide it to disenfranchised communities. Republicans are unwilling to listen to that because they give away their game if they acknowledge the truthfulness of that."

The party's long distrust of the news media also creates an easy justification for lying. Conservative pundits and politicians were quick to label the rise of fact-checking just another overreach by the liberal media. Republican voters, already skeptical of the mainstream media, had a new watchdog they didn't believe. "They're naturally going to care less about elites tut-tutting over the truth," said Miller. "And some of it is top-down because they've been told not to trust the 'arbiters of truth.'" Eric Jotkoff, a communications strategist in many Democratic campaigns, said the Republicans prefer to use outlets such as Facebook, Fox News, and talk radio stations, which seldom check their claims. "Increasingly you have one party that strives to be factual and accurate and one party who actually takes pride in not being factual or accurate."

There's some irony here. Conservatives adopted an underdog mentality about the media and continue to invoke it—even though they have the No. 1 cable news channel and dominate talk radio. Kevin Madden, a former Republican communications aide, said they believe "that they're outnumbered and that they're never going to get the benefit of the doubt from the biased media," and therefore, "you're going to throw some more elbows."

That mentality in turn makes them willing to accept and spread ridiculous claims. They don't care what the media says. Getting called out for a falsehood "is a badge of honor," said Dowd. That enables the party's elected officials and their media enablers to push preposterous claims like "The Ministry of Truth is going to censor Biden's opponents" and feel no guilt.

Anita Dunn, a White House adviser to President Biden, told me that while Democrats sweat the details on a speech or talking point, the Republicans blithely ignore the facts because they know they get away with it and score easy points. "And they also know that especially given the way social media works now when they put something out there, it becomes a fact very quickly," she told me.

WHAT THEY LIE ABOUT

With such a rich database now at our fingertips, our Duke team decided to explore another question: What subjects do politicians lie about?

To answer that, our Duke team used 1,016 PolitiFact claims that had been rated Mostly False, False, or Pants on Fire. The team once again used our database of all claims by politicians, leaving out Trump so he would not have a disproportionate influence on the results. They tagged those claims in two categories— the nature of the lie and the issue.

The nature of the lie involved three broad aspects that included self/personal record, legislation, and opponent's record. An easy way to think of these is through the prism of the campaign ads you see. The nature of the lie is if the ad attacks an opponent's biography/record or if it boasts about the candidate or legislation they've passed.

The issues involved topics ranging from abortion to religion to voting/elections. Their prevalence reflected the parties' main narratives and what was relevant in the time period we studied, 2016–2021, the first five years of ClaimReview (which also largely matched the years of Trump's campaign and presidency). Our analysis of the topics showed how issues ebb and flow. For example, there were not as many falsehoods about abortion as we expected. (Abortion became a major campaign issue in the 2022 election after the Supreme Court's decision in the Dobbs case.) We also noticed waves of popularity for other topics as parties used them in talking points and attacks. For example, immigration surged as a topic in 2017 after Trump took office and began talking about building a border wall. Health, a category that included falsehoods about Obamacare, was not as high as we expected because other issues had replaced it by 2016 when our ClaimReview database began.

The most common topic for both parties was a category we called government operations, which included claims about bureaucracy, excessive spending, impeachment, and executive orders. Some typical examples: a false attack ad from then-Rep. Ted Budd that said a North Carolina Democrat got $30 million in tax money to build a luxury hotel and a false claim from Democratic Sen. Cory Booker, who cited a nonexistent Congressional Budget Office study to back up some far-fetched math about Medicare.

Next highest for Republicans (it ranked lower for Democrats—fifth) was law/crime/policing, a subject that the GOP has long used to energize its base. A typical falsehood: a Texas official's Pants on Fire claim that the state has had over six hundred thousand crimes and twelve hundred homicides committed by undocumented immigrants between 2011 and 2018. (Those numbers were about 400 percent greater than the actual ones.)

Immigration, which ranked third for Republicans, provides a case study in how a single issue can be weaponized in different types of lies. Besides using it to scare their base with ridiculous falsehoods about crime, Republicans also use it to brag about their accomplishments, attack Democrats, or attack other Republicans. They often claim their GOP opponent supported "amnesty" for immigrants. Or they use it to boast about their actions "to stop illegal immigrants from voting," or to portray Democrats as immigrant-coddling softies who let criminals and terrorists run rampant in the United States.

WHAT DEMOCRATS LIE ABOUT

This book focuses on the lying that Republicans do, but Democrats do not deserve a pass. Our analysis showed they earned a False or Pants on Fire nearly 15 percent of the time from PolitiFact and earned Four Pinocchios in nearly 34 percent of the *Washington Post* fact-checks. The bottom line is that Democrats lie a lot too.

When Kessler and I think of the most common lies by Democrats, we first think of Medicare and Social Security. Those topics have been part of the Democratic playbook for many years as the party tries to keep older voters from defecting to the GOP. You may recall the commercials, which usually relied on a grainy black-and-white photo and an ominous voice-over: *Congressman Bob voted to cut/slash/end Medicare/Social Security. We can't trust Congressman Bob with* our *future....*

There was usually a grain of truth because Bob voted for some nonbinding Republican plan to bring some fiscal responsibility to the chronically underfunded programs. Bob's vote wouldn't affect current beneficiaries, but it would require a reckoning down the road. When PolitiFact chose "Republicans voted to end Medicare" as the 2011 Lie of the Year, Kathleen Hall Jamieson, the co-founder of FactCheck.org, told me it was the longest-running Democratic deception—with roots that went back to at least 1952.

But times have changed. When our Duke team ran the numbers for Democrats in our 2016–2021 database, falsehoods about Medicare and Social Security were not at the top of the list. As noted earlier in this chapter, the No. 1 category was government operations (which included claims about bureaucracy, excessive spending, nominees, impeachment, and executive orders). Social welfare, which included Medicare and Social Security, was tied for seventh. That reflected the nature of Democratic tactics in the Trump years, when the party was focused on attacking Republicans on an array of topics ranging from budget cuts to Trump's impeachment.

When Democrats earned a False or a Pants on Fire, it was for unfounded attacks on Trump (such as one that he was "morbidly obese"), bogus claims about priorities (that his administration was "raiding money" from military pensions to pay for the border wall), or wild exaggerations about policy ("the president is cutting the CDC's budget by 80 percent"). The Democrats' falsehoods tracked their passions—overreaches about guns (a concealed-carry bill would allow residents of certain states "to walk right into a school zone with a loaded weapon"), ridiculous tax breaks for the rich ("Hedge fund managers and others in private equity pay much lower [tax] rates on their income than do truck drivers and teachers and nurses"), and voting ("There are 43 states that have now passed voter suppression laws").

When Biden earned a False/Pants on Fire or Four Pinocchios, it was for a hodgepodge of historical fumbles, ridiculous brags, policy goofs, and bad predictions. Sometimes he just seemed to dream things up. A few of his big ones from 2020–2021 ranged from his claim that "McDonald's [makes] you all sign noncompete contracts that you cannot go across town to try to get a job at Burger King" (False), to his boast that he got arrested on the way to see Nelson Mandela (Pants on Fire), to his claim that the Second Amendment prohibits people from owning a cannon (Four Pinocchios).

FEAR

Lies that use fear tap into our worries about safety, money, and freedoms. Some of these lies are from Republicans about immigrants who sneak across the border, commit violent crimes, and take American jobs. Others are from Democrats about how we might lose Medicare, Social Security, and our medications. Politicians skillfully stoke our deepest fears, raising alarm bells about school shootings and rampant crime and terrorists trying to get into the United States.

Fear isn't a new weapon, but it's perfectly suited for our modern ecosystem. Politicians take advantage of social media algorithms and the insatiable appetite of partisan cable to spread shadowy questions about the subjects of fear—and then appear as the saviors who will protect people from harm. Writing in *The Atlantic*, Molly Ball said Donald

Trump is a master of tapping into this interconnected network of rage and worry: "Trump channels people's anger, but he salves their fear with promises of protection, toughness, strength. It is a feedback loop: He stirs up people's latent fears, then offers himself as the only solution."

Fear works. A 2015 review of more than fifty years of research found that appeals that tapped into fear were more than twice as effective than those that did not. Some of the most famous political ads use scare tactics, such as the one that supporters of George H. W. Bush ran against Michael Dukakis in 1988 that came to be known as the Willie Horton ad. It appeared to be a commercial comparing the two candidates' positions on crime. But its use of race—showing a photograph of Horton, a Black man who had raped a white woman and stabbed her partner while furloughed from prison when Dukakis was governor—triggered white voters' racial anxieties.

COULD THE LYING BE EQUAL?

As I finished writing this chapter, I considered a fundamental question: Was I wrong? Could my data be skewed by selection bias by the fact-checkers? Was it possible that lying was more equal than I believed? Some conservatives say that's the case.

Neil Newhouse, the Republican pollster, was blunt with me that fact-checkers were biased. "Both sides stretch the truth," he said in an interview. "It's not like Republicans have a fucking monopoly on stretching the truth in advertising or what they say. So for fact-checkers to find an overwhelming number of instances where it's Republicans over Democrats, my argument is, well, they're obviously not looking at the right places, or [Republican campaigns] are not doing a good enough job pointing them in the right places."

He summed up: "I think there are inaccuracies on both sides; both sides will stretch the truth in order to make a point and that both sides do this equally."

John Feehery, a longtime Republican operative on Capitol Hill, told me that the disparity I found in the fact-checking data does not reflect reality: "More fact-checkers are Democrats. . . . It's about their bias." Madden told me the same thing. He thinks fact-checkers give a distorted depiction of reality by choosing more false claims for Republicans. He said, "Democrats get off too easy."

Many conservatives said PolitiFact was biased. To reach that conclusion, critics could simply add up our Truth-O-Meter ratings. A May 2013 news release from George Mason University's Center for Media and Public Affairs examined 100 PolitiFact fact-checks from early 2013 and found that Republicans were rated False three times more often than Democrats. (A similar GMU tally a year earlier found PolitiFact gave Republicans False ratings by a two-to-one margin compared with a roughly even count for the *Post* Fact Checker.) The release called it "a study," but it does not appear to have been published in any academic journal. The release included a quote from Robert Lichter, then the director of George Mason's Center for Media and Public Affairs, that suggested PolitiFact was out of step with reality: "While Republicans see a credibility gap in the Obama administration, PolitiFact rates Republicans as the less credible party." But Lichter offered no details to back up that quote and did not explore what else PolitiFact could have checked.

At the University of Minnesota, Eric Ostermeier wrote a post in 2011 on his Smart Politics website that was titled "Selection Bias? PolitiFact Rates Republican Statements as False at 3 Times the Rate of Democrats." Ostermeier counted the ratings for 511 fact-checks in 2010 and early 2011 and found that Republican statements earned False or Pants on Fire ratings 39 percent of the time, compared with just 12 percent for Democrats.

But like Lichter, Ostermeier did not offer any significant analysis to back his allegations. He noted some comments I made to C-SPAN and the *New York Times* about the importance of our work and my explanation of how we chose claims to check, and he focused on a quote I made that while it was politics, we treated it like a sport. He concluded his post by saying: "By levying 23 Pants on Fire ratings to Republicans over the past year compared to just 4 to Democrats, it appears the sport of choice is game hunting—and the game is elephants."

When people have raised questions about possible bias, PolitiFact editors for years have explained the criteria for choosing what gets checked:

- Is the statement rooted in a fact that is verifiable? We don't check opinions, and we recognize that in the world of speechmaking and political rhetoric, there is license for hyperbole.

- Does the statement seem misleading or sound wrong?

- Is the statement significant? We avoid minor "gotchas" on claims that are obviously a slip of the tongue.

- Is the statement likely to be passed on and repeated by others?

- Would a typical person hear or read the statement and wonder: Is that true?

> We select statements about topics that are in the news. Without keeping count, we try to select facts to check from both Democrats and Republicans. At the same time, we more often fact-check the party that holds power or people who repeatedly make attention-getting or misleading statements.

The fact that PolitiFact editors don't keep count by party is important because it reduces the pressure for false balance. Although we would occasionally glance at the home page and say, "We haven't checked a Democrat [or a Republican] in a while," it helped make sure that our editors and reporters never felt pressure to even the score. The daily decisions about what to check were based on the most significant claims that readers would be curious about.

Another suspicion by conservatives is that we employed an army of liberal fact-checkers. (In 2012, Republicans claimed a PolitiFact Virginia reporter was biased because he had voted in Democratic primaries.)

Actually, I hired about a half-dozen reporters and editors, and I never asked any of them about their political viewpoints, their voting history, or their party affiliation (we permitted reporters and editors to register by party). I believe it's probably true that fact-checkers, like other journalists, are more likely to be liberal. But all political journalists are expected to put aside their own viewpoints, and it seemed ours always did. We made it clear they were expected to be nonpartisan in their work—and I found they were.

It's important to note that Democrats and their own allies in the media saw an opposite reality about our work. They said fact-checkers were so afraid of being called biased that they awarded unwarranted False or Four Pinocchio ratings to show they were balanced. Dan Kennedy, a longtime media critic in Boston, wrote that the fact-checkers' false equivalency became a serious problem in the age of Trump. "Despite the media's admirably tough-minded stance on Trump's falsehoods, they are nevertheless holding Democrats to a much higher standard," he wrote in a commentary for WGBH.

Democrats complained about Kessler doing this, particularly in his fact-checks on Bernie Sanders. They said he nitpicked to an extreme. Likewise, they complained when PolitiFact chose the Democratic line that "Republicans want to end Medicare" as the 2011 "Lie of the Year." In a blog post titled "PolitiFact, R.I.P.," *New York Times* columnist Paul Krugman said: "The people at PolitiFact are terrified of being considered partisan if they acknowledge the clear fact that there's a lot more lying on one side of the political divide than on the other. So they've bent over backwards to appear 'balanced'—and in the process made themselves useless and irrelevant."

So were we biased against the Republicans? Or were we practicing false equivalency against the Democrats? Many days I felt like a basketball referee. Neither team would be happy unless I called the entire game in their favor. Both sides were right that we occasionally made a bad call with individual Truth-O-Meter ratings. I edited thousands of fact-checks and, as with any profession that requires many judgments, days or weeks later I would sometimes have qualms that a small number were off, usually by a notch.

But weighing all the complaints—I've read and considered lots of them since I started PolitiFact in 2007—I have never seen sufficient evidence that we missed enough False or Pants on Fire claims by Democrats to make a difference. Selection bias doesn't cause the difference. Our ratings simply reflect what's happening in the real world.

I noticed the trend of more GOP falsehoods when I was covering Congress in the late 1990s, long before I became a fact-checker, and the disparity has simply become more pronounced. In fact, looking at the data from Kessler's Pinocchios and PolitiFact's Truth-O-Meter, I believe the numbers actually *understate* the magnitude of the lying from Republicans and their supporters in the partisan media.

Take, for example, the many lies told about Nina Jankowicz and the Disinformation Governance Board. There were hundreds told by Republican members of the House and Senate, by people on Fox, by hosts on talk radio, and by people on Facebook and Twitter. How many of those claims got examined by fact-checkers and others in the news media?

One.

The Associated Press checked the claim that Jankowicz wanted to edit people's tweets. Kessler and PolitiFact produced no fact-checks on that or any other claims about Jankowicz or the board. (PolitiFact published a Q&A about the controversy, but there were no Truth-O-Meter ratings.)

Or take the hundreds (thousands?) of lies about the 2020 election told by Republicans in the House, where 139 of the members voted not to certify the election. Relatively few of those House Republicans got called out by national or local fact-checkers. That's because the national organizations do relatively little local work and there are few local fact-checkers. In a typical year, only a small percentage of rank-and-file members of Congress ever get fact-checked on anything, according to a 2023 report by my team at the Duke Reporters' Lab.

I truly wish that Newhouse was correct that the number of lies from Republicans and Democrats was equal. Imagine how that would improve our political discourse! It would help us have genuine discussions about important topics like climate change and immigration—topics with such disparity in lying that the parties now cannot have a serious conversation.

No, the problem in our political journalism is not the bias of the fact-checkers, but that there are too few of them for the gusher of falsehoods that spews from the mouths of our politicians every day.

The reality is clear: Republicans lie more, and they lie worse.

CHAPTER 10

The Jeep Lie

On a mild evening in October 2012, Mitt Romney bounded onto a stage to the upbeat chords of Kid Rock's "Born Free." He was in Defiance, Ohio, a town with a long history in auto manufacturing and a nicely metaphorical name for telling a whopper. He gave man-hugs to Gov. John Kasich and Sen. Rob Portman, fellow Republicans who had been warming up the crowd, and then launched into a twenty-two-minute speech. He accused President Obama of lying—and told a lie of his own. "I saw a story today," he said, "that one of the great manufacturers in this state, Jeep—now owned by the Italians—is thinking of moving all production to China."

That sentence, which Chrysler, Jeep's corporate owner, had declared hours earlier was untrue, was a calculated move by Romney to win a crucial state in the final days of a tight race. And his campaign kept it up: For days, they repeated the lie in TV ads despite statements from Chrysler, despite quadruple Pinocchios and Pants on Fire Truth-O-Meters and countless other debunks by fact-checking journalists—not to mention a barrage of attacks from the Obama campaign and even an internal "conscientious objector," a senior Romney aide who pleaded with the campaign's top strategist to stop the ad.

The story of the Jeep ad is a case study in how political operatives make a calculated decision to lie and try to justify it. It also reveals the inner workings of a presidential campaign that was staffed by talented people but at times could be dysfunctional. It begins, like so many political lies, with a grain of truth.

* * *

Demand for Jeep SUVs in Asia was so strong in 2012 that the company wanted to start producing them there. On October 22, three days before Romney's rally in Defiance, Bloomberg broke the news that the company was considering adding an assembly plant in China to build all its models. (A note on the nesting-doll organization of the companies: Fiat was majority owner of Chrysler, which owned the Jeep brand.) The Bloomberg story said Fiat "plans to return Jeep output to China and may eventually make all of its models in that country." The story noted that "Chrysler currently builds all Jeep SUV models at plants in Michigan, Illinois and Ohio" and clarified that this move would be "adding Jeep production sites rather than shifting output from North America to China."

On October 25, the lie sprouted. Paul Bedard, a columnist at the conservative *Washington Examiner*, took the accurate Bloomberg story and twisted it into a false attack on Obama. "In another potential blow for the president's Ohio reelection campaign, Jeep, the rugged brand President Obama once said symbolized American freedom, is considering giving up on the United States and shifting production to China," Bedard wrote. "Such a move would crash the economy in towns like Toledo, Ohio, where Jeeps are made and supplied, and rob the community of the economic security they thought Obama's auto bailout assured them." It got amplified by the Drudge Report, the influential aggregator that in 2012 could boost an article's traffic by hundreds of thousands of pageviews. The Drudge link said: "JEEP eyes shifting production to China."

Chrysler spokesman Gualberto Ranieri quickly debunked the column with a snarky statement on the company's blog:

> Let's set the record straight: Jeep has no intention of shifting production of its Jeep models out of North America to China. It's simply reviewing the opportunities to return Jeep output to China for the world's largest auto market. U.S. Jeep assembly lines will continue to stay in operation. A careful and unbiased reading of the Bloomberg take would have saved unnecessary fantasies and extravagant comments.

But Bedard's fantasy was too good for the Romney campaign to resist. It was a perfect line to use in Defiance because General Motors had long been the largest employer in the area, and Romney needed to regain some cred after he had opposed the bailout of the auto industry in 2008. In Defiance, Romney vowed that he would "fight for every good job in America. I'm going to fight to make sure trade is fair, and if it's fair America will win."

In repeating the lie, Romney hid behind a fig leaf of attribution, starting his sentence with "I saw a story today that said . . ." But that gave him little cover when journalists began a thorough debunking. "Romney cites incorrect auto-manufacturing claim in Ohio," said CBS. "Romney Repeats False Claim of Jeep Outsourcing to China; Chrysler Refutes Story," said the *Detroit Free Press*. The story said that "Romney's comments were immediately skewered by auto industry observers and Romney's political opponents because Chrysler added about 7,000 workers in the U.S. and Canada since emerging from Chapter 11 bankruptcy in 2009."

There was lots of harrumphing from the Obama campaign and its allies. Obama spokesmen called Romney "blatantly false" and said he "shamefully tried to scare voters." MSNBC host Al Sharpton said, "That's not even remotely true." Ed Schultz, another host, began the night's *Ed Show* by saying, "Mitt Romney tells his biggest lie to date. You won't believe this one." *Washington Post* columnist E. J. Dionne Jr. seemed flabbergasted. "I've been around campaigns for a long time and I honestly haven't seen somebody push beyond the edge of the truth so often and say things that are just so flatly untrue." Democratic Sen.

Sherrod Brown called it "incredibly irresponsible for a presidential candidate to scare people up there by telling them, 'I just read the other day that all of your jobs are going off shore' when just the opposite is true." The president of the United Auto Workers union chimed in: "It seems that every time Mitt Romney attempts to talk about the auto industry and how much he cares about American workers, he fumbles."

The timing and location of this skirmish was important. Nationwide the race was close, and Ohio was considered a toss-up. Romney's nightly tracking polls showed the race so tight that it was within the margin of error. On the electoral map, there was virtually no way he could win the election without Ohio. So despite the blowback, the campaign decided to go even bigger with the Jeep lie.

* * *

In a profession full of characters with odd habits and big personalities, Stuart Stevens still managed to stand out. He was so much more than a "political consultant," the catch-all term for the spinmeisters and image-meisters who advise candidates and write and produce the ads that have been the staples of modern political campaigns for sixty years. Stevens, who was then in his late fifties, also has been a novelist, a food critic (he and a friend wrote a book about eating at all of Europe's twenty-nine Michelin three-star restaurants), and a TV producer and writer (his credits include *Northern Exposure* and the short-lived *K Street*, among others). He was a lover of endurance sports who skied and competed in Ironman triathlons.

He had straw-blond hair and a face weathered from hours in the sun and wind. He was called senior strategist in the Romney campaign, which gave him lots of influence in an organization that some Republicans worried had become dysfunctional. Mike Allen and Jim VandeHei wrote in *Politico* that Stevens had too many duties: "In what many in the campaign now consider a fundamental design flaw, Stevens is doing three major jobs: chief strategist, chief ad maker and chief speechwriter."

In Ohio, a state with auto plants in thirteen counties, Stevens had a big challenge. Romney had family ties to the auto industry—his father had been the president of American Motors Corporation—but he had struggled to win support from autoworkers and their allies because he had opposed the 2008 government bailout of GM and Chrysler. Another sore point: His 2008 op-ed in the *New York Times* had been headlined "Let Detroit Go Bankrupt," which conjured an image that the companies would go belly-up. The full article was actually a nuanced argument for a managed bankruptcy with a few government protections. But the Obama campaign had used the headline in countless TV ads and mailings.

To Stevens, the Jeep news was a juicy opportunity. If he played it right, the campaign could regain some ground on Obama and erase memories of that stupid headline. Romney could mention it in Defiance and then Stevens would rush it onto the air as a commercial. He wasn't deterred by the blowback from journalists and the Obama campaign. He didn't bother showing the ad to a test audience. He just charged ahead.

Stevens had Hollywood cred, but the Jeep ad was not particularly cinematic. It was a standard-issue political commercial with a mishmash of people driving cars and being stuck in traffic and cars being crushed in a junkyard, plus a familiar-sounding narrator. The ad said Romney would do more for the auto industry than Obama, it cited PolitiFact to claim that Obama's attacks on Romney had been wrong, and it contained an artful sentence that essentially said Jeep was moving all production out of the United States: "Obama took GM and Chrysler into bankruptcy, and sold Chrysler to Italians who are going to build Jeeps in China."

* * *

As chief strategist/chief ad maker/chief speechwriter, Stevens had lots of freedom to write and produce the ad with little oversight. He put it together in about a day, writing the ad on his laptop and producing it the day after Romney's speech in Defiance. But at some point as it was about to air, Kevin Madden saw a preview and warned him that it was going to backfire.

Madden, then forty years old, was a longtime spokesman for Republican politicians and campaigns. Before Romney, he worked for House Republican leaders Tom DeLay and John Boehner as well as President Bush's 2004 reelection campaign. He was widely respected by the Washington press corps because he was considered a truth teller in a job where many others weren't. He had anchorman good looks and had been No. 2 on *The Hill*'s "Most Beautiful" list. He dropped f-bombs like a longshoreman, which further endeared him to political reporters, who wished they could say those things in print and on the air. He took the truth-teller part seriously. His reputation was on the line as much as the campaign organization, because if Stevens lied in an ad, it was Madden who had to go on television and try to explain it, a practice he called "eating a shitburger."

At this particular moment in the roller-coaster ride of the Romney campaign, he was blunt with Stevens, whom he regarded as an egotistical lone wolf. He thought Stevens was focused too much on the daily headlines and not enough on the broader themes that should power the campaign's message. The Jeep ad seemed particularly hypocritical because Romney had been hammered for investing in businesses that moved operations to other countries to reduce labor costs. But this was a case of a U.S. product being so successful that the company was expanding production in another country, not shifting its operations offshore.

Stevens held his ground, claiming that any new Jeep production in China meant they weren't being produced in the United States and therefore those jobs were lost to U.S. workers. Madden told him reporters covering the campaign wouldn't buy that. "The facts don't actually support what you're saying. You fucking made a mistake. Admit it. We're going to take a hit on this."

They went back and forth. Madden recalled that at one point Stevens said, "It's an ad, not a white paper." Madden was incensed. "I can't defend this ad," he said. "I've got to go fucking eat this shitburger." But with Stevens's lofty triple title, there was no opportunity to appeal. Madden resigned himself to a miserable forty-eight hours responding to reporters.

When they asked, he dodged the question. "I remember just going round and round with the press on it saying, 'Look, we believe that we have a better manufacturing policy, we have a better plan for Detroit and growing Detroit and expanding Detroit' . . . whatever. I never really answered the question because I didn't believe that the ad was smart, and I fucking said that internally. But the ad's already out. We're going to pay a huge price on this because this ad sucks, and it's not true." He later referred to himself as a "conscientious objector."

How could Stevens be so clueless? Madden had predicted exactly what was going to happen. The false ad—another blunder by the Romney campaign!—would be *the narrative* for the political media for the next few days rather than anything Romney said or did. The campaign would be back on its heels playing defense.

The fact that Stevens could create the ad with little collaboration illustrated the dysfunction of the campaign, Madden recalled. It had not emerged from voter surveys, nor was it suggested by the campaign's pollster, Newhouse. Indeed, when I asked Newhouse about it, his reply was something like, "What ad?"—because he wasn't even in the loop about it. No, it just emerged after Stevens saw the Bloomberg story. Romney must have approved of the strategy since he uttered the line in Defiance, and his approval message is on the ad. And after Defiance, Stevens decided to double down and defend the ad.

Said Madden, "This is what happens when you have an ad guy who's also serving as your lead strategist dream something up and then thinks he's got an 'Aha!' moment. And when it doesn't come together, you have a very disjointed team effort trying to contain the damage. . . . A winning campaign on that would be like, 'We fucked up. Let's minimize this. Let's go do something else here.' It did not happen that way."

* * *

The ad first aired on Saturday, October 27, two days after the rally in Defiance. Unlike many TV spots, which are announced to the media and often previewed on *Morning Joe*, this one wasn't—a strong clue that Stevens knew he was about to get pummeled.

He did. The Obama campaign saw the ad in Toledo and quickly distributed it to reporters. That led, as the Obama campaign had hoped, to a series of fact-checks and opinion columns that called out the Romney campaign for the Jeep lie.

Glenn Kessler, the *Washington Post* Fact Checker: "The series of statements in the ad individually may be technically correct, but the overall message of the ad is clearly misleading—especially since it appears to have been designed to piggyback off of Romney's gross misstatement that Chrysler was moving Ohio factory jobs to China.... Four Pinocchios."

Michael Tomasky in The Daily Beast: "There's basic dishonesty and then there's f-you dishonesty—dishonesty so blatant, so consciously abusive of facts that everyone knows, that it deserves a category of its own.... Romney's new ad about Jeeps and Italy is f-you dishonest."

PolitiFact: "The ad ignores the return of American jobs to Chrysler Jeep plants in the United States, and it presents the manufacture of Jeeps in China as a threat, rather than an opportunity to sell cars made in China to Chinese consumers. It strings together facts in a way that presents a wholly inaccurate picture... Pants on Fire."

Jonathan Cohn in the *New Republic*: "Of course, this kind of deception is emblematic of the campaign Romney and his supporters have waged in the last few days. They insist Romney never thought government should let Chrysler and GM collapse. But Romney's vague and inconsistent rhetoric included statements that he would have opted for a 'private sector bailout'—something that was not possible in 2009, because private investors were in no position to make the necessary loans."

The editorial board of the *Cleveland Plain Dealer*: "In one sentence, Romney presses hot buttons about bankruptcy—though he, too, favored that route, albeit without direct federal investment—foreigners and outsourcing. It's a masterpiece of misdirection."

Chrysler Group chief executive Sergio Marchionne issued a statement: "I feel obliged to unambiguously restate our position: Jeep production will not be moved from the United States to China." He cited numbers to illustrate the company's commitment to U.S. production and concluded by saying, "Jeep assembly lines will remain in operation in the United States and will constitute the backbone of the brand. It is inaccurate to suggest anything different."

Only a handful of Republicans piped up in favor of the ad. The campaign issued a statement from running mate Paul Ryan, and Republican Rep. Jason Chaffetz of Utah appeared on Andrea Mitchell's show on MSNBC and called the ad "one hundred percent correct and accurate. The Romney campaign stands behind it. The reality is, what Fiat is doing and the way they're going to outsource and put Jeep and others overseas, it's accurate."

Donald Trump got into a dustup on Twitter with Chrysler executive Ralph Gilles. "Obama is a terrible negotiator. He bails out Chrysler and now Chrysler wants to send all Jeep manufacturing to China—and will!" he tweeted. Gilles replied: "You are full of shit!" In a second tweet, Gilles added: "I apologize for my language, but lies are just that, lies."

The fact that there weren't more defenders says a lot about the lie. At a time when the Romney campaign needed reinforcements, it appears from the news coverage that it was primarily Madden and an occasional unnamed campaign spokesperson who were defending the Jeeps-in-China narrative. The response was weak and failed to match the muscular Democratic effort.

The Obama campaign pounced on the unforced error. "Ladies and gentlemen, have they no shame?" Vice President Biden asked during a campaign rally with Bill Clinton in Youngstown. He said Romney's claims were "bizarre" and that "this guy pirouettes more than a ballerina."

Meanwhile, Madden's fears had come true. As he predicted, the campaign was spending hours responding to reporters who wanted to know how this ad could be so wrong, particularly since Chrysler had been so clear with its denial. Madden's comment to reporters showed how he tap-danced around the lie: "The ad makes the point that the governor believes that we need a strong auto industry and that he'd have a better policy that would help the auto industry be a strong part of a growing American economy. And the ad speaks for itself."

The Obama team had been using Romney's "Let Detroit Go Bankrupt" headline in every attack they could—in countless speeches, ads, and mailings. The stumble by Stevens had not only given them another opportunity; it allowed them to call Romney a liar. "We really saw it as an opportunity," recalled Jim Margolis, the head of Obama's ad team. "We were playing heavy, heavy in Ohio, and we had the firepower to do that." Margolis's team quickly made a response ad that said: "Chrysler itself has refuted Romney's lie."

Madden doesn't recall when Romney's ad stopped running but said it probably just got replaced after a couple of days, as ads typically do. He was happy to move on.

* * *

A week later, Ohio went blue.

Obama, who carried the state by three points, won counties with major auto plants but did not win Defiance, a GOP stronghold. The brouhaha over the Jeep lie and Romney's comments on the auto bailout seemed to have a modest dampening effect in the Republican areas where he might have performed better. University of Akron political science professor Daniel Coffey said the issue "probably prevented the Romney campaign from doing better among white working-class voters."

In December, when senior editors at PolitiFact chose the 2012 Lie of the Year, our deliberations didn't take long. There were a few other contenders (such as Romney's claim that Obama went on "an apology tour" and an Obama claim that Romney backed a bill that outlaws all abortions), but none had been so reckless as the Jeep lie.

"People often say that politicians don't pay a price for deception, but this time was different: A flood of negative press coverage rained down on the Romney campaign, and he failed to turn the tide in Ohio, the most important state in the presidential election," then–deputy editor Angie Drobnic Holan wrote in our announcement story.

Holan noted that fact-checkers had unanimously called out Romney for the false ad and his remarks in Defiance. The episode was, in many ways, an early triumph for fact-checking journalists. She pointed out that Newhouse, Romney's pollster, had made headlines during the summer's Republican National Convention when he said, "We're not going to let our campaign be dictated by fact-checkers." In the case of the Jeep ad, the Romney team followed that script and doubled down to defend the lie—and found virtually no support.

Obama strategist David Axelrod said the ad was overtaken by the counter-message from Chrysler and fact-checkers saying it was false. "The controversy surrounding the ad became a focus of news coverage," he told PolitiFact. "At the end of the campaign, when everybody is watching everything closely . . . They just weren't going to get away with it. It was a very high-risk strategy, and it backfired."

Kessler named the ad in his list of biggest Pinocchios of 2012, noting it was "a sign of desperation." He recounted the facts and said, "Even more remarkable, the Romney campaign fiercely defended the ad, even as it came under harsh criticism from, among others, Chrysler." FactCheck.org included the Defiance speech and the ad in its annual list of "Whoppers." Managing Editor Lori Robertson quoted the ad that "Obama took GM and Chrysler into bankruptcy, and sold Chrysler to Italians who are going to build Jeeps in China" and then said, "That's a lot of misinformation in a single sentence."

* * *

Stevens created the whole mess but managed to keep his head down and let Madden take the incoming fire. Yet when I reached out to talk with Stevens for this book, he not only was willing to explain the ad, he wouldn't stop talking.

He began by saying he was wary of the auto industry's promises and amazed that reporters would take Chrysler at its word. "Call me skeptical if I don't exactly believe the auto industry, which has a record of consistent mendacity, dating from its origins," he said. He then made his argument, which can be summed up as this: By starting any production in China, Jeep was missing an opportunity to expand its production in the United States and export the vehicles to China. That meant the jobs were not being added in the United States.

Of course, that's not what Romney said in Defiance, nor what the ad implied. Here's an excerpt from our interview:

Me: Let's be honest here. What you were trying to do was scare people into thinking that because of Obama, Jeep was moving all of its production to China.

Stevens: What I was trying to do is say in the context of it, they're taking these tax dollars to expand. First of all, they sold it to an Italian company, which they didn't say they were going to do when they got the bailout. And now they were expanding it and they were making a decision. So if I had written an ad [that said]: "Instead of hiring you, your neighbor, or extending your hours on the line, they decided to hire a Chinese [worker]." That would've been a true statement.

Me: (Amazed at his relentless spinning) You're so good at this. I do admire you.

Stevens: Well, I'm right! I'm right! . . .

Me: Why is it the case that every fact-checker said that the ad was false?

Stevens: Because, what was their source? Fiat. You had a situation where the people who had been in the business of calling the Big Three liars for decades went to the Big Three as a credible source of information. I find that embarrassing.

I reminded him that the ad was rated Pants on Fire by PolitiFact. If he were checking it, what rating would he give it? Mostly True? Half True? He ducked the question and said it depended on what percentage of Jeeps is made in the United States today. (Of course, the percentage of domestic production in the future wasn't known when the ad was shown in 2012, and fact-checkers have a general rule that they assess a claim on the knowledge available at the time it was made.)

He summed up with the not-quite-definitive, "I still don't know that the ad wasn't one hundred percent right."

CHAPTER 11

Working the Refs

In a 1992 meeting with the *Washington Post*, Republican National Committee chair Rich Bond revealed one of his party's secrets to manipulating the news media. The strategy, Bond said to the room full of reporters and editors, was to *constantly* complain that the coverage was unfair. He likened it to lessons he'd learned coaching his kids' basketball and baseball teams. He said great coaches "work the refs" after an unfavorable call so that "maybe the ref will cut you a little slack on the next one."

For decades, that's been a key part of the Republican strategy with the media: complaining about bias so much that journalists cut some slack the next time. It's worked. The party has been so relentless with its *you're-biased-against-us* refrain that political reporters have pulled their punches. Fearful of blowback, journalists have packed their stories with false balance and failed to point out the glaring disparity in how the parties lie. They've ignored hypocrisy and underplayed the GOP's growing threat to democracy, all because the Republicans have been so good at working the ref.

Lately, the GOP and its allies have boldly expanded this strategy by taking aim at government, academia, and major tech companies so they can neutralize even more institutions that threaten to call out the party for its lies. By using lawsuits, a new panel from Rep. Jim Jordan called the Select Subcommittee on the Weaponization of the Federal

Government, and support from conservative media and elected officials around the country, the Republicans have shrewdly applied the lessons they learned from decades of bullying the media. They've used an impressive arsenal of lawsuits, congressional hearings, subpoenas, Freedom of Information requests, and supportive howls from right-wing journalists to expand their strategy of intimidation.

Jeff Jarvis, a journalist and media researcher, said the party has been smart and effective. "Republicans and authoritarians know how to exploit the weak underbelly of enlightened democracy," he told me. "They recognized, more than anything else, the weaknesses in mainstream mass media—which is to say that our obsession over the years with 'balance' was easy to exploit."

Emboldened by the success of media intimidation, the Republicans are aiming bigger. To see where they're headed, just follow their use of quotation marks, which they use to belittle and discredit things. Ten years ago when the fact-checking movement picked up momentum, conservative sites responded by putting "fact-checking" in quotes to signal its illegitimacy. Now conservatives have begun doing that with "misinformation" and "disinformation":

> *Jim Jordan launches "misinformation" investigation to uncover Biden "censorship" scheme —Washington Examiner*

> *Left-Wing Groups Urge Congress to Help Censor "Climate Disinformation"* —Daily Caller

> *US Dept. of Defense to Detect "Disinformation" with The Help of AI—Will Crack Down on Conservatives in Social Media despite Current Lawsuits* —The Gateway Pundit

The Republican strategy is energized by themes the party has used for years: "Big Tech wants to censor us"; "academia is too liberal"; and "government meddles too much." With Republicans and their allies repeating those themes as part of a sprawling, sustained campaign, it can have a powerful effect in clearing the landscape to allow more lying.

* * *

To put their new strategy in perspective, it helps to look back and see how the right's perception of media bias began. Today, many people associate the bias complaints with Roger Ailes and his early work with Richard Nixon. But the complaints actually started in the 1940s and '50s, and they built as more of a simmer than the full-volume outrage that we are accustomed to today.

In *Messengers of the Right: Conservative Media and the Transformation of American Politics*, historian Nicole Hemmer shows how the movement gradually built momentum over several decades. The conservative journal *Human Events* was founded in 1944 by veteran editors from the *Washington Post*, the *New York Post*, and the *Christian Science Monitor* who believed the mainstream media was slanting the news to downplay criticism about U.S. involvement in World War II. *Human Events* evolved into a journal of conservative thought with a mission statement that said the publication's goal was "accurate representation of the facts. But it is not impartial. It looks at events through the eyes that are biased in favor of limited constitutional government, local self-government, private enterprise and individual freedom."

Back then, conservatives felt they were stymied by liberals who did not want to give a platform to ideas from the right, so the conservatives had to be scrappy and innovative in their efforts to build a large audience. Hemmer said they used shorter shows on the radio, which gave them an opportunity to reach people in their cars, and they launched their own publishing houses to work around the existing liberal-owned publishers and get their books in front of more readers.

They were aided by an influential writer at *TV Guide*, Edith Efron, whose articles and data analysis confirmed conservative suspicions about liberal bias. Using the techniques of a social scientist, she assessed the bias of the TV networks' coverage of the 1968 election by counting whether words spoken were favorable or negative for Richard Nixon and Hubert Humphrey. The results were striking: About half were positive for Humphrey. But for Nixon, only 8.7 percent were.

As the movement for a right-wing media grew, it shaped conservatives' identity in an important way, Hemmer says. They weren't just idealogues. They also were *outsiders*, rebels fighting to overturn the status quo. They began to think of themselves as "an oppressed minority," which sunk in and became part of their DNA. That underdog belief continues today even though there is much more parity. The right dominates talk radio and has the top cable news network, Fox.

Conservative media also provided a friendly home for conspiracy theorists. Some outlets became connected with the John Birch Society, which warned of the threat of a global communist takeover; others said that President Johnson had been involved in murders. That coziness between right-wing media and the conspiracy believers laid the foundation for the way unfounded theories about the death of Vince Foster and President Obama's birthplace sprouted in right-wing media and then got mainstream coverage—and the way that bogus claims from Pizzagate to QAnon continue to sprout today.

When Roger Ailes came onto the scene to advise President Nixon and other Republicans, he found lots of frustration with the mainstream media. By then, there was a strong belief that liberal bias was making it difficult for Nixon to get fair treatment from the journalists covering the White House. As Nixon put it once to his aides, "The press is the enemy. They are all against us."

When Ailes ran Fox from 1996 until 2016, he had a big stage to attack liberal bias . . . with *conservative* bias. At his kickoff news conference, Ailes even had the chutzpah to claim that he was going to use objective journalism to respond to the lefty mainstream media. At the news conference, he said his "fair and balanced" coverage was going to "unblur" the lines between opinion and news. He said on-screen graphics would clearly label news and opinion (a promise that wasn't kept).

Instead, Ailes built a network on the lie of fairness and fooled millions of viewers that their diet of right-wing opinion was actually a balanced, nutritious meal of news. Today, Fox is a daily pep rally against the liberal media, from digs in the morning on *Fox & Friends* ("the corrupt and complicit mainstream media") to full-frontal attacks from Hannity ("If Donald Trump had this history, do you think the mainstream media mob would give him a pass?").

That pep rally leads to pressure on mainstream political journalists suggesting that they are too liberal. Every day they hear complaints—some vague, some specific—that "the media" is too liberal. (The villain is usually *the media*, even though that term could encompass everything from a liberal site such as that of *The Nation* to a conservative one like Breitbart.) When I covered campaign rallies, I heard it from voters who said they were tired of biased media and wanted just the facts. On Capitol Hill, I heard it from Republican members and staffers who were cordial but often sneaked in a dig about how the MSM was out to get them.

Said Eric Alterman, a longtime media critic and a professor of English and journalism at Brooklyn College–CUNY, "They've terrorized the mainstream media into being afraid to call candidates on their lies."

* * *

In 2020, as Donald Trump's lies about voting by mail and absentee ballots began to swirl, researchers launched a bold project to identify the falsehoods and try to reduce their spread on social media. The idea originated with four Stanford University students who did internships at the Cybersecurity and Infrastructure Security Agency, a DHS group that helps to coordinate cybersecurity for government and the private sector. When they returned, the students convinced Stanford researchers to create the project, which was launched with the University of Washington and other groups one hundred days before the 2020 election. They called it the Election Integrity Partnership.

Two well-respected academic centers led the project: Stanford's Internet Observatory, a small, influential center in Silicon Valley that produced timely reports on trust and safety, and the University of Washington Center for an Informed Public, a hub for studying misinformation.

Researchers studying misinformation often do their work by conducting controlled experiments and then sit back like they're watching a specimen grow in a petri dish. But the teams from the University of Washington and Stanford were led by a unique group of computer scientists and former tech executives who wanted to take action in the real world. The result was a remarkable effort that managed to stop dozens of election lies. The project worked like this:

Organizations ranging from local election offices to the AARP would pass along a report of something they saw or heard, usually from social media, that they believed would give people inaccurate information about voting. It might be a post on Twitter or Facebook about dead people voting or ballots allegedly marked with Sharpies that were not being counted. Rumors based on the posts often had spread rapidly. A team of analysts at the EIP assessed the relevance, severity, and accuracy of each claim. The most significant false claims were tagged for possible action.

The analysts would talk with journalists or sometimes make a recommendation to the social media companies about whether the post should be deleted or demoted so it was seen by a smaller audience, or they would suggest that a fact-check label be added to it. The social media companies took action for 35 percent of the posts that were reported—21 percent were labeled; 13 percent were removed; and 1 percent were soft-blocked, which meant they could be found only by searches. No action was taken for 65 percent of the posts that the EIP reported to the companies.

The Long Fuse, the hefty 273-page report that described their work, might have been ignored by Jordan and his allies if it weren't for its central finding: The election lies came overwhelmingly from the right.

And the report named names, the people and publications that were the biggest offenders at spreading the lies: Donald Trump, his family, and conservative sites such as The Gateway Pundit, FoxNews.com, and Breitbart. Unlike many academic papers, which often rely on euphemisms or dodge controversy by avoiding the partisan labels, a chart listing the twenty-one top spreaders was clear about their political orientation. In the column "Left or Right," all were from the right.

That's why, years later, the partnership was still being attacked by Jordan's new weaponization subcommittee and its pals in the conservative media—and why the owner of The Gateway Pundit filed a lawsuit in federal court in Louisiana (a friendly venue for conservatives) against the researchers and groups involved in the EIP. In November 2023, Jordan's committee released a report titled "THE WEAPONIZATION OF 'DISINFORMATION' PSEUDO-EXPERTS AND BUREAUCRATS: HOW THE FEDERAL GOVERNMENT PARTNERED WITH UNIVERSITIES TO CENSOR AMERICANS' POLITICAL SPEECH" (note that the committee put "Disinformation" in quotes). The Gateway Pundit suit began: "This case challenges probably the largest mass-surveillance and mass-censorship program in American history." (The Gateway Pundit suit was filed by America First Legal, a group headed by Stephen Miller, a senior aide in the Trump White House.)

Put aside that over-the-top language for a moment, and the report and lawsuit actually raise some questions worth discussing: How should social media companies moderate their content when people post lies, particularly about elections and public health? What role should the government play in raising questions about misinformation? How should those entities interact when there are false claims circulating? Brendan Nyhan, a political scientist at Dartmouth College, told me the Stanford-UW partnership did good work but that it relied on too much coziness between the academics, the government representatives, and the tech companies and did not provide enough transparency about the process.

Unfortunately, those are topics for a serious policy conversation, which of course is something that our political leaders rarely have these days. The lawsuit and Jordan's report were not about starting a serious conversation. They were a part of the growing effort to work the ref, to neutralize the broad array of players who call out the lies. In fact, Renée DiResta, who helped lead Stanford's effort in the election partnership, reminded me about the political history of Jordan and other 2020 election deniers who are involved: "All of these people who perpetuated the Big Lie in very direct ways are now also attacking the researchers who studied the Big Lie."

* * *

Of the people involved in the partnership, no one knew the ins and outs of working a ref better than Kate Starbird, a highly regarded computer scientist and misinformation expert who headed the University of Washington's portion of the project. Starbird was remarkable for many reasons. After she earned her doctorate in technology, media, and society (her dissertation was a hopeful study about "digital volunteerism" during disruptive events such as earthquakes), she embarked on her second career studying and combating misinformation. But her experience with refs came from her first career, when she was a professional basketball player.

Starbird, a six-foot-one shooting guard, had played at Stanford, where she earned her computer science degree and scored 2,215 total points, a school record she held for eleven years. She was named the Naismith College Player of the Year in 1997 and helped the team get to three Final Fours. After graduation, she played for professional teams in the United States and Europe. When I asked her whether Jordan and his allies were working the ref with their subpoenas and hearings, she quickly saw the parallels to basketball—and her answers shed great insight on the Republicans' new tactics.

First, she said, working a referee in basketball can be effective, particularly for teams that play dirty and are trying to persuade a less-experienced ref. It can be done effectively by coaches and even a crowd, but less often by players. "Working the ref works all the time," she said. "You've been in the game where the other team's playing super-dirty, and the refs eventually are like, 'Oh, we're calling too many fouls on one team. We've got to stop calling fouls' . . . and it becomes a very physical game. That's why physical teams can sometimes use that to their advantage."

She addressed the political comparison: "Where this metaphor really works is working the ref where you've got one team that's really dirty and they're trying to get the ref to call it equal by calling it balanced and the same number of infractions on each team," she said. (Hmmmm. That sounded to me like what Republicans have done with the media.) In basketball (and perhaps in political journalism?), it's about trying to get the ref to "stop calling infractions on the more physical team." She said weak referees "can be easy targets."

The Stanford team included two well-known researchers, former Facebook chief security officer Alex Stamos and DiResta, a computer scientist who eventually got fed up with the conspiracy theories that right-wingers pushed on social media. The theories weren't just falsehoods about the partnership's work in the 2020 election—although there were plenty of those—there also were ridiculous personal attacks about her, including one about a college fellowship she did at the CIA. She'd been labeled "#DeepStateDiResta," likened to Hitler, and called "pure evil."

DiResta tried to maintain a sense of humor about the attacks, declaring in her bio on Threads that she was the "Main character of 5 Twitter Files fantasy epics" (a reference to the Elon Musk document dump known as the Twitter Files, which had fueled many right-wing conspiracy theories) and that she "runs the world" from the Stanford Internet Observatory. In real life, she was a computer scientist who had worked for tech start-ups and got interested in disinformation when she was a new mom who noticed how anti-vaxxers were using social media to exaggerate their influence. She ended up at the observatory.

DiResta had a wry outlook on the silly lies told about her and would even call herself by the nickname some conspiracy theorists used—CIA Renée. Yes, she had been a college intern for the CIA, but in response to the conspiracy claim that "you never really *leave* the CIA," she would say, "My God! You do in fact *leave*! They take away your clearance and they stop paying you." "I don't know where this bullshit comes from," she told me. "People watch too many movies."

She was weary of "the right-wing crankosphere" that had twisted the facts about her work and her life. She said the conservatives relied on innuendo and simply regurgitated the same suspicions over and over. They had twisted the truth so much that "facts don't matter" to their audience. "They're propagandists who created a cinematic universe and made me a character."

One example: The EIP had analyzed 22 million tweets that had words or URLs relevant to the group's work about the election. But the critics grossly distorted that, saying the EIP "censored" or "flagged" those 22 million for removal by Twitter. DiResta said that ultimately Twitter decided to remove only a couple of hundred tweets because they violated the company's policies.

Both DiResta and Starbird had been attacked by trolls on social media and faced a blizzard of requests and subpoenas from Jordan's committee for emails and interviews. Starbird had been called "Comrade" and a Stalinist and smeared for her gender presentation, among other things. Because she worked for a public university, she also received dozens of public records requests that were clearly more harassment than legitimate inquiry. Starbird sat for a closed-door interview with the committee (as Nina Jankowicz had done), but DiResta declined to be interviewed. She wanted her entire testimony to be public.

The panel was indeed a weaponization committee—using the muscle of a congressional inquiry to try to silence the researchers. Said DiResta, "Harassment is designed to shut you up and intimidate you."

Starbird and DiResta had some things in common with Jankowicz. They all had been attacked by Republicans and conservative media, they all had endured personal attacks and threats, and they all worked for large institutions that had responded sluggishly to the conservative barrage. Just as the Department of Homeland Security and the Biden White House were clueless and ill prepared for the onslaught about the "Ministry of Truth," Stanford and the University of Washington also were slow to respond. "Whether they're universities or other kinds of institutions, they are incredibly vulnerable targets, and in terms of the communications strategies, they're not up to this moment," Starbird told me. "I think, in part, that's because the playbook for how to deal with these is broken."

In the summer of 2022, when the attacks began, Starbird said she wanted to "get our truth out into the world. And I was told repeatedly by just about everyone, 'Don't do it. Silence is better. It's going to go away.' And I was like, 'This is not going to go away. I can tell this is going to have legs.'"

That's a frequent disagreement about how to respond to political lies. Some people believe that it's not worthwhile to respond because it just prolongs the controversy. DiResta agrees it's not worth engaging directly with the critics but says it's still vital to get the facts out quickly and clearly for other audiences. She knows they won't persuade the hard-core believers on the far right, but they need to be available for "the bulwarks," people such as Mike Pence and former attorney general Bill Barr. They had been dependable supporters of Trump, but after the 2020 election they played crucial roles in resisting the Big Lie.

The Republicans, always clever about the words and phrases they used, were quick to redefine the most ordinary actions as censorship. It was a brash move to put academic researchers and the tech companies on the defensive. "'Censored,' to them, does not mean taken down. It does not mean disappeared from the Internet. It does not mean the account is actioned," said DiResta. "It simply means that it did not have the sort of mass distribution that they think it should have or it had a fact-check appended to it. . . . A fact-check is censorship in this cinematic universe." Any effort to combat misinformation was often considered part of the broad conspiracy they called the "Censorship Industrial Complex."

* * *

One key to the Republicans' effectiveness is that they appear to be so coordinated, like there's a commander back in some headquarters watching giant TV monitors and making sure they all use the same (false) talking points and that everyone pursues parallel strategies to harass the researchers and the government. Is there a single leader here? How coordinated is all of this?

When I asked Starbird this, she noted her expertise: She studies conspiracy theories. But . . . she uses that term sparingly. "I'm always a little hesitant to over-ascribe coordination in terms of explicit coordination when things are more like a flock of birds (in which they keep an eye on others, and if a few birds start to go in one direction, often the whole group follows). In this case, it's somewhere in between. There's some coordinated things. There's some funders that are doing things [to support the effort]." They're aided, but not necessarily coordinated with, "some random Substack superstars who are making a living putting this stuff out there, and they're doing it for a different set of reasons than some of these politically funded folks, but it's beneficial." Some of the people involved are true believers in the lies and others are political opportunists, Starbird said.

Everyone has a slightly different motivation, some political, some financial, but they are all in sync, all working toward a common purpose. So, yes, there's evidence of coordination, enough to justify a Netflix series (you can picture the conspirators meeting in a diner), but maybe not enough to call it a conspiracy.

(It's worth noting that the Republicans and their allies often target women. In the same way they unleashed a relentless blitz against Jankowicz, they chose to go after DiResta and Starbird far more than a man with a similar high-profile role in the partnership, former Facebook security chief Alex Stamos.)

Lawsuits have also become a formidable weapon of intimidation, particularly one filed by the attorney general of Missouri against the

Biden administration. It claimed the federal government had pressured the social media companies to censor conservatives. (The case was originally known as *Missouri v. Biden,* but when it reached the U.S. Supreme Court, it was renamed *Murthy v. Missouri.*) The case was initiated by Missouri's litigious attorney general, Eric Schmitt, who had filed many suits against the Biden administration before he was elected to the U.S. Senate. Jim Hoft, the owner of The Gateway Pundit, joined this suit, too.

Starbird and DiResta said the lawsuits were all part of the right wing's "lawfare," a broad but loosely coordinated effort to delegitimize misinformation research. When you combine the suits with the subpoenas and hyperbole-filled reports from Jordan's committee, they could have a long-lasting impact on researchers at universities around the nation.

As DiResta noted, there is an immediate one: Researchers of the Big Lie are being grilled by a partisan committee and having to defend themselves in the courts. But the effort seems to have a wider goal of intimidating all misinformation researchers. Although Stanford and the University of Washington have provided legal support for DiResta and Starbird, other universities may not have the resources or the willingness to put up with subpoenas and possible legal fights. Nyhan said he is "worried about the potential chilling effect" of the congressional action and the lawsuit. Ultimately, the universities could discourage research into misinformation. Why go through the hassle?

But Starbird was defiant, writing in a *Seattle Times* op-ed: "We're not buckling and we won't be bullied."

* * *

Government, though, *can* be bullied.

Legislators can simply pass a law that puts restrictions on what an agency can do. They can defund the agency or put limits on how money can be spent. When the Disinformation Governance Board was still alive, that's exactly what a host of Republicans threatened to do—to strip the agency's funding. The "Ministry of Truth" would simply disappear.

So as Republicans issue subpoenas and hold hearings and file lawsuits to ultimately create a frictionless landscape for their lying, neutralizing government is the easiest piece. They also can mobilize their voters to say they don't want government to fight "disinformation." Sometimes all it takes is repetition to intimidate officials at all levels, as their work with Biden's Department of Homeland Security showed. The administration caved under pressure, even though the criticism was built on lies.

At the local level, Republicans have so thoroughly cowed elections officials that some are afraid to utter the word "misinformation." Marion County, Florida, elections supervisor Wesley Wilcox, a Republican, has stopped using the word because people in his party see it as code for censorship of conservatives. "In Republican circles, 'misinformation' is a dog whistle," Wilcox told NPR. "All of a sudden, man, you got skewered if you even mention the word."

Not only is the word toxic, but local officials don't even want to acknowledge that the *problem* of misinformation exists. NPR reported that officials were so worried about a conservative backlash that an election partnership that Wilcox helped manage stopped promoting a service that allowed local officials to report false voting information online.

Republican officials and conservative websites also have taken aim at the Global Engagement Center, a small State Department agency that monitors disinformation outside the United States, by claiming, with hardly any evidence, that the agency is censoring conservative sites inside the United States. Texas attorney general Ken Paxton and the conservative sites The Daily Wire and The Federalist claimed in a lawsuit that the agency, through some distant connections with other organizations, was engaged in "one of the most audacious, manipulative, secretive, and gravest abuses of power and infringements of First Amendment rights by the federal government in American history."

The lawsuit had more hyperbole than specifics. It relied on some pretty tenuous connections between groups that didn't seem to be doing what the suit alleged they were doing. And James Rubin, the head of the agency, had been emphatic that his group was exclusively focused on disinformation *overseas*. But that didn't matter because the Republicans' exercise seemed to be all about working the ref, stirring up a fuss about a legitimate effort to combat misinformation and disinformation.

My Duke colleague Philip M. Napoli, a communications scholar, said the whole approach is an exercise in agnotology (politically induced ignorance) and pointed out the ridiculous irony of their actions. In a 2024 paper, he wrote that they are supposed to be pushing back against the weaponization of the federal government, but in the process, they are actually weaponizing the First Amendment. Jarvis said Republicans have achieved something that in the past would have been unimaginable. They've made the simple concept of a fact into something partisan:

> The right wing has gotten to the point that defending fact is becoming de facto left wing. Defending facts becomes a forbidden behavior. That's one matter to go after you and the media. It's another matter to say government can't do it, because if government defends facts, then they're attacking the right wing, they're taking a side.

* * *

After the January 6, 2021, attack on the Capitol, social media companies took action to stop Donald Trump from spreading lies. Meta kicked him off Facebook and Instagram. YouTube suspended his account, and Twitter, then publicly owned, stopped him from tweeting. "After close review of recent Tweets from the @realDonaldTrump account and the context around them we have permanently suspended the account due to the risk of further incitement of violence," Twitter wrote. The companies took similar action against other people and groups that were spreading election lies.

But Trump's "permanent suspension" wasn't very permanent. Elon Musk, who bought Twitter in April 2022 and then renamed it X, restored Trump's account later that year. Meta allowed him back on Facebook and Instagram, though with heightened penalties if he violated the rules. "The fact is people will always say all kinds of things on the internet. We default to letting people speak, even when what they have to say is distasteful or factually wrong," Nick Clegg, Meta's president of global affairs, wrote in a statement. "Democracy is messy and people should be able to make their voices heard." YouTube, owned by Google, not only reinstated his account but also announced it would no longer remove videos that promote election falsehoods.

Collectively, the social media companies have backed away from the aggressive stance they took in early 2021. They seem to have adopted Clegg's approach that lying is okay and somehow readers will sort it out. I wish that were the case. Take Meta, for example. It has the most extensive fact-checking program of the social media companies, but that didn't stop the lies that infect people such as Eric Barber.

Starbird said the tech companies are now afraid to experiment with ways to curtail the spread of falsehoods. The ones that are doing it "won't even talk about it anymore. The folks that don't want to be stopped in spreading misinformation . . . have been very effective at making that kind of work toxic."

It is, she said, "working the ref, so the ref just stops."

CHAPTER 12

The Ministry of Truth, Part 3

DECEMBER 2022: RAGE CLEANING

As Christmas neared, Jankowicz found herself in cycles of frustration and anger. It had been a chaotic year, with epic highs and lows. She loved being a new mom to her son, who was now an adorable and amazing six-month-old. For a few months, she was in an exciting new job. But that job had quickly become the worst experience she'd ever had, subjecting Jankowicz to constant ridicule and making her fear for her life.

The house was a mess because she had spent so much of her time dealing with the latest incoming attacks. A new letter from Josh Hawley had stirred up a fresh round of harassment against her (it peaked on Thanksgiving, of all days). And now that Republicans had narrowly won the House, Rep. Jim Jordan, likely to be the new chairman of the Judiciary Committee, was making noise about calling her to testify. Jankowicz threw herself into some rage cleaning to get the house ready for the Christmas tree and try to cleanse her frustrations from the year. But she was still frustrated and bitter.

"I don't even know if it would qualify psychologically as PTSD, but I'm not normal at work anymore," she told me in early December. "Every little thing that happens to me, I think that everything is about to blow up and I have screwed something up."

To no one's surprise, the Homeland Security Advisory Council, which was charged with reviewing the Disinformation Governance Board, had reported back that the board was not necessary. That gave Mayorkas the green light to finally make the pause permanent and kill the board. The Department of Homeland Security issued a statement that read like the inscription on a tombstone: "In accordance with the HSAC's prior recommendation, Secretary of Homeland Security Alejandro N. Mayorkas has terminated the Disinformation Governance Board and rescinded its charter effective today, August 24, 2022."

In its statement, the advisory council said the board's mission still mattered. It said DHS "must be able to address the disinformation threat streams that can undermine the security of our homeland," citing falsehoods about computer updates or foreign-influence efforts to undermine U.S. elections. The report called for more coordination within DHS—essentially, having a Disinformation Governance Board without having a Disinformation Governance Board. (The committee had interviewed nineteen "subject matter experts and other witnesses" for its report but did not talk with one obvious choice: Jankowicz.)

Despite the termination of the board, attacks against Jankowicz had resumed on Twitter and Fox and elsewhere. They stemmed partly from a new letter Hawley had sent to Mayorkas, complaining that the secretary had not answered the questions from the letter he and Grassley sent back in June. The letter confused the steering committee that set up the Disinformation Governance Board with the actual board and used classic techniques of conspiracy theorists, such as mixing theories with facts and putting scary phrases in quotation marks to suggest there were shenanigans when there was no actual evidence. "The documents further show that the Disinformation Board's Executive Director, Nina Jankowicz, repeatedly pushed for DHS to establish an 'analytic exchange' with 'industry partners'—possibly a portal for Big Tech companies to coordinate speech suppression with the government." (Note the "possibly" in that sentence.)

The fresh harassment also was prompted by Jankowicz's new job with the Centre for Information Resilience, a London-based organization that conducts research and highlights the global problems of disinformation, particularly from Russia. Jankowicz planned to focus on attacks on women and minorities. Because she was working with a group based in the U.K., she had to register with the U.S. Justice Department as a foreign agent, a routine requirement for anyone who "acts as a foreign principal's public relations counsel, publicity agent, information-service employee, or political consultant."

Cue the outrage! She was a *foreign agent*! The headline on MediaBusters made it sound like she was betraying her country: "Benedict Arnold: Nina Jankowicz Registers as Foreign Agent to Fight So-Called Disinfo." Most of the stories in conservative media accurately recounted the dry facts of her registration but failed to explain that the registration was routine for anyone doing that kind of work for a company outside the United States.

"White House's former 'disinformation czar' Nina Jankowicz registers as a foreign agent" screamed the bold headline on the Fox News website. It included the usual photos of her singing as Mary Poppins and an archived one from an MSNBC appearance with the chyron "DISINFORMATION AGENCY FACES OWN DISINFORMATION CRISIS." (Fox, in a rare gesture of fairness, reached out to her for a quote—and then didn't include it.)

On BlazeTV, host Pat Gray (whose show on YouTube had thirty-eight thousand subscribers) mentioned the registration without explaining why it was required or how it worked. He made it sound like she was now an enemy: "She now has been registered as a foreign representative under the Foreign Agents Registration Act on behalf of the Center for Information Resilience, which is a British organization. It's good to know. That could have been our disinformation czar right there. Talk about dodging a bullet. Wow."

Jankowicz's biggest antagonist was now Jordan, one of the most hard-line conservatives in the House. (Former Speaker John Boehner, a fellow Republican, once said of him, "I just never saw a guy who spent more time tearing things apart—never building anything, never putting anything together.") He had written to Jankowicz on December 1 signaling his plans to seek her testimony when he became chairman of the Judiciary Committee. He complained she hadn't responded to a May letter he'd sent and said: "Since then, new information has come to light about the Biden Administration's embrace of government-driven censorship and its effort to 'police disinformation.'" He reiterated his request for her to be interviewed by the committee. It was time for Jankowicz to lawyer up.

Her winter gloom was compounded by the feeling that she was just a convenient villain for their moneymaking schemes. The Republicans raised money by claiming they were crusading against her (remarkable because she'd been out of government for six months); Fox and other media platforms used her for ratings and clickbait. The truth didn't matter. They just kept lying.

"It's very profitable for them to continue to smear me," she said in our interview. "I'm just an easy target. The administration put up no fight. Fox News brought me up again this morning in regard to these continued discussions of anti-conservative bias at Twitter and all this stuff. It makes a great narrative for them and it's just easy." Lying about her also was easy for Jordan and the Republicans taking control of the House because they now had more power. "They know that they've caught me between a rock and a hard place because if I don't comply with their investigations—even if I'm the most boring version of myself—they're going to find something to rip apart."

She felt abandoned by the Biden administration and her bosses at DHS, who had offered no support during the ongoing attacks. "Yeah, I'm screwed up for life. Thank you, DHS. All because I decided to do something in my area of expertise and serve my country."

* * *

Photos and screengrabs of Jankowicz—as herself in front of the DHS flag, as Mary Poppins, as the cabaret singer, and every other unflattering photo they could find—had been published in hundreds of places and been seen by millions of people. Between her appearances on Twitter, conservative websites, prime-time television, YouTube, Newsmax, the One America News Network, and C-SPAN, she had become a recognizable figure to much of conservative America.

She realized this when she was meeting one of her lawyers at Northside Social, the trendy coffeehouse in Arlington where I had first interviewed her. Some random guy took a photo that she initially presumed was just a picture of the whole room. But that evening, her husband saw it on social media with a caption like "Just having coffee with Nina Jankowicz right now." He introduced himself in the coffeehouse by saying, "Oh, I'm such a fan." But when she and Mike later looked him up on social media, he had said horrible things about her. Another post they found, by someone else, said something like "I just passed Nina Jankowicz on Capitol Hill, and I had to resist the urge to accost her."

One man, a self-styled "journalist," harassed her so much that she sought a protective order. In her request to the judge, she wrote: "I never know if he will show up at an event I'm attending or speaking at for my work. I never know when the material he shares will spawn a new violent threat—recently one of his viewers created their own video saying I should be 'tried for treason and hung until I'm dead.'" The protective order was granted. The whole thing was draining and cost her time and a lot of anguish—not to mention legal costs. The man then appealed, which took her additional time to fight. (She won again.)

Her husband worried about the encounters and wanted her to be more cautious—to wear a COVID mask when she traveled and use a fake name when she ordered coffee or a burger. It seemed insane what the lies had done to her life: The barista would shout, "Nina J.!" and she'd look around, scared that someone would know it was her.

Jankowicz wasn't alone. Other targets of Republican lying (and the companion smear campaigns on conservative media) have told similar stories of harassment. The Georgia election workers who won a $148 million judgment against Rudy Giuliani for his bogus claims received hundreds of racist texts, emails, and letters with messages such as "We know where you sleep" and "I'm coming for you."

SPRING 2023: A RAY OF LIGHT

For months, she thought about suing Fox. No other organization had done more to hurt her. The company had continued to villainize her long after the board had been paused and she had quit. Tucker and Hannity and Ingraham had mocked her and lied about her over and over. She wanted them to pay—not to make her rich, because she had never cared much about wealth (if she had, she wouldn't have gone into public service and wouldn't be in this predicament). No, this was about accountability, about making them pay for all the pain they had caused her. She had talked with lawyers about filing a lawsuit, but the conversations were not encouraging. The law provided lots of protections for Fox, and a lawsuit was likely to fail. The lawyers weren't interested.

Then, in early 2023, another lawsuit against Fox signaled there might be an opening. The suit had been filed in Delaware state court after the 2020 election by Dominion Voting Systems, a company that made the voting machines used in twenty-eight states. Its first sentence summed up the case: "Fox, one of the most powerful media companies in the United States, gave life to a manufactured storyline about election fraud that cast a then-little-known voting machine company called Dominion as the villain." The suit sounded similar to what Jankowicz had gone through: It claimed that for months, hosts and guests on Fox repeated falsehoods about Dominion and its products. The company's defamation suit faced a high bar to win. Dominion needed to prove that Fox employees on the shows acted with "actual malice," meaning they knew the claims were false or that they recklessly disregarded the truth.

But the suit's chances improved as Dominion's attorneys gathered emails and text messages from Fox employees, including hosts such as Carlson and Hannity. The emails and messages showed that many people at Fox, including the hosts, were aware they were airing falsehoods.

As the Dominion case picked up momentum, Jankowicz decided she would try a suit of her own. She didn't have money to hire an attorney, so she started a GoFundMe campaign. It was titled "Help Nina Hold Fox News Accountable for Its Lies." She recorded a video that explained her case with a montage of Fox segments interspersed with her own comments directly to the camera. "Fox News irrevocably changed my life when they force-fed lies about me to tens of millions of their viewers," she said. "Tens of thousands have harassed me online; hundreds have violently threatened me."

Her goal was to raise $100,000. That would help cover her legal costs for the lawsuit, get the protective order against the man who was harassing her, and pay for an attorney to help her prepare for testimony to the House committee. It was likely to be part of the new Select Subcommittee on the Weaponization of the Federal Government (Jordan and other party leaders apparently didn't see any irony in that name) that was going to investigate favorite Republican/Fox targets such as Jankowicz, the Disinformation Governance Board, and Hunter Biden's laptop.

One week after she launched the fundraising effort, donors had contributed about $40,000—a substantial amount, but far short of her $100,000 goal. Monica Showalter, a writer at the conservative site The American Thinker, belittled that as a paltry showing, saying that Jankowicz had failed as a censor and was now failing to raise enough to file a lawsuit. But then Fox and Dominion suddenly settled their lawsuit, giving Jankowicz hope. Fox agreed to pay the company $787.5 million, a staggering amount of money that showed the strength of Dominion's case. The text messages, emails, and depositions of the Fox employees had indicated that Dominion, which sought $1.6 billion in the suit, stood a high chance of prevailing if the case went to trial. Fox settled just before the trial began.

The week after the Dominion settlement, Fox fired Tucker Carlson. Jankowicz celebrated his departure on Twitter:

> Good riddance, Tucker. You have contributed more to the degradation of our democracy and the hell my family has endured for the past year than anyone else. Without any basis, you claimed I would be "policing speech" and had "men with guns" at my disposal to do so. That was the night the death threats against me and my family started. We almost had to flee our house. I was weeks away from giving birth. Your departure from Fox doesn't undo the permanent damage you have done to individuals like me who you have recklessly lied about for your personal enrichment. I hope Fox continues to face high costs for the disinformation you knowingly spread, Tucker.

For Jankowicz, the settlement was a ray of light. It signaled that Fox was vulnerable, even with the substantial burden of proof in a defamation suit. Still, she had difficulty finding lawyers willing to write and file the suit. The firm she initially hired wanted a big payment up front that she couldn't afford. She kept looking and finally found two lawyers who were committed more to the cause of getting her justice than making money.

The lawsuit, filed in Delaware state court, began: "In the spring of 2022, Defendants Fox News Network, LLC, and Fox Corporation, which hold Fox out as a trusted news organization, began a malicious campaign of destruction against Plaintiff Nina Jankowicz because hounding her was good for Fox's bottom line." In clear, powerful prose, the suit told the story she'd been aching to tell for months. It said Fox defamed her with its lies in three ways: by repeatedly saying she wanted to censor Americans' speech, by claiming she was fired by the Department of Homeland Security, and by saying that she wanted to give verified Twitter users, including herself, the power to edit others' tweets.

The suit explained the limited role of the Disinformation Governance Board and that it had "no operating authority or capability" and "no ability to intervene, respond to, or prevent the spread of disinformation. Nor did it have any power or purpose to silence speech or surveil citizens."

It documented Fox's lies in great detail and noted the smear campaign that continued long after she resigned. It said hosts and commentators referred to her as "low IQ," "illiterate," "Miss TikTok meets America's Got No Talent," "disinfo overlord," "disinformation czaress," "minister of truth," "Scary Poppins," a "useful idiot," "janko-half-witz," a "lunatic," and "the wicked witch." The suit said the network mined Jankowicz's social media and publications for material to use against her—not for balanced reporting but to smear her. "It was often deliberately misleading and at times objectively false. Fox knew exactly what it was doing."

The lawsuit said Fox had a motive for its meanness:

> And what was the point of bullying Jankowicz day in and day out? Fox's coverage was calculated to ridicule and embarrass Jankowicz because doing so reinforced a caricature of Jankowicz that fit Fox's fabricated narrative that she was an "unhinged" Orwellian "Minister of Truth," intent on policing what ordinary American citizens could and could not say.

The suit included graphic details about the harassment she'd endured. Videos from Fox segments were included in many of the online threats, the lawsuit said, and the network's content fostered an atmosphere that led to some of the most violent tweets and Facebook messages. "Kill yourself you subhuman sack of shit," said one message she received on Facebook. "Go hang yourself you leftist cunt," said another. An analysis of about 50,000 tweets that referred to her Twitter handle @wiczipedia, showed more than 350 included anti-Semitic or misogynistic attacks against her; 131 tweets threatened violence, hostile action, or advocated the use of her personal information to target her. She also received death threats by email and voicemail.

The lawsuit noted a great irony inside the headquarters of Fox. The network has a "Brainroom," a fact-checking unit that is supposed to make sure the content aired by the network is accurate. "And yet, even when the Brainroom gets the facts right, Fox will disregard its work, choosing ratings—delivered through increasingly pitched, inflammatory content—over integrity."

The suit made it clear that the network puts profits ahead of integrity. "When a conflict between ratings and the facts arises, the ratings win," the suit said. "What happened to Jankowicz was no accident; Fox has created a monster, churning out increasingly venomous content in a desperate play to retain control of the outrage machine."

Jankowicz gave the scoop about her lawsuit to the *New York Times*. The story was headlined "New Defamation Suit against Fox Signals Continued Legal Threat." She took a screengrab of the headline and made it her Twitter background.

* * *

Jim Jordan had big goals for the Judiciary Committee and its Select Subcommittee on the Weaponization of the Federal Government. Now that his party was in charge of the House (a narrow majority, which would later make finding a Speaker of the House difficult), the Ohio Republican with the square jaw and thin gray hair planned to use the Judiciary subcommittee to investigate the many misdeeds of Joe Biden and his administration—Hunter Biden's laptop, censorship of social media, and of course, the Disinformation Governance Board. (Never mind that the board had been killed six months earlier. It was still great for Fox segments and fundraising emails.) When Democrats criticized his new effort, Jordan took to the House floor to respond. "This is about the First Amendment, something you guys used to care about," he said. "And I'd actually hoped we could get bipartisan agreement on protecting the First Amendment. . . . The five rights we enjoy as Americans under the First Amendment. Your right to practice your faith, your right to assemble, right to petition the government, freedom of the press, freedom of speech. Every single one's been attacked in the last two years."

He launched the subcommittee with a promise of explosive findings. "I have never seen anything like this. Dozens and dozens of whistleblowers, FBI agents, coming to us," Jordan said at the first hearing. But after a few weeks with no bombshells, the reviews for his crusade were tepid. "Jim Jordan's Weaponization Subcommittee Keeps Firing Blanks," read a headline in the conservative site The Bulwark. A former staff investigator for Republican Sen. Charles Grassley put it bluntly: "Jordan's 'weaponization' panel is all conclusions, no evidence."

* * *

Jankowicz got called to testify in a closed session of the full House Judiciary Committee on April 10, 2023. The stakes were high. For the Republicans, this was a fishing expedition to see if they could find enough material to score some points in a public hearing. So Jankowicz had to squelch their Ministry of Truth narrative and persuade them that she was a sympathetic figure. She hired an attorney who was an expert in the unique Washington showcraft of congressional testimony. They settled on the topics she would decline to discuss: anything to do with her qualifications, any hypotheticals about what the board would have done, anything about her previous statements prior to government, anything about her hiring—questions about those should be referred to the Department of Homeland Security and the White House.

She had two requests for the committee. She was concerned the man she'd gotten the protective order against would be there to harass her, so she asked for a Capitol Police officer to escort her to the committee room. She also wanted a room where, as a nursing mother, she could pump her breast milk. The Republican staff agreed to both.

She usually did not wear a lot of makeup, but she was testifying before a congressional committee, even behind closed doors, so she had her hair done and took a lot of time so her makeup looked really good. ("I had my armor on," she told me.) She also tipped off a news photographer she knew so he'd get a favorable photo. Her arrival went well. The guy she called "my stalker" didn't show up, and the photographer got a nice shot of her striding confidently through the hallway, Starbucks in hand.

She testified for five hours, split between the Republicans and Democrats. Staffers asked most of the questions, but members of the committee, including Jordan, asked some too. She told them about the mundane work of the board. No, it wasn't about censorship. The mission was coordination, to do dull but important things like train people to recognize and respond to disinformation and make sure that different agencies within DHS weren't wasting taxpayer dollars on the same services. Also: The board *never actually met*. The whole effort was paused before anything was done.

Of course, this being a congressional committee, there were theatrics. A woman who was one of the staff attorneys for the Republicans had been kind when Jankowicz arrived and even ushered her down to the mothers' room, but she then turned into an attack dog and implied that they could hold Jankowicz in contempt of Congress when she declined to answer questions about why she was a foreign agent. (Jankowicz's attorney assured her that wasn't a realistic possibility.)

She showed poise under pressure. With direct answers and occasional humor, she described herself as a senior bureaucrat "herding cats" to get disparate agencies to work together. When a Republican committee staffer tried to land a blow by citing one of her tweets, Jankowicz replied, "This is one tweet, less than 240 characters, of my body of work, which includes two books, four congressional testimonies—some at the behest of your Republican colleagues in the Senate. I would suggest that, if you want to look at my work and my commitment to civil liberties and disinformation, [you] look at the rest of my work and not cherry-picked tweets that have been used to defame me, and frankly have led to significant threats to me and my family because they've been taken out of context and without nuance."

The most important development of the day was that Jankowicz finally got support from some friendlies—Democratic staffers who had been briefed ahead of time by her attorney. They asked helpful questions that enabled her to tell what she'd endured in the past year. She recounted the lies, the harassment, the death threats. She felt she told a compelling story that neutered their silly falsehoods and showed the personal toll of their lying. She was hopeful that she'd quashed their desire to call her back for a public hearing. The only way they could do that would be if they sliced and diced the video recording to totally distort her testimony.

One big lesson in all this: She should speak for herself. She had shown that when she did, she could tell a persuasive story. If only DHS had realized that! But instead, they had silenced her and relinquished the narrative to the Republicans and their lies. For future jobs, she vowed that she would control her own communications.

* * *

In June 2023, Fox's attorneys fired back with a muscular motion to dismiss her lawsuit. They had moved the case to federal court in Delaware to get a more friendly venue, and in their new motion told the court that Jankowicz's case was so weak it should be thrown out. Their thirty-five-page brief, written in a smart-alecky "we-can't-believe-such-a-lame-suit-ever-got-filed" tone, sought to poke holes in every aspect of her case.

It began with the basic point that employees of the network and its guests were engaged in free speech by discussing the controversy about the Disinformation Governance Board: "Hosts and guests on Fox exercised their First Amendment rights to join the public debate and voiced their opinions and predictions that the Board and Plaintiff would police speech, be arbiters of truth, and thereby censor speech. Apparently oblivious to the irony, Plaintiff now brings a defamation action to censor Fox—for saying that Plaintiff would censor speech. Her lawsuit is a broadside attack on bedrock First Amendment principles."

Her case was flimsy, the brief said. Nearly half the claims Jankowicz cited were *about the board*, not herself, and therefore were not defamatory. (You can't defame a government agency.) It said all of the claims were statements of opinion, a distinction that would be clear to any Fox viewer.

It said she was splitting hairs over her definition of getting fired and that the description of her departure was "substantially true" for someone whose agency had been paused. It said her complaint about Twitter had no merit because Fox hosts were fairly summarizing the proposal and her reaction to it. The Fox motion also repeatedly cited a letter to Mayorkas from twenty state attorneys general that attacked the board and Jankowicz, making it sound like the letter was a legal document when it really was just political hyperbole from twenty Republicans.

The otherwise smartly written Fox motion strangely brought up her singing and love of musical theater. It said: "Her 'cringeworthy' Mary Poppins video was widely mocked." The relevance of that was unclear. The brief also tried a long-shot approach based on a technicality. It claimed that any statements made before May 10, 2022 (which would be most of the statements) should be disallowed because of a one-year time requirement before the case was filed.

When I spoke with Jankowicz two weeks after the motion to dismiss was filed, she was in a great mood (she joked that she was "very committed to sticking it to the man") and she was optimistic about her prospects of winning a settlement. "We're going to totally eviscerate them when we file the amended complaint," she said. Both sides were expected to be finished filing briefs within a few months, she said, which would clear the way for settlement conversations. She was optimistic because Abby Grossberg, a former producer for Tucker Carlson, had recently gotten a $12 million settlement from Fox for a suit that accused the network of operating a hostile and discriminatory workplace and coercing her into false testimony.

"People are telling me that I should expect one to five [million dollars]. Like, no! I want twenty!" Jankowicz told me. But she said she wasn't sure that was realistic. "So I have to think about a number that I'm comfortable with and then the terms of that settlement." But regardless of the money, one condition was key: She wanted to be free to speak about her case after a settlement.

She had gotten accustomed to seeing herself pop up on conservative websites and didn't pay much attention, even when they kept lying about her. A typical one: Sharyl Attkisson, a video journalist whose website promised "FEARLESS, NONPARTISAN REPORTING," mentioned her in a TV segment about *Missouri v. Biden*, a lawsuit about coordination between government and the tech companies. That would have been fine because Jankowicz had been a named party in the suit (though she was in the process of trying to get her name dropped because she was not relevant to the case). But Attkisson also shoehorned in a gratuitous mention of the Disinformation Governance Board that repeated the lie that it would "crack down further on speech that it didn't like" and (of course) played a clip of Jankowicz singing.

In 2023, she was traveling again—to Britain, where her job was based, and even back to Ukraine, where she had spent a year during her Fulbright fellowship. She returned in the late summer because her new employer, the Centre for Information Resilience, was doing a project for the Ukrainian government analyzing sentiment in the country's territories that were occupied by Russia. She loved Ukraine and wasn't sure what it would be like in the midst of the long war. Kyiv was lovely—better than ever. There was some evidence of the repeated bombings, but people in the city seemed resolute and they repaired damage quickly. Otherwise, it was surprisingly normal. People were out shopping, enjoying the city, eating in restaurants. She found it was wonderful to see old friends she met during her fellowship.

Yet the Republicans' lies and Fox's demonization of her continued to cause pain and problems. In the summer, a Google Alert revealed that someone had made deepfake porn using her face. She then discovered at least three videos, all artificially generated, that were faked to make it look like she was engaged in sex acts. Writing about the video in *The Atlantic*, she said: "Although they may provide cheap thrills for the viewer, their deeper purpose is to humiliate, shame, and objectify women, especially women who have the temerity to speak out."

Jankowicz also found there were fewer opportunities to give speeches. She was a recognized expert on misinformation and disinformation and frequently got paid for speeches at colleges and other groups. She still got those invitations for speeches outside the country (though the economics of those wasn't always worthwhile with a time-consuming trip), but they had largely dried up inside the United States.

She had some low moments that summer. She and Mike had to euthanize Jake, their fourteen-year-old dog. He was part shepherd, part husky, adopted from a shelter, and was famous for howling along with NPR's *All Things Considered* theme song. (He even appeared on the show and howled on cue in 2019.)

She had a dream about Jim Jordan—not someone she liked to be dreaming about! Did it mean something? She remembered it like this:

> *She was back at the Capitol and was brought back into the Judiciary Committee room to testify again—a real possibility. She was sitting in the audience ready to go up, but then they ended the session and then somebody in the room was handing out pamphlets that summarized her closed deposition and included photographs of her that she didn't know existed... but then she discovered the pamphlets were not from the committee but were paid for by some weird group—and that group had a motto:*
>
> *"Delete all women."*

* * *

Sometimes she wondered why she was so tired all the time, and then she'd realize she had three jobs. She was the mom to an adorable but energetic toddler; she was the U.S. representative for the Centre for Information Resilience; plus, she spent countless hours on her legal matters—the lawsuit against Fox and her never-ending battle against her stalker. The Fox lawsuit was so time-consuming because there were so many lies and she had to document them all. She kept a master spreadsheet, with details on each one. So if someone asked, "Has the new Speaker of the House ever said anything about you?" she could pull it up and tell you what he said and when.

One remarkable phenomenon in all this: She was still a great villain for the conservatives. Months after the Disinformation Governance Board was dissolved—and even longer since she left the Department of Homeland Security—she continued to have tremendous value for Republicans and their media allies. About once a week she would get mentioned by them or on a right-wing website—not because anything new had happened, but because they just wanted to remind readers of the famous Biden blunder and censorship escapade. They still couldn't say "Ministry of Truth" enough.

The lawsuit had reached a lull. After firing briefs back and forth with Fox's lawyers, they now were waiting for U.S. District Court Judge Colm Connolly to hold a hearing on Fox's motion to dismiss. Connolly was a former U.S. attorney who once prompted a criminal defendant to exclaim in court that Connolly was a "heartless, gutless, soulless disgrace of a human being!" But Jankowicz's lawyers thought he was fair-minded and might be inclined to rule in their favor.

His ruling on Fox's motion to dismiss would be big. If they cleared that hurdle, it seemed likely that Fox would go into settlement talks with them. As the final briefs were filed in late 2023, they were looking for every possible clue about how he might rule: Fox had left some typos in one brief . . . and Connolly supposedly hated typos. Maybe that would work in their favor!

Jankowicz seemed resigned that Connolly was likely to throw out one of the three pillars of their case, the one that said Fox defamed her by saying she wanted to censor Americans' speech. That argument seemed to be on the weakest footing because of the right Fox had to criticize government. But even if she lost that one, the other two pillars—that Fox defamed her by falsely saying she was fired and by saying she wanted to edit people's tweets—still seemed solid.

In November 2023, Jankowicz spoke by Zoom with my journalism class. The students spent much of the hour asking her to reflect on the previous two years and discuss whether she had any regrets or things she would have done differently.

Would things have turned out differently if the board had a better name?

"It could have been called the Kittens' Governance Board or something, and [Republicans] still would have been like, 'This is the Ministry of Truth!' I don't think it had that much to do with the name. I think it was more about the fact that DHS communicated poorly—or not at all."

If you had the power to turn back time, what would you change about the announcement?

She said it would be much more extensive than a simple leak to *Politico*. It would involve "briefing the Hill, briefing journalists, briefing industry, briefing academics and think tanks ahead of the actual public rollout." That plus something that was missing for days after the original rollout . . . a fact sheet.

Do you think any of the conservative criticism about the Disinformation Governance Board was justified or fair?

"No. It would be different if we were saying, 'This individual American's tweet is wrong, and we're going to try again to take it off the Internet.' But that's not what it was about. . . . My job was getting different parts of DHS to talk to one another. So yeah, everything that was said about the board pretty much was bullshit."

Toward the end of the class, one student asked about the impact the attacks have had on her and how she views the future of social media. Jankowicz turned melancholy.

"I don't regret any of it. I don't regret the TikTok video. I still think it's pretty catchy and funny. I wish I didn't have to hear it ten million times, and I wish that more Americans appreciated the art of musical theater. But what makes me sad is just that everything I post now goes through like a lot of filters and ping-pongs around in my head and I often just say, 'It's not worth it, right?' I have to think about my kid. I get really upset when I see often male colleagues posting these adorable pictures of their children without a second thought. And I would love to show everybody my son—I think he is the most delightful creature on the planet. But I can't do that because I don't want to endanger him. . . . I just spoke at my alma mater last week at Bryn Mawr, and my old thesis adviser had to ask me, 'Is it okay if we advertise this publicly?' And I said, like, 'Well, nobody's shown up yet, but there's always a chance that somebody will. And I suggest that you inform Public Safety.' And I didn't tweet about it or share it ahead of time or let anybody in the area know publicly except on a one-on-one basis, because my stalker might show up or somebody else might show up. So, yeah, I mean, like there's all these calculations that I don't think anybody should have to think about. And I . . . I really lost something."

CHAPTER 13

How Can We Stop the Lying?

The situation looks bleak. Liars, once just a nuisance in American politics, now seem to have the upper hand. The digital age has given them new powers to spread their malarkey far and wide. The watchdogs can't keep up. The situation seems especially dire because our journalism has become so polarized and fueled by tasty falsehoods.

When we launched PolitiFact in 2007, I naively thought that it would be effective at persuading people what was true or false. I didn't think we'd necessarily get them to change their votes if their candidate was caught saying something wrong, but I was hopeful that our scorecards would strike a chord and might eventually change how they voted, or that our journalism would nudge politicians to reduce their lying. It didn't turn out that way. I underestimated the strength of the partisan media. I thought Rupert Murdoch and Roger Ailes might offer their own version with a name like Fox Facts. But instead, the Fox announcers just smeared our work. (A typical insult: "The fact-checkers are basically just a P.R. arm of the Democrats at this point.")

The repetitive attacks and corrosive language took a toll, and Republican voters ignored or distrusted our journalism. PolitiFact and many other media organizations published thousands of valuable fact-checks, but they didn't reach the people who really needed them: the Republicans hearing the most lies. We also relied on an old-school approach. We waited for readers—people repeatedly told they couldn't trust us—to seek out our websites. We must find new ways to reach a broader audience and nudge politicians to be more truthful.

The 2020 election and its aftermath revealed the consequences of the lies. Many people were fooled by falsehoods about ballots thrown in dumpsters, Sharpie-marked ballots, ballots burned, ballots counted under "a shroud of darkness," ballots counted late, and countless others. We can't just blame Donald Trump. Although he is the nuclear core who fuels the Big Lie, he is aided by co-conspirators who each have something to gain. Republican officials support his lies out of fear. If they don't play along, they're afraid he will seek revenge by withholding an endorsement. They also profit by using the lies in their fundraising. And conservative media is afraid of losing its audience, as Fox News did in the days immediately after the election.

In short, the lying worked. Three years after Joe Biden was inaugurated as president, more than one-third of Americans still believed he had not legitimately won the 2020 election, according to a *Washington Post*–University of Maryland poll. Likewise, lies on other issues continue to raise doubts. In 2023, more than one-fourth of Americans believed climate change was mostly caused by natural patterns, and 7 percent did not believe it was happening at all. The digital age has made facts more available than ever, but the truth is not getting to the people who need it.

Solving the lying problem—even putting a substantial dent in it—is a massive challenge. It's not just a matter of getting fact-check journalism accepted by an audience that has been conditioned to reject it. We also need to persuade politicians to change a behavior that has paid them dividends for years. We need to convince them that if they lie, there will be consequences.

That sounds impossible, doesn't it? But I am hopeful. Social movements can surprise us. In the early 2010s, marriage equality seemed to be a distant dream. But through increased media representation, Pride parades, and eventually a landmark Supreme Court decision, the environment changed rapidly. The same thing can happen with lying if enough people tell leaders that they won't tolerate it.

In *Network of Lies*, a book that examines how the Fox News Channel found a business model in mendacity, journalist Brian Stelter discusses recent developments that could change the network's culture. He cites promising signs such as challenges to license renewals of local Fox affiliates, the willingness of former Fox personalities to speak up about the network's tactics, and indications that some Murdoch family members are challenging the cynical approach at the heart of the network. Those ideas represent some wishful thinking and optimistic tea-leaf reading. Fox has weathered many storms, including the ouster of Ailes, a $787.5 million settlement in the Dominion lawsuit, and the sudden departures of big stars such as Bill O'Reilly and Tucker Carlson. But still, changes happen, and it's not too farfetched to think that some combination of the things Stelter cites could, indeed, change the Fox culture.

Though Fox News has played an outsized role in spreading falsehoods, it's important to recognize that lying is not just a Republican problem. As I showed in chapter 9, nearly a third of Democrats' claims rated by PolitiFact were rated Mostly False or lower. Or considered another way: 34 percent of all the False and Pants on Fire claims come from Democrats. So, we need approaches that address Democrats as well as Republicans.

Many of the approaches discussed in this chapter involve fact-checks, a journalistic genre thoroughly examined by researchers over the past two decades. Those studies have generally shown fact-checks are effective at correcting people's misinformed beliefs, particularly in the short term. The studies have found mixed results about longer-term effects. Also, the right-wing media environment is hostile to fact-checks. A 2017 study that I co-authored titled "Heroes or Hacks: The Partisan Divide over Fact-Checking" found that conservative websites often belittled fact-checking while liberals celebrated it. The conservative outlets don't publish fact-checks very often, so their audiences aren't exposed to them.

The most famous fact-checking study involved the discovery of a phenomenon dubbed the "backfire effect." Political scientists Brendan Nyhan and Jason Reifler found that after people hear a correction, they double down to support a false belief. That finding was debunked by a 2016 study by Thomas Wood and Ethan Porter, who determined the backfire effect was not a common occurrence. The Wood-Porter finding was confirmed by other researchers and then acknowledged by Nyhan himself in 2021 when he published a paper called "Why the Backfire Effect Does Not Explain the Durability of Political Misperceptions." But despite all that debunking, many people still cite the backfire effect, probably because it is what Nyhan says is "a sticky idea," and it fits what many people believe: that humans stubbornly hold their beliefs, even in the face of contradictory evidence.

We need to think big in addressing the lying problem and address it at both ends: persuading the politicians to change their behavior and alerting the audience when the claims are not true. Let's take those separately.

CHANGING HOW POLITICIANS BEHAVE

In more than forty years as a journalist, I never heard a reporter ask a politician, "Why do you lie?" In fact, I had not asked that question myself until I began interviewing people for this book. Although individual falsehoods occasionally get addressed when journalists ask about scandals or a campaign statement, the overall practice of lying is rarely discussed. Likewise, at the many voter town halls I've covered, I can't recall a voter ever asking about it. It is an elephant in the room that gets overlooked in the everyday grind of politics and governing.

It's time to elevate lying to be a key attribute that's regularly discussed in campaigns. A politician's score with fact-checkers should be as much a part of their record as how they voted on key issues. If they get a lot of False ratings, they should be asked about it at town halls and in questionnaires from civic groups. Journalists should mention the record in candidate profiles and opponents should bring it up during debates.

There are encouraging signs that truth telling matters to voters and politicians. A 2019 survey by the Pew Research Center found that 91 percent of Americans believe it is essential for politicians to be honest and ethical. A study called "Counting the Pinocchios" by Nyhan and his undergraduate students at Dartmouth College found that people are more affected by an aggregate report card of a candidate's record than individual fact-check articles. It found no difference by party, an encouraging sign that suggests report cards might overcome Republican resistance to fact-checking. A 2013 study by Nyhan and Reifler found that politicians who were reminded in a letter that their statements would get scrutinized by PolitiFact were less likely to make false statements than those who did not get the letter.

Together, the research suggests there is fertile ground for a citizen movement to hold politicians accountable for lying, to make it as relevant in campaigns as a voting record or the candidate's platform on critical issues. I believe politicians will respond if enough people speak up. As always, elected officials will act in their own interests. That's why they lie—and that's why they will stop.

Here are some ideas, including several proposed by students in my Lying in Politics courses, that could provide incentives or disincentives to get politicians to change their behavior:

A PLEDGE AGAINST LYING

This would be similar to the Taxpayer Protection Pledge, the promise by many Republican candidates and elected officials to oppose tax increases. Candidates could be asked to sign the lying pledge when they announce they are running for office. It's an idea that should appeal to politicians of both parties. A nonpartisan group could keep a database of the signers the same way that Grover Norquist's Americans for Tax Reform keeps one of the candidates and officials who've pledged not to raise taxes. Those who chose not to sign the lying promise would have to explain why during the campaign. Opponents might run ads against them for failing to sign the pledge, and signers could be called out for violating their promise if fact-checkers caught them in falsehoods. This could be an expanded version of the Pro-Truth Pledge, a project launched in late 2016 that asked people to check the accuracy of information before sharing it.

Pledges aren't perfect. Candidates will surely break them and dispute them. But simply having them be part of a campaign will elevate honesty into the political discourse and make voters and campaign operatives more aware that lying matters. As a pilot project, the pledge could be scaled down for some local races. A news organization or civic group could get all candidates in a race to agree to a lying-free campaign.

LOWER AD RATES FOR TRUTHFUL POLITICIANS

This idea sounds a little farfetched, but if social media companies have the courage to try it, it could have an impact. It aims for the sweet spot for American politicians, their desire to be reelected, by changing the rates they pay for ads on Facebook and other social media platforms. Advertising on social media has many advantages over conventional television and radio because it enables them to micro-target their audience. They can zero in on the voters they really want without wasting a lot of money reaching people who aren't likely to vote for them. Politicians will pay to reach the voters they need—but they'd love to pay less.

Facebook and other social media companies would raise or lower ad rates depending on the politician's record with fact-checking organizations. The ratings would be aggregated into a single score that would determine the ad rates. The savings or increase would be substantial, which would give politicians an incentive for honesty. The companies would use multiple fact-checkers to ensure there were many sources to determine the rates.

Social media companies have generally avoided deleting or restricting posts from politicians because the companies don't want to inhibit political speech. This approach would enable them to stay consistent with that position. They would simply be offering incentives for politicians who are judged to have the most accurate records.

A "TRUTHFULNESS BADGE" ON SOCIAL MEDIA

Another way to encourage better behavior by politicians would be to award them badges on their social media accounts, like the blue "verified user" checks that show their accounts are authentic. Under this idea, they would be rated on a scale such as gold, silver, and bronze that would reflect their fact-checking records. It would allow people to see at a glance how they compare with others. As with the idea of lower ad rates, this would use a variety of fact-checkers to ensure no single organization determined the badge.

Both of the preceding ideas would require the leaders of social media companies to be bold and to endure the inevitable blowback from Republicans, who would claim it was censorship. But the leaders of Meta showed they were willing to prioritize accuracy when they responded to false news problems after the 2016 election by setting up their Third-Party Fact-Checking program, which demotes false content. Although Meta has not been willing to use that program on politicians, if pressured by customers they could show that kind of boldness once again. X, formerly Twitter, has experimented with a promising crowdsourcing effort to fact-check content, initially called Birdwatch and then called Community Notes. But in 2024, under the ownership of Elon Musk, the platform was overrun with false content.

TRUTH TELLERS GET MORE TIME AT DEBATES

Candidates want to talk as much as they can during debates, so several of my students proposed giving bonus time to the ones with the best fact-checking records. The idea is simple: The better a candidate's aggregate score with PolitiFact, FactCheck.org, and the *Washington Post*, the more bonus they would get for their total speaking time. Likewise, candidates with the worst records would get less time (under one student's estimate, a candidate with the most falsehoods would lose as much as ten minutes of talking time).

This concept faces significant hurdles. Debate organizers, particularly the commission that oversees presidential debates, have historically been quite cautious and would probably be reluctant to try something so audacious. Candidates also would be hesitant to participate if they knew they were going to be penalized. Still, the approach might work for a local race such as a congressional or mayoral race with candidates whose records were roughly even.

THE NEED FOR MORE FACT-CHECKING

Many of the ideas in this chapter rely heavily on fact-checking—far more than organizations currently provide. (Skeptical readers might ask if this is my solution to every problem: *more fact-checks!*) But there is tremendous need: Our own 2023 Duke study, known as the "Fact Deserts" report, found there was so little scrutiny of state and local politicians that most never got checked a single time. Lying is as easy as speeding on the autobahn.

We need an infusion of money to pay for this important journalism. Foundations, which have periodically provided generous grants for sites such as FactCheck.org and PolitiFact, should provide sustained funding the same way they do for PBS and NPR. Fact-checks not only contribute to an aggregate sense of a politician's record (the more news organizations checking them, the better); they provide an important ground truth that is necessary for our political discourse. Tech companies should provide sustained funding too. Fact-checks improve search engine results and make artificial intelligence more intelligent.

"FAIR AND BALANCED"—FACTS FROM THE RIGHT

Despite the conservative narrative against fact-checking, some right-leaning media organizations have seen its value. The Dispatch and the *Daily Caller*'s "Check Your Fact" are part of Meta's program to check posts on Facebook. The organizations are paid by Meta, but Steve Hayes, the editor of The Dispatch, says that's not the only incentive. The fact-checks are popular with readers who appreciate finding out what's true and what's not. His journalists "are not looking for conservative facts or liberal facts or, as Kellyanne Conway once famously said, 'alternative facts.' We're just looking for facts," Hayes told me. "We can have big fights about what the facts mean, and how we should interpret them, and what policies in the context of political debates should flow from those facts. But we should be very clear on establishing the facts."

It's a strength-in-numbers approach. The presence of more conservative fact-checkers would further legitimize the practice. Instead of seeing the sites as tools of the liberals in the mainstream media, conservative readers would realize that fact-checking makes for a better discourse.

CHANGE THE DEBATE, LITERALLY

If you've watched debates lately, you've seen that the candidates don't try to have a substantive discussion. They just want to deliver zippy insults that will be repeated on the news and social media, regardless of whether the insults are true. Vox, the left-leaning explanatory journalism site, has experimented with a debate format that holds tremendous promise for political races. Vox produced unique debates on euthanasia in Canada and legalizing cannabis that are calm and substantive and make viewers smarter about the issues.

The format is quite structured: Vox producers got representatives for each side to agree on six facts. There was no moderator, and they avoided the cheesy lecterns and patriotic colors of campaign debates. Instead, the stylish bare-bones set, with a few pieces of plain furniture, was designed to foster a conversation. Each spokesman had an opportunity to elaborate on their opponent's facts. There was no grandstanding. The format provided a revealing discussion of the topics. In the debate about weed, for example, they had a polite exchange about the relevance of a study on driving under the influence.

A similar approach could bring some calm and helpful discourse to campaign debates. Candidates would have to agree on a topic such as immigration or education policy and then submit a handful of facts they want to cite. Each one would be verified ahead of time as accurate by the debate organizers. The candidates would then discuss each fact and use it to explain their positions and reveal contrasts with their opponent, who would have time to respond. The format would elevate the caliber of the discussion, make everything more truthful, and reduce the likelihood that the candidates would sling mud at their opponents. The sessions would be recorded and edited, so unsubstantiated charges could be removed.

When I suggested this plan to Laura Bult and Joss Fong, who produced the debates for Vox, they were skeptical that candidates would be willing to follow the rules and devote the necessary time to the structured debate. Bult said their format is designed to minimize the very thing that motivates many politicians—the opportunity to get an advantage with charisma or zingers. "This format really strips that away, and it's just down to the bare evidence and facts that support a side," Bult said. "But I would love it if that happened and if that was how political debates were formatted. I think it would be a huge public service."

I think it's worth a try in a campaign where the candidates have enough self-confidence that they're willing to experiment and don't feel the need to grandstand. It could work in a race for Congress or state attorney general as long as candidates stay focused on a single issue such as immigration or climate.

EXPERIMENTING WITH NEW FORMS

The formats that fact-checkers use to publish and broadcast their work have changed little in twenty years. Most organizations still publish traditional articles on websites, or, in the case of TV stations, broadcast their segments on news shows. The TV stations also post the videos on their websites, but the segments are rarely collected in one place where viewers can compare candidates or elected officials.

Part of the reason for this cautious approach is that journalists don't think like marketers. They're producing journalism the way they've made it for two decades. But if they want to reach elusive audiences, they need to try new story forms such as short-form video. Also, they need to serve a reader I never envisioned fifteen years ago: search engines from Google and Microsoft and a new generation of AI tools. We don't know how those tools will evolve, but they will need a corpus of accurate content so they can provide people with reliable results.

Another reason for the careful approach to fact-checking is journalists' long-held belief that they should not be activists. When I was PolitiFact editor, people often asked if I got discouraged when politicians kept repeating falsehoods. My standard reply was, "We just provide the information. It's up to voters to decide how to use it." But as misinformation has grown into a more serious problem that threatens our democracy, I've become convinced that we need to modernize the delivery of our work.

That doesn't mean we should be public crusaders against liars. We should let others tally our Pinocchios and Pants on Fires (which I explain later in this chapter). But we should not passively sit back while an entire political party lies about an election. We should correct misinformation, call attention to large trends, and continue publishing and broadcasting fact-checks that convince people of the truth.

Another easy way to broaden the audience: News organizations should use their email newsletters and news alerts for fact-check summaries. They could produce a daily notification that summarizes a fact-check in a few words and allows users to click to see the full version.

DON'T BE AFRAID TO KEEP SCORE

KEEPING THE STANDINGS

I began this book describing my lie to Brian from Michigan. When he asked if Republicans lied more, I falsely said that we didn't keep score. PolitiFact actually did keep report cards for individual politicians, and all it took was some simple math to figure out that he was right about Republicans overall. But PolitiFact still doesn't keep a global tally of politicians by party, nor do any of the major fact-checkers or journalism organizations. Someone should.

I've discussed this idea with journalists and people in academia. I initially took the position that the fact-checkers and news organizations should get over their hang-ups and just be honest about the score. If Republicans or Democrats are the biggest overall liars, I believed editors should be honest about saying so. But after talking with them, I've realized that the dynamic hasn't changed since I answered Brian's question: There's no way that fact-checkers could be seen as impartial if they are proclaiming one party as the biggest liar. Still, that information should be collected and available. Voters should have an easy way to know the overall tallies so they can hold officials from that party accountable.

One solution is to have a single website—we could call it The Political Standings—that aggregates the results from all sites and publishes combined scores. Although it's difficult to combine ratings from multiple fact-checkers to get a single "truth score" because they have different methodologies and different thresholds for what they check, there still are ways to display the data to show how politicians and parties compare. The site could highlight the latest checks and provide the running tally of party totals. Voters can just check The Standings. You could even call attention to the politicians with the worst score by putting a leaderboard in a public place, like one of those signs that shows the running total of the national debt. The websites and public displays could serve two purposes—informing people who aren't seeing fact-checking content and exposing the records of the politicians with the worst records to pressure them to improve.

PRESS THE ISSUES

ISSUE-CENTRIC FACT-CHECKING

Tom Rosenstiel, co-author of the widely read ethics book *The Elements of Journalism*, has advocated a new approach to publishing fact-checks. He says research has found people are turned off when their favorite politicians are awarded a Pants on Fire or Four Pinocchios. He believes people will respond better if the fact-checking is packaged to address the misconceptions people may have about an overall issue rather than whether their congressman deserved a zinger for getting something wrong. "The purpose becomes helping the audience understand the issue," he told me in an interview. "It depoliticizes this in that the first orientation is not, 'Is this a lie?,' but 'what is true and what is not true.'"

He envisions broad topic areas such as immigration or abortion rights that would be distilled from many individual checks. Some might be on politicians, but they also could come from widely circulated posts on social media. Another advantage is that fact-checkers wouldn't have to be so literal. The format would also allow more flexibility to check things such as themes, which could be collected in the big issue areas.

Rosenstiel's idea would not require dramatic changes by the fact-checkers. They're already checking the politicians. They just need to check a wider cast of characters and sources, distill the findings, and present them in a more user-friendly way.

JOURNALISM AS DATA

Fact-checkers produce their work for humans, but that's not the only audience. Search engines and large language models, the brains of artificial intelligence, also read it, and we should structure our work to serve them too.

I stumbled across this inadvertently after we created PolitiFact. We structured each fact-check more like data than a traditional article. We had separate fields for the politician, the claim, the Truth-O-Meter rating, et cetera. That made it possible to create our unique website. It also made it easier for readers (and our critics) to count fact-checks and analyze the ratings, which was a positive thing. When I got to Duke, I shared the concept by partnering with Google to create ClaimReview, the data standard that is now used by about half the world's fact-checkers. ClaimReview is read by search engines so they can more easily point readers to relevant content. Instead of having to read an entire article and use an algorithm to guess what it's about, ClaimReview enables the search engine to be sure who is being checked, what they said, and how it was rated. It was used by Google, Microsoft's Bing, the Internet Archive, and anyone who wanted to access the open data.

ClaimReview has great potential that hasn't been fully tapped. It can tip off search engines when there's a falsehood that has been checked by many news organizations. Social media companies and search engines can then make wiser decisions because the claim has been debunked by a diverse group of fact-checkers so the false claim should not be prominently displayed in a news feed or in search results. This is not a radical idea, nor is it censorship. Facebook already does a scaled-down version of this with its Third-Party Fact-Checking. It's just smart moderation to provide customers with more accurate content. ClaimReview makes that possible.

* * *

Every year, the World Economic Forum produces a gloomy report about the risks facing the planet. The report, based on a survey of leaders from academia, business, government, and civil society, ranks the global forces that could cause major disruptions in coming years. The experts' choices for the past twenty years have been the sort of mayhem you would expect: war, climate change, natural disasters, and infectious diseases. In January 2024, a new duo suddenly appeared at the top of the list of short-term threats: "Misinformation and disinformation."

The report said those problems weren't new, but it noted that a convergence of factors made the risks from them more urgent than ever. Advances in technology made it easier for people to create everything from cloned voices to counterfeit websites. A steady diet of falsehoods has bred cynicism and dark thoughts. "When emotions and ideologies overshadow facts, manipulative narratives can infiltrate the public discourse," the report said. "Falsified information can also fuel animosity, from bias and discrimination in the workplace to violent protests, hate crimes and terrorism."

The report was a major topic of discussion at the group's annual meeting in Davos, Switzerland, and it got lots of news coverage, some quite bleak. Said CNN: "Humanity faces a perilous future, marked by an explosion of disinformation turbocharged by artificial intelligence and the devastating effects of climate change."

Conservatives reacted predictably with columns and blog posts that pooh-poohed the results, howled about possible censorship, and put "misinformation" in quotes to suggest it's not a real thing. Their reaction was a reminder there's still a giant gulf between the people who recognize the threat of lies and those who spread them or want to pretend they're not a problem.

Yes, disinformation *is* a thing and its atomic unit is the political lie. The WEF report rightly speaks of the problem in dire terms. If anything, the WEF warning sounds too much like countless other reports about the impending climate disaster. That makes it easy for liars and their enablers to distract from the problem with snark and cries of censorship. As I've shown in this book, lying is an epidemic that threatens our trust in government, our ability to hold fair elections, and our civil discourse.

In the four years I've worked on this book, I've been amazed at the sheer volume of falsehoods that go unchecked, the callous way that campaigns and media organizations profit from them, and the stony cruelty of the liars. Reflecting on all that I've seen and heard, the moment that typifies that cruelty is an episode I included in chapter 6 when Nina Jankowicz sent a personal letter to Sens. Josh Hawley and Charles Grassley. In the letter, she described the ordeal she endured from the lies spread about her. "As a result of this warped narrative, tens of thousands of my fellow Americans, by the most conservative estimate, so strongly believe I am a threat to their freedom that they took time to defame, harass, stalk, and threaten me," she wrote. She asked Hawley and Grassley to condemn the attacks against her and stop promoting the false narratives. "As Senators, you have the power to set a different tone and example."

Hawley, who replied in just ninety minutes, ignored the substance of her letter, falsely claimed she wanted to shut down questions that were based on "whistleblower revelations," and said she should testify under oath. He didn't take time to reflect on the damage he and others had done to her. He didn't pause to think whether he had lied, or whether he'd gone overboard with his attacks. He had severely damaged her career to advance his false narrative, and his response made it clear that he didn't care. This was just another battle in the partisan war. Hawley had won.

* * *

Hawley might have behaved differently if he had different incentives. Politics is a complex marketplace, and ultimately the actors do what's best for themselves. Change the incentives, and they will change how they behave.

There's no intrinsic link between lying and the foundational beliefs of Republicans, so they could stop or drastically reduce that behavior and reposition themselves as the party of honesty. It's not a stretch to think that some principled conservatives could set up an organization that establishes a pledge against lying. If party leaders and big donors decide it's important, there could be significant peer pressure to sign. A vow against lying eventually could be as important as being pro-gun or anti-abortion. Facebook, no longer subject to the silly rhetoric about censorship (because Republicans now identify themselves as being in the honest party!), would be willing to try a market-based system that adjusts ad rates based on fact-checking records. That would create further incentives for honesty.

Democrats, now lagging behind the new party of honesty, would have to scramble to show they cared about truth too. They would rush to sign the pledge and burnish their records with fact-checkers. (They'd quibble even more when they earned a Half True because now it had consequences for their ad rates!)

Then, if the Biden administration introduced a new panel in the Department of Homeland Security such as the Disinformation Governance Board, Hawley could still criticize it as a boneheaded idea with a terrible name that, yes, sounds Orwellian. But he wouldn't have to lie, particularly about the woman in charge. He could tell the truth and still win this round.

Epilogue

In June 2023, **Eric Barber** was back in federal court making a tearful plea to stay out of prison. Judge Christopher Cooper wasn't buying it.

Barber had been arrested in Tennessee for possession of marijuana and drug paraphernalia. He hadn't told his probation officer he was going to be out of state for that trip, so he ended up with four probation violations. That meant Cooper could revisit Barber's sentence, which had been forty-five days in prison and two years of probation. The resentencing had turned out to be surprisingly complicated. His public defender, Ubong Akpan, tried every angle to reduce the new sentence. She called attention to a discrepancy between the laws of the two jurisdictions and noted that Barber's wife, Chastity, "is very pregnant with their third child" and needs his support at home. (Akpan later clarified to the judge: "They're not technically married" but live together with their children, and "she's very dependent upon him, as you can probably imagine.")

Left unsaid in the two hearings was the reason for Barber's sentence in the first place. Barber had been fooled by Donald Trump's election lies to the point where he had driven three hundred miles to take part in a *Gangs of New York* fight, complete with battle gear. The whole episode could have been avoided if Barber hadn't fallen for the lies he'd seen on Fox and Facebook.

Akpan, Judge Cooper, probation officer Ian Bates, and prosecutor Eric Boylan spent about forty-five minutes discussing how the new sentence could comply with laws from the two jurisdictions. Once that seemed to be settled, Barber was invited to plead his case about a new sentence, which seemed likely to involve more prison time.

Barber began by explaining the arrest: "I am a medical marijuana patient in my state. This is a decision me and my physician made to keep me off of opiates where I've had two back surgeries, shoulder surgeries. I've worked construction my entire life." He said after he served his most recent jail term he lost his job and has had difficulty finding anything since then.

"Very few people will even interview me because I'm so well-known," Barber said. "Positions such as cleaning out the porta-johns, working at fast food, I've been able to secure a few interviews, but when I inform them I am on probation for January 6th, they sometimes even light up like, 'Oh, I do remember you . . .' [and he doesn't get hired]. I live in a very small community, so employment's been extremely difficult." He said his best hope is racing stock cars. "You can go to the track and compete, and depending on where you finish, you will receive winnings. And that's what I've been doing since the season started in May."

He told the judge about all the apologies he'd made and how he'd taken responsibility for his actions on January 6.

"I've made many statements to the media that what we did was wrong, and we should not have rioted. It was—what we did was a dark day for America. And I have to live with the fact that I was part of that for the rest of my life. And my children will know, when they get older, that I was there that day. And [my] community standing— you know, as a city councilman, my political career is garbage now. It's never going to happen." He told the judge that he knowingly violated probation with the hope of winning a car race and taking home the prize money. He said he calculated the risk to be seven days in jail if he was caught, but he now realized the jail term could be much longer.

Barber closed with an emotional plea: "Many people may not believe that I've been punished enough, but not only have I been punished greatly outside of the courtroom, I'm going to be punished for this for the rest of my life. And I just ask for mercy of the court and a chance to demonstrate my ability to abide by the probation rules. And I assure you, Your Honor, if given another opportunity, I can."

"Thank you, sir," Cooper said.

The judge was frustrated by the story he just heard. He'd read about Barber's criticism after the initial sentencing, when Barber called himself "a political prisoner" and complained that he got jail time because Cooper was an Obama appointee.

Cooper, an African American Stanford Law grad who joined the federal bench after stints with the Justice Department and several big law firms, reminded Barber that his initial sentence wasn't as harsh as federal prosecutors had recommended. But Cooper still felt some jail time was warranted. He noted that on January 6 Barber had come ready to fight.

"You know, you weren't just on the lawn or on the steps of the Supreme Court. Okay? You were prepared for battle, not just for self-defense. You indicated your desire to punch somebody in the face, if I remember. You were one of the ones relatively early in the building. You stayed a fair amount of time. You went into nonpublic sensitive areas. You minimized your role in your public interviews afterwards, and you had some prior criminal history and prior probation violations."

Cooper said Barber should remember what he said at the initial sentencing:

> You stood in front of me, and you shed tears like you're doing now, and you told me that you were wrong, and you shouldn't have done it. You talked about the officers that were affected and the congressional staff members who didn't know whether they'd go home that night. And while I find it difficult sometimes to separate true remorse from crocodile tears, I believed you. And that affected the sentence that I gave you. . . . And what do you do? You go out, if not the next day, a couple of days later and you say that a stolen phone charger is nothing compared to a stolen election. . . . And that you were a political prisoner.

Cooper now seemed convinced he'd seen two performances of crocodile tears.

> That might be emotional, but that doesn't sound like remorse to me, okay? You disrespected this process and this court. You also said some things about me, but, you know, that doesn't matter. . . . That's— I don't take it personally. And now you're telling me the same thing. You fooled me once, shame on you. Fool me twice, shame on me.

Cooper said Barber's violation "was willful" and occurred just a few months after he began probation. "I refuse to believe that there's no place in the state of West Virginia that will employ you. I see plenty of folks who have gone back to their jobs or have found new jobs or gone in the want ads or whatever, okay? And it doesn't sound like this racing thing is all that lucrative, anyway."

"It's not," Barber said.

Cooper said he could sentence him to the maximum, 180 days in prison, but would give him credit for the 45 days he'd served plus an additional 75 days. Cooper noted that the various laws made it "a very novel issue" and could change. He said Barber would not have to report to prison until he got a chance to appeal, and he extended Barber's probation for another twelve months.

"Mr. Barber," Cooper said, "I don't want to be here. It's nothing personal, all right? But you know, you're not taking this seriously. I don't think you're remorseful. I think you played me, and I think that's a shame. So with that, good luck."

* * *

After Barber appealed the new sentence, prosecutors agreed with his public defender that D.C. law took precedence. So Judge Cooper ended up reinstating the original sentence—forty-five days in prison and two years of probation.

As I finished work on this epilogue, I asked Barber in a Facebook chat if he had any closing thoughts. He quickly replied that January 6 "clearly wasn't an insurrection." He said it was "a rowdy protest" and "the people's filibuster" because citizens simply interrupted the legislative process to show they objected to what their government was doing. He said that was no different than many protests by liberals that had been supported by the liberal media.

I asked if he still believed that Trump had won the election. He puckishly switched to a racing metaphor, portraying Biden as a driver who broke the rules. "In racing you can win even if you're cheating," he said. "You get the check and the trophy, plus the victory lane photos." He added that "it helps if the tech inspectors are sympathetic to you." When I asked his reasoning, he rattled off many of the same suspicions that Trump supporters have long cited—large numbers of mail-in ballots, that he wasn't satisfied with the integrity of internal ballot certifications, and that many lawsuits were dismissed on the plaintiffs' standing rather than the merits of the cases.

As for his future, though, that phase of his life is over, he said. "I'm done politicking."

* * *

In his memoir, *So Help Me God*, **Mike Pence** wrote that he boldly stood up to Trump even when the president said he would go down in history as a wimp. When Trump tweeted during the Capitol siege that he lacked courage, Mike came up with a quote he loved—"It doesn't take courage to break the law, it takes courage to uphold the law"—and then turned to his daughter Charlotte and said, "Write that down." But missing from Mike's account of that day, and from the 542-page book overall, is any hint that he was outraged by Trump's thousands of lies over the four years they served together.

The book and Mike's careful explanations of January 6 are testament to his long history as Trump's enabler. For years, he was so eager to kowtow to Trump and his supporters that he not only looked the other way when Trump lied; he joined in. He tried to walk a tightrope by certifying the electoral count on the grounds he didn't have the constitutional authority to do otherwise, but he never became a prominent voice against Trump's wildly false claims that were (and still are) undermining our democracy. In fact, he joined the chorus of Republicans echoing lines about worries of "election integrity."

The "courage" he bragged about to his daughter doomed him with a party that wanted him to be an even bigger sycophant. When he ran for president in 2023, the party's base was still under the spell of the Big Lie and voters had no interest in the guy who abandoned the president in his moment of need. One party official in Iowa told *Politico*, "There are some Trump supporters who think he's the Antichrist."

As Mike's presidential hopes faded, his campaign oddly tried selling shirts and hats that highlighted why his party disliked him. The merch referred to an episode a few days before January 6 when Mike told Trump that he did not believe he had the power to decide which votes to accept. Trump replied, "You're too honest," and said that "hundreds of thousands are gonna hate your guts." In August 2023, after that quote was included in an indictment against Trump, the Pence campaign decided to sell hats and shirts with "Too Honest" on them. Mike got publicity from the sales, but given the lack of enthusiasm for him at that point, it's doubtful the campaign sold many, and the stunt only reminded GOP voters that he had abandoned Trump.

Two months later, the too-honest candidate withdrew.

* * *

Tim Miller's LinkedIn page reflects the itinerant life of a political activist—and now a media personality. You have to click "Show all 19 Experiences" to get the full list, and even that does not include his latest pundit roles. After his time with the Republican National Committee and the Romney campaign (there were no lingering effects from the Orca debacle), he worked for a group that conducted opposition research "by cataloguing every Democrat utterance" and then joined Jeb Bush as communications director. After Bush was beaten by Trump, Miller became communications director for Our Principles PAC, an anti-Trump group, until Trump won and some of the founders decided to support him. Miller said that felt like something straight out of the HBO series *Veep*: "Our principle is that Donald Trump can't be president. . . . Oh wait, he's president? Our principle is that we need Donald Trump!"

As he grew disenchanted with his party, he found he liked the opportunity to speak up about its silliness as a pundit. He became a regular contributor for MSNBC and began doing podcasts for The Bulwark, a conservative site, and irreverent short videos for Snapchat. He wrote *Why We Did It: A Travelogue from the Republican Road to Hell*, a best seller about how his party came unglued and fell in love with Trump. A theme in the book was party leaders' shameless willingness to lie.

He also became something of a journalist, a title he is uncomfortable with. He did occasional reporting gigs for the Showtime political program *The Circus*, including one in which he confronted Steve Bannon, who was backing Kari Lake in the 2022 Arizona governor's race, and asked him about promoting the Big Lie about the 2020 election. When Bannon replied that a Republican House of Representatives would seriously "adjudicate" the unresolved questions, Miller said, "Oh c'mon. You don't really believe this shit? People stormed the Capitol over this shit, dude. These are lies, over the lies. If you weren't lying about it, that wouldn't happen. You don't believe this, man. . . . I'm not doing this anymore," and ended the interview. (*The Circus* was canceled in late 2023.)

What makes Miller so good in his new role of pundit/interviewer is that he is not beholden to anyone. He was willing to truly question Bannon. Other political journalists won't because they depend on him as a behind-the-scenes source for insights into Trump. But Miller doesn't want to go back into politics and he doesn't have to protect sources or worry about offending a future boss.

"I'm very unshackled," he told me.

I asked if he thought the Republican culture of lying was likely to change.

Miller said he was pessimistic. He said Trump was a powerful role model for GOP officials who showed them to be unapologetic with their lies. The media, increasingly separated into partisan silos, rarely holds them accountable for their exaggerations and falsehoods. "So no, I don't think it's going to get any better. I think it's going to get worse."

* * *

After the Romney campaign in 2012, **Kevin Madden** became a consultant for a D.C. public affairs firm and a pundit for CNN. He was still able to use his wit and political wisdom, but he wasn't in the heat of the partisan wars. When Trump came on the scene in 2016, he drifted away from politics because he felt his party had drifted away from him. He now works for Penta, a big firm that provides strategic consulting for large companies and associations.

As someone who toiled in politics for many years and still watches with interest from the sidelines, he is disappointed about the magnitude of lying and he's not especially optimistic that it can be tamed.

"The most challenging thing about combating misinformation is just how badly some audiences in the public realm want to believe information that's not true. . . . They *want* to believe it," Madden said.

He got philosophical for a moment. "But I think as far as my role and what we can still do, all it takes for evil to prevail in the world is for good people to do nothing. . . . I think the people who are trying to combat it have to be much more vigilant. They have to be much more organized; they have to be much more engaged. . . . You can never really take a day off."

* * *

Nina Jankowicz struck back against Jim Jordan and his allies in April 2024 when she launched a new nonprofit, the American Sunlight Project. The group was created to fight Jordan and other politicians like him who were trying to intimidate researchers, tech companies, and government agencies that dared to combat misinformation.

She gave the scoop about the project to the *New York Times*, which provided a nice splash in its pages ("New Group Joins the Political Fight Over Disinformation Online"), featuring a photo of Jankowicz and noting the failure of any formal entity to forcefully address the disinformation crisis. The same day, Jankowicz sent a letter to Jordan and other Republican committee chairmen challenging them to release unedited transcripts and recordings from hearings like the one she had endured after the cancellation of the Disinformation Governance Board. In the letter to the committee chairs, she and group co-founder Carlos Alvarez-Aranyos said the Republicans had selectively released "out of context testimony as a retaliatory and chilling tactic" to intimidate people in academia and social media who wanted to research and reduce falsehoods that were infecting the political discourse.

"Disinformation knows no political party. Its ultimate victim is democracy," they wrote. "This threat is growing more acute each day, and you have become the primary obstacle to addressing it."

The mission of the American Sunlight Project is to "expose the infrastructure and funding behind the disinformation campaigns that are attempting to undermine American democracy, beginning with the campaign against disinformation research." Jankowicz said the group planned to use a variety of media, including ads and digital outlets like podcasts to share findings with the voters and government officials that needed to hear about them. She told the *Times* that contributors had committed $1 million for the effort.

The announcement, which came almost two years to the day after her life was turned upside down by lies, seemed to mark a turning point. Jankowicz told me she felt she could now have the impact she'd always wanted. "It feels like finally, rather than just watching the world burn down, I'm at least trying to put out the fire."

About a month later, Jordan surprisingly gave in to one of her demands and released her transcript. It showed the Republicans had fished for possible angles of attack, but she calmly batted away their leading questions and reminded them that their lies had taken a personal toll. Hours after the release, Jankowicz issued a statement headlined "Jordan Caves to Jankowicz." The statement called Jordan's release "a major victory for transparency and truth." She vowed to keep fighting.

* * *

On July 22, 2024, Judge Colm Connolly dismissed Jankowicz's case, siding with Fox on every claim. In an eighteen-page memo explaining his ruling, the judge did not discuss the attacks that she had endured and essentially said he wasn't buying her arguments. He said all but one of the alleged defamatory statements in her lawsuit were about the government, not Jankowicz—and the one that *was* about her wasn't false. He also noted that the statements were made on Fox shows "dedicated to opinionated commentary" where viewers "would likely have understood the challenged statements to be opinion."

That afternoon, I spoke to Jankowicz, who said she was disappointed the ruling did not mention the tremendous harassment she had experienced. She said she planned to appeal. "I'm trying to fight for the truth," she said. The court's decision "is not a reflection of the truth. I think that another court might see through the arguments that Fox has made. I feel like I need to get to the end of the line and exhaust all of my options before I give up on this. I didn't go into this thinking it would be easy."

Author's Note

When I began work on this project four years ago, I envisioned writing a book that would rely heavily on political analysis and fact-checking data, with a few case studies. But the more I focused on the case studies—the tales about Nina Jankowicz, Eric Barber, Stuart Stevens, and Kevin Madden—the more I got caught up in their stories. I realized the best way to explain lying in politics was to show how it affected the people involved.

Fortunately, the people I chose were willing to spend time with me and discuss their episodes and their lives in great detail (that includes Barber, who, after trying to get me to pay him, eventually chatted with me on Facebook at no charge). A few were unwilling to be interviewed. Rob Silvers, Samantha Vinograd, and other officials of the Department of Homeland Security declined or did not reply to many inquiries. Mike Pence also did not reply to several emails.

I often told friends that my book had great characters, which probably sounded a little unusual for a work of nonfiction. I meant that they were smart people whom I enjoyed spending time with. Their individual stories reveal larger truths about victims of lies, the strategic lying by campaigns, and how people can be fooled by lies they want to believe.

If there are significant updates to their stories, I'll publish them on my website, billadair.com.

One note about chapter 3, "The Lying Hall of Fame." My goal was to present a lively tour through the modern history of political mendacity through the stories of the biggest liars. I felt this approach would be more interesting than a traditional history. In discussions with my student researchers, I realized I could write an entire book about the hall of fame. For this book, I chose a sample of politicians, people in the media, and groups. But as with any hall of fame, readers may disagree with my choices. (*Why didn't you include the Whigs for all the lying they did in 1840?!*)

* * *

As I explained in the book, I've been deeply involved not just in PolitiFact but also in the global movement of political fact-checking. A few disclosures about my employment and other activities:

When I came to Duke in 2013, I continued to work for PolitiFact as a contributing editor. I occasionally edited national fact-checks and helped set up and edit PolitiFact North Carolina. But once I decided to write this book after the 2020 election, I ended my PolitiFact work. I never had any personal financial stake in PolitiFact, which is now owned by the Poynter Institute.

My salary comes from Duke University for serving as the Knight Professor of the Practice of Journalism and Public Policy, which was endowed by the Knight Foundation. I direct the Duke Reporters' Lab, which conducts research in fact-checking and the future of journalism. Major supporters have included the Google News Initiative, Meta, Craig Newmark, the Online News Association, and the Knight Foundation.

I am the co-founder of the International Fact-Checking Network, the global association of fact-checking organizations. I serve without pay on the group's advisory board.

Acknowledgments

My first working title for this book was *The Lying Project*, a reminder that this was bigger than one author writing a single volume. Although my name is on the cover, many talented students at Duke University helped extensively with research, interviews, and advice.

For three semesters I taught a course called Lying in Politics that was part lecture and part lab. It gave me an opportunity to conduct interviews, develop ideas, and explore theories with some of the sharpest undergrads in the nation. The students were wonderful collaborators whose assignments provided ideas that I've mentioned throughout the book. I also hired students as research assistants who nudged me, questioned me, and challenged my assumptions. Students are often the best teachers.

Research assistants Sevana Wenn, Grace Abels, Nicole Kagan, and John Lee all played important roles in the project. Sevana was a masterful researcher and editor who tracked the lies about the Disinformation Governance Board, read court documents, and helped me find the truth about the Ministry of Truth. Grace led the data analysis (and filled up the whiteboards in the Reporters' Lab with her nonstop ideas). Nicole read lawsuits, dug into the background of historical liars, and conducted a creative analysis of Tucker Carlson's tricky way of lying. John stepped in to double-check Grace's data and helped me piece together details about the Jeep lie.

Sara Israelsen-Hartley, a public policy grad student and a veteran journalist, traveled to Phoenix to explore the Big Lie in Arizona and wrote the deeply reported account of Paul Boyer's vote in chapter 8.

Other students on the team contributed in many other ways. Sofie Buckminster and Nina Moske sacrificed some of their winter break to keep me on track. Jothi Gupta helped me understand the backstory and obsessions of Stuart Stevens. Belen Bricchi and Sofia Bliss-Carrascosa helped crunch the numbers for the analysis in the "Patterns of Lying" chapter. Etan Zeller MacLean and Gabrielle Lazor were late draftees to help fact-check the manuscript. Michaela Towfighi had the dreadful task of watching all my C-SPAN appearances to find my lie to Brian from Michigan. Thanks also to Leigh Marshall, Rose Wong, Rebecca Torrence, Akiya Dillon, and Maddie Wray.

Many thanks to all the students who took my Lying in Politics course: 2021: Sean Blank, Alexandra Gara, Ann Gehan, Fernanda Herrera, Claire Kraemer, Carley Lerner, Elana Levitan, Zoe McDonald, Caroline Petronis, James Toscano Jr., Trinity Wenzel Wertheim, Brennan Zook, and TA Natalie Meltzer; 2022: Diya Chadha, Lily Coll, Brendan Driscoll, Lana Gesinsky, Chloe Hubbe, Jaiden Kaplan, Jamie Kramer, Jordan Laster, Jonathan Mah, Julia Murphy, Chase Pellegrini de Paur, Ryann Richter, Hanna Rumsey, Lauren Steele, Hana Stepnick, Ryan Thompson, Luke Vermeer, Mylie Walker; 2023: Mele Buice, Jacqueline Cole, Derek Deng, Anna Goldberg, Esme Fox, Nabile Hoque, Leslie Kang, Izzy Kohn, Chloe Nguyen, Milla Surjadi, Jillian Vordick, Storey Wertheimer, Max Wilkey, Viktoria Wulff-Andersen, and Kellie Young. And thanks to the News as a Moral Battleground students who also contributed ideas: Hannah Pechet and Riya Sharma.

I am grateful to friends who read chapter drafts and provided feedback along the way. Thank you to Tom Rosenstiel, Kyle Villemain, Ryan Thornburg, Phil Napoli, and David A. Graham. I also got tremendous assistance and advice from the hardworking staff of the Duke Reporters' Lab, including Joel Luther and Asa Royal. Joel and Asa provided datasets and automated tasks that would have taken our team many additional hours. I am thankful to Mark Stencel for sharing his archive on the early history of fact-checking, which helped me get the details right about David Broder and other key players who launched the movement in the late 1980s and early '90s.

This book would not have been possible without the many elected officials, congressional staffers, White House aides, and political operatives who spoke candidly with me about a subject that is often taboo. Special thanks to Tim Miller and Kevin Madden for their candor about the Romney campaign. It might look like that campaign was a nexus of lying. But I suspect it actually lied less than others. The rich details about the Jeep and Orca lies are testament to Tim's and Kevin's honesty about a sensitive topic. I wish there were more people like them in American politics.

I'm especially thankful to Nina Jankowicz for sharing her story and enduring my frequent questions over the past two years. I also appreciate Eric Barber for his willingness to talk candidly with someone he considers part of the liberal media. He initially balked at my interview request, but we ended up having many conversations over Facebook about politics, his jail time, and stock car racing.

I appreciate the assistance I got from many colleagues at Duke and elsewhere, including Frank Bruni, Shelley Stonecipher, and Alison Jones of the DeWitt Wallace Center for Media and Democracy, and Judith Kelley, Peter Feaver, Bruce Kuniholm, Kristin Goss, and Asher Hildebrand of the Sanford School of Public Policy. Shane Stansbury helped me understand the details of federal sentencing. Thanks to Brendan Nyhan for helping me sort out the academic research on fact-checking.

At Atria, editor Nick Ciani was enthusiastic about this book from the start. Thank you, Nick, for embracing my vision and helping me make it sharper and smarter. Thanks also to Hannah Frankel for keeping me on track and helping me get the endnotes right, and to copyeditor Barbara Wild and production editor Jason Chappell. At the David Black Agency, thanks to Gary Morris for suggesting this book and for tremendous persistence in helping me publish it.

My family provided tremendous love and support through the time I worked on this project. Thank you, Molly, Annie, and Miles for keeping me going. And most of all, thanks to my wife, Katherine, who read drafts, provided valuable advice, and left me wonderful notes that greeted me when I started work at 4:00 a.m. Your love and support made this possible.

—Bill Adair
Durham, North Carolina
April 2024

Sources

This book is the result of four years of interviews with current and former elected officials, political aides, campaign consultants, journalists, historians, and academics. Most quotations in the book come from those interviews. I also relied on video of congressional hearings, cable news shows, political ads, and C-SPAN call-in programs. I reviewed thousands of pages of documents—transcripts of court proceedings and Capitol Hill hearings, legal filings, reports from think tanks and congressional committees. The interviews and books are listed below, followed by individual citations.

Interviews

Eric Alterman, Professor of English and Journalism at Brooklyn College–CUNY
Eric Barber, former City Council Member, Parkersburg, West Virgina
Robert Bauer, former White House Counsel, President Barack Obama
Jocelyn Benson, Michigan Secretary of State
Paul Boyer, former Arizona State Senator
Laura Bult, Producer, Vox
Marcus Childress, Investigator, House Select Committee to Investigate the January 6th Attack on the United States Capitol, U.S. House of Representatives
Damon Circosta, former Chair of the North Carolina State Board of Elections
Cal Cunningham, candidate for U.S. Senate in North Carolina, 2020
Kert Davies, Director of Special Investigations, Center for Climate Integrity

Renée DiResta, Technical Research Manager at Stanford Internet Observatory
Matthew Dowd, political consultant to Republican and Democratic candidates
Anita Dunn, Senior Advisor, President Joe Biden
Steve Ellis, President, Taxpayers for Common Sense
John A. Farrell, Author, *Richard Nixon: The Life*
Anthony Fauci, former Director of National Institute of Allergy and Infectious Diseases
Peter Feaver, Professor of Political Science, Duke University; former Special Advisor for Strategic Planning and Institutional Reform on the National Security Council Staff, White House, 2005–2007
John Feehery, Partner, EFB Advocacy, a lobbying and strategy firm; former aide to Republican members of Congress
David Folkenflik, NPR media correspondent, author of *Murdoch's World*
Joss Fong, Producer, Vox
Al Franken, Senator from Minnesota, 2009–2018
Lucas Graves, Professor of Journalism and Mass Communication, University of Wisconsin
Steve Hayes, Editor, The Dispatch
Brian Lamb, Founder, C-SPAN
Jeff Jackson, Member of Congress from North Carolina, 2023–2024
Kathleen Hall Jamieson, Professor of Communication, University of Pennsylvania, and founder, FactCheck.org
Nina Jankowicz, former Executive Director of the Disinformation Governance Board, U.S. Department of Homeland Security
Valerie Jarrett, former Senior Advisor to President Barack Obama
Jeff Jarvis, former professor, CUNY's Craig Newmark Graduate School of Journalism
Jillian Johnson, City Council Member, Durham, North Carolina
David Jolly, Member of Congress from Florida, 2014–2017
Eric Jotkoff, Senior Communication Strategist, National Education Association
Glenn Kessler, Editor and chief writer of "The Fact Checker," *Washington Post*
Jim Kolbe, Member of Congress from Arizona, 1985–2007
John Koskinen, former U.S. Commissioner of Internal Revenue
Kevin Madden, former spokesman for Mitt Romney's 2012 U.S. presidential campaign
Jim Margolis, Partner, GMMB, Inc.; adviser to 2008 and 2012 Obama presidential campaigns and 2016 Clinton presidential campaign
Mike McCurry, White House Press Secretary, President Bill Clinton
Tim Miller, former spokesman, Republican National Committee and various Republican candidates; now podcast host for The Bulwark

Neil Newhouse, Partner and Co-founder, Public Opinion Strategies; pollster for 2012 Romney campaign

Brendan Nyhan, Professor, Department of Government, Dartmouth College

Chris Quinn, Editor, Cleveland.com

Denver Riggleman, former Member of Congress, Virginia

Jon Roozenbeek, Postdoctoral Fellow, University of Cambridge

Jay Rosen, Associate Professor of Journalism, New York University

Rob Schaul, former Analysis and Resilience Policy Lead, Cybersecurity and Infrastructure Security Agency, U.S. Department of Homeland Security

Dan Shelley, President and Chief Executive Officer, Radio Television Digital News Association

Michael Steele, former Lieutenant Governor of Maryland and former chair of the Republican National Committee

Kate Starbird, Associate Professor in the Department of Human-Centered Design & Engineering at the University of Washington and Director of the Emerging Capacities of Mass Participation Laboratory.

Stuart Stevens, political consultant, chief strategist, Romney 2012 campaign

Olivia Troye, former Special Advisor to the Vice President for Homeland Security & Counterterrorism

Wendy Tuck, City Council Member, Parkersburg, West Virginia

Henry Waxman, Member of Congress from California, 1975–2015

Julian Zelizer, Professor of History and Public Affairs, Princeton University

Selected Bibliography

Alterman, Eric. *Lying in State: Why Presidents Lie—and Why Trump Is Worse.* New York: Basic Books, 2020.

Alterman, Eric. *When Presidents Lie: A History of Official Deception and Its Consequences.* New York: Viking, 2004.

Applebaum, Anne. *Twilight of Democracy: The Seductive Lure of Authoritarianism.* New York: Doubleday, 2020.

Bok, Sissela. *Lying: Moral Choice in Public and Private Life.* New York: Vintage Books, 1978.

Caro, Robert A. *The Years of Lyndon Johnson.* Vol. 3, *Master of the Senate.* New York: Alfred A. Knopf, 2002.

Cialdini, Robert B. *Influence: How and Why People Agree to Things.* New York: William Morrow, 1984.

Danesi, Marcel. *The Art of the Lie: How the Manipulation of Language Affects Our Minds.* Amherst, NY: Prometheus Books, 2020.

Farrell, John A. *Richard Nixon: The Life.* New York: Doubleday, 2017.

Finchelstein, Federico. *A Brief History of Fascist Lies.* Berkeley: University of California Press, 2020.

Fisher, Max. *The Chaos Machine: The Inside Story of How Social Media Rewired Our Minds and Our World.* New York: Little, Brown, 2022.

Franken, Al. *The Truth: With Jokes.* New York: Dutton, 2005.

Frankfurt, Harry G. *On Bullshit.* Princeton, NJ: Princeton University Press, 2005.

Gladwell, Malcolm. *Talking to Strangers: What We Should Know about the People We Don't Know.* New York: Little, Brown, 2019.

Graves, Lucas. *Deciding What's True: The Rise of Political Fact-Checking in American Journalism.* New York: Columbia University Press, 2016.

Haidt, Jonathan. *The Righteous Mind: Why Good People Are Divided by Politics and Religion.* New York: Vintage Books, 2013.

Halperin, Mark, and John Heilemann. *Double Down: Game Change 2012.* New York: Penguin Press, 2013.

Jamieson, Kathleen Hall. *Dirty Politics: Deception, Distraction, and Democracy.* New York: Oxford University Press, 1992.

Jankowicz, Nina. *How to Be a Woman Online: Surviving Abuse and Harassment, and How to Fight Back.* London: Bloomsbury Academic, 2022.

Jankowicz, Nina. *How to Lose the Information War: Russia, Fake News, and the Future of Conflict.* London: I.B. Tauris, 2020.

Kessler, Glenn, Salvador Rizzo, and Meg Kelly. *Donald Trump and His Assault on Truth: The President's Falsehoods, Misleading Claims and Flat-Out Lies.* New York: Scribner, 2020.

Kovach, Bill, and Tom Rosenstiel. *The Elements of Journalism: What Newspeople Should Know and the Public Should Expect.* New York: Crown, 2001.

Levine, Timothy R. *Duped: Truth-Default Theory and the Social Science of Lying and Deception.* Tuscaloosa: University of Alabama Press, 2020.

Miller, Tim. *Why We Did It: A Travelogue from the Republican Road to Hell.* New York: HarperCollins, 2022.

Oborne, Peter. *The Assault on Truth: Boris Johnson, Donald Trump and the Emergence of a New Moral Barbarism.* London: Simon & Schuster, 2021.

O'Connor, Cailin, and James Owen Weatherall. *The Misinformation Age: How False Beliefs Spread.* New Haven, CT: Yale University Press, 2019.

Pfeiffer, Dan. *Battling the Big Lie: How Fox, Facebook, and the MAGA Media Are Destroying America.* New York: Twelve, 2022.

Rauch, Jonathan. *The Constitution of Knowledge: A Defense of Truth.* Washington, DC: Brookings Institution Press, 2021.

Riggleman, Denver. *Bigfoot... It's Complicated: A Congressman and Former Intelligence Officer Explores the Politics of True Believers: Bigfoot and Otherwise.* Denver, CO: Outskirts Press, 2020.

Riggleman, Denver, and Hunter Walker. *The Breach: The Untold Story of the Investigation into January 6th.* New York: Henry Holt, 2022.

Sherman, Gabriel. *The Loudest Voice in the Room: How the Brilliant, Bombastic Roger Ailes Built Fox News—And Divided a Country.* New York: Random House, 2014.

Stelter, Brian. *Hoax: Donald Trump, Fox News, and the Dangerous Distortion of Truth.* New York: One Signal Publishers/Atria, 2020.

Stelter, Brian. *Network of Lies: The Epic Saga of Fox News, Donald Trump, and the Battle for American Democracy.* New York: One Signal Publishers/Atria, 2023.

Stevens, Stuart. *It Was All a Lie: How the Republican Party Became Donald Trump.* New York: Alfred A. Knopf, 2020.

United States Congress House Select Committee to Investigate the January 6th Attack on the United States Capitol. Preface by David Remnick and epilogue by Congressman Jamie Raskin. *The January 6th Report: The Report of the Select Committee to Investigate the January 6th Attack on the United States Capitol.* New York: Celadon Books, 2022.

Wallace, Lewis Raven. *The View from Somewhere: Undoing the Myth of Journalistic Objectivity.* Chicago: University of Chicago Press, 2019.

Notes

PROLOGUE

xi *Under the glare*: *Washington Journal*, "2012 Election Ads," C-SPAN, June 4, 2012, https://c-span.org/video/?306378-3/2012-election-ads.

INTRODUCTION

xiv *One of the first lies*: Iris Lav and James Sly, "Estate Tax Repeal: A Windfall for the Wealthiest Americans," Center on Budget and Policy Priorities, June 21, 2000, accessed through the Wayback Machine, https://web.archive.org/web/20000815070755/http://www.cbpp.org/5-25-00tax.htm.

xv *Massachusetts senator had* : Brooks Jackson, "Zell Miller's Attack on Kerry: A Little out of Date," FactCheck.org, September 3, 2004, https://www.factcheck.org/2004/09/zell-millers-attack-on-kerry-a-little/.

xv *I turned my attention*: Bill Adair, "Cheney Turns Up Heat on Kerry," *Tampa Bay Times*, September 2, 2004, https://www.tampabay.com/archive/2004/09/02/cheney-turns-up-heat-on-kerry/.

xvi *Bush would later claim*: Peter Baker, "Bush Doesn't Second-Guess Himself on Iraq. Even if Everyone Else Does," *New York Times*, March 20, 2023, https://www.nytimes.com/2023/03/20/us/politics/george-w-bush-iraq-war.html; Glenn Kessler, "The Iraq War and WMDs: An Intelligence Failure or White House Spin?," *Washington Post*, March 22, 2019, https://www.washingtonpost.com/politics/2019/03/22/iraq-war-wmds-an-intelligence-failure-or-white-house-spin/.

xvi *In her famous essay*: Hannah Arendt, "Lying in Politics," in *Crises of the Republic* (New York: Harcourt Brace Jovanovich, 1972), 1–118.

xviii *Edelman, the global communications*: Richard Edelman, "Breaking the Vicious Cycle of Distrust," January 18, 2022, Edelman.com, https://www.edelman.com/trust/2022-trust-barometer/breaking-vicious-cycle-distrust.

xviii *A Yale study found*: Jacob Wallace et al., "Excess Death Rates for Republican and Democratic Registered Voters in Florida and Ohio during the COVID-19 Pandemic," *Journal of the American Medical Association*, July 24, 2023, https://jamanetwork.com/journals/jamainternalmedicine/fullarticle/2807617.

xviii *In the fall of 2023*: John Davis, "Gov. DeSantis and Florida Surgeon General Warn against New COVID-19 Restrictions and Vaccine," WGCU, September 14, 2023, https://news.wgcu.org/health/2023-09-14/gov-desantis-and-florida-surgeon-general-warn-against-new-covid-19-restrictions-and-vaccine.

xx *They just kept repeating*: "53% of Republicans View Trump as True U.S. President," Reuters, May 24, 2021, https://www.reuters.com/world/us/53-republicans-view-trump-true-us-president-reutersipsos-2021-05-24/.

xx *I saw this in a discovery*: Ciara O'Rourke, "Dewhurst Says Phoenix Has More Kidnappings Than Any Other City in the World except for Mexico City," PolitiFact, June 18, 2010, https://www.politifact.com/factchecks/2010/jun/18/david-dewhurst/dewhurst-says-phoenix-has-more-kidnappings-any-oth/.

xx *falsely portraying them*: Miriam Valverde, "Florida Congressman Misrepresents Data on Murders Attributed to Immigrants in the Country Illegally," PolitiFact, February 19, 2019, https://www.politifact.com/factchecks/2019/feb/19/matt-gaetz/gaetz-misrepresents-federal-data-murder-immigrants/.

xx *even as carrying*: W. Gardner Selby, "Rick Perry Claim About 3,000 Homicides by Illegal Immigrants Not Supported by State Figures," PolitiFact, July 23, 2014, https://www.politifact.com/factchecks/2014/jul/23/rick-perry/rick-perry-claim-about-3000-homicides-illegal-immi/.

xxiii *After the polls closed*: "President Donald Trump & Vice President Mike Pence Election Night Remarks," C-SPAN, November 4, 2020, https://www.youtube.com/watch?v=duE8tnrSmNc.

xxiii *They quickly disproved*: Bill McCarthy, "No, Biden Did Not Receive Thousands of Mysteriously Surfaced Votes in Michigan," PolitiFact, November 4, 2020, https://www.politifact.com/factchecks/2020/nov/04/tweets/no-biden-did-not-receive-thousands-mysteriously-su/.

xxiii *close ties to Venezuela*: Glenn Kessler, "Giuliani's Fantasy Parade of False Voter Fraud Claims," *Washington Post*, November 16, 2020, https://www.washingtonpost.com/politics/2020/11/16/giulianis-fantasy-parade-false-voter-fraud-claims/.

xxiii *ballots being burned*: Angelo Fichera, "Viral Video Shows Burning of Sample Ballots, Not Trump Votes," FactCheck.org, November 5, 2020, https://www.factcheck.org/2020/11/viral-video-shows-burning-of-sample-ballots-not-trump-votes/.

xxiii *Three years after*: Rachel Weiner et al., "Republican Loyalty to Trump, Rioters Climbs in 3 Years after Jan. 6 Attack," *Washington Post*, January 2, 2024, https://www.washingtonpost.com/dc-md-va/2024/01/02/jan-6-poll-post-trump/.

xiii *commencement address at Warren Wilson*: Bill Adair, "Facts, Community, and Bears," Commencement Address, Warren Wilson College, May 11, 2019, https://dewitt.sanford.duke.edu/facts-community-and-bears/.

CHAPTER 1 The Ministry of Truth

1 *The three-sentence scoop*: Eugene Daniels et al., "Fauci Pulls out of WHCD. Is Biden Next?," *POLITICO Playbook*, April 27, 2022, https://www.politico.com/newsletters/playbook/2022/04/27/fauci-pulls-out-of-whcd-is-biden-next-00028131.

1 *Still, she was happy*: Unless noted otherwise, quotes and thoughts attributed to Jankowicz in Chapters 1, 6, and 12 come from our interviews, July 2022 to April 2024.

2 *Twitter*: Twitter was renamed X by owner Elon Musk in July 2023.

2 *"Cat's out of the bag"*: Nina Jankowicz (@wiczipedia), "Cat's out of the bag: here's what I've been up to the past two months, and why I've been a bit quiet on here. Honored to be serving in the Biden Administration @DHSgov and helping shape our [. . .]," X post, April 27, 2022, 7:50 a.m., https://twitter.com/wiczipedia/status/1519282822158110721.

2 *two-hour appearance*: "Mayorkas Announces Disinformation Board," C-SPAN, April 27, 2022, https://www.c-span.org/video/?c5013090/user-clip-mayorkas-announces-disinformation-board.

3 *"BREAKING: Biden Admin"*: Jack Posobiec (@JackPosobiec), "BREAKING: Biden Admin Department of Homeland Security to create a 'Disinformation Governance Board' dedicated to 'countering misinformation' [. . .] What could go wrong," X post, April 27, 2022, 2:13 p.m., https://twitter.com/jackposobiec/status/1519379124070068224, Jack Posobiec (@JackPosobiec), "The DHS board will be headed by Nina Jankowicz, who once claimed militarized Trump supporters would show up to the polls with weapons to intimidate voters," X post, April 27, 2022, 2:20 p.m., https://x.com/JackPosobiec/status/1519381022592352257, Jack Posobiec (@JackPosobiec),

"Jankowicz formerly worked as an advisor to the Ukrainian government under a Fulbright-Clinton Fellowship," X post, April 27, 2022, 2:47 p.m., https://x.com/JackPosobiec/status/1519387795877502976, Jack Posobiec (@jackPosobiec), "Here's Nina in 2020," X post, April 27, 2022, 2:34 p.m., https://x.com/JackPosobiec/status/1519384442934022145, Jack Posobiec (@JackPosobiec), "Jankowicz is also known for forming a Harry Potter 'wizard rock band' known as the Moaning Myrtles," X post, April 27, 2022, 2:24 p.m., https://x.com/JackPosobiec/status/1519382023147827204.

3 *In a profile*: Andrew Marantz, "The Far-Right American Nationalist Who Tweeted #MacronLeaks," *The New Yorker*, May 17, 2017, https://www.newyorker.com/news/news-desk/the-far-right-american-nationalist-who-tweeted-macronleaks.

4 *She again urged*: Nina Jankowicz, "FYSA-DGB announcement blowback," email to Espinosa, Marsha; Peck, Sarah; Waters, Erin; Clemens, Ruth; Seidman, Ricki, April 27, 2022, https://www.dhs.gov/sites/default/files/2023-06/9%20Citizens%20United%20v.%20DHS%20%2822-cv-02019%29%282022-HQLI-00057%29%28Jan%202023%20Release%29%28Part%201%20of%202%29.pdf.

4 Kirkus Reviews *praised her*: "A Successful Codification of Practical, Occasionally Fiery Methods of Protection and Means of Attack," *Kirkus Reviews*, April 17, 2022, https://www.kirkusreviews.com/book-reviews/nina-jankowicz/how-to-be-a-woman-online/.

5 *"Just revealed"*: Eric Schmitt (@Eric_Schmitt), "Just revealed: Biden's DHS is creating a 'Disinformation Governance Board' dedicated to 'countering misinformation.' . . . The same people who lied about COVID [. . .]," X post, April 27, 2022, 2:45 p.m., https://twitter.com/Eric_Schmitt/status/1519387332700516352,

5 *Jankowicz gave a*: Katelyn Caralle, "Biden Sets Up 'Disinformation Board' Headed by Russia Expert Who Called Hunter's Laptop a 'Trump Campaign Product' and Said She 'Shudders to Think' about Elon Musk Taking over Twitter," DailyMail.com, April 28, 2022, https://www.dailymail.co.uk/news/article-10760907/Biden-starts-Disinformation-Board-led-Russia-expert-called-Hunters-laptop-Trump-product.html.

6 *"would be led by political hack"*: "U.S. House of Representatives House Session, Part 2," C-SPAN, April 27, 2022, https://www.c-span.org/video/?519700-5/house-session-part-2.

7 *She sought to*: Nina Jankowicz (@wiczipedia), "For those who believe this tweet is a key to all my views, it is simply a direct quote from both candidates during the final presidential debate. If you look at my timeline, you will see

I was livetweeting that evening," X post, April 27, 2022, 6:09 p.m., https://twitter.com/wiczipedia/status/1519438518551994369.

9 *The memo said*: Robert Silvers, Samantha Vinograd, Organizing DHS Efforts to Counter Disinformation, U.S. Department of Homeland Security (Washington, D.C., September 2021), 1–2, https://www.hawley.senate.gov/sites/default/files/2022-06/2022-06-07%20DOCS%20ONLY%20CEG%20JH%20to%20DHS%20%28Disinformation%20Governance%20Board%29%5B1%5D.pdf.

10 *A point of clarification*: "Foreign Influence Operations and Disinformation," Cybersecurity and Infrastructure Security Agency, https://www.cisa.gov/topics/election-security/foreign-influence-operations-and-disinformation#.

15 *"A* disinformation *board"*: "Biden Admin Creates 'Disinformation Governance Board,'" *Outnumbered*, Fox News, April 28, 2022, https://www.foxnews.com/video/6305328854112#sp=show-clips.

15 *"a far-left radical Democrat"*: "Hannity: I Don't Think the Disinformation Governance Board Will 'Fact-Check' Themselves," *Hannity*, Fox News, April 29, 2022, https://www.youtube.com/watch?v=C6VUDj7QJBM&t=336s.

15 *Mark Levin, a radio*: Mark Levin, "Mark Levin Audio Rewind," April 29, 2022, in *Mark Levin Podcast*, produced by Cumulus Podcast Network, podcast, 16:50, https://podcasts.apple.com/us/podcast/mark-levin-audio-rewind-4-29-22/id209377688?i=1000559161061.

16 *Carlson declared*: Tucker Carlson, "Tucker: This the Point Where We Have to Draw the Line," *Tucker Carlson Tonight*, April 28, 2022, https://www.youtube.com/watch?v=e4inJSblCUY.

16 *Said Clay Travis*: Clay Travis (@ClayTravis), "This is the new Biden administration head of Ministry of Truth, Nina Jankowicz. She is in charge of what's truth and fiction in America. Every time you think the Biden administration can't get more ridiculous, they do," X post, April 29, 2022, 8:00 a.m., https://twitter.com/ClayTravis/status/1520010169769500672.

17 *Knudsen cherry-picked*: Hannah Bleau Knudsen, "Biden Disinformation Chief Sang about Boys in Girls' Bathrooms Being 'Creepy,'" Breitbart, April 29, 2022, https://www.breitbart.com/politics/2022/04/29/biden-disinformation-chief-sang-about-boys-in-girls-bathrooms-being-creepy/.

17 *The* New York Post *seemed*: Jon Levine, "Biden 'Disinfo' Boss Nina Jankowicz Once Belted Out a Raunchy Parody Christmas Song," *New York Post*, April 30, 2022, https://nypost.com/2022/04/30/another-music-video-of-biden-disinfo-boss-nina-jankowicz-surfaces/.

18 *"She's off-key in a really bad Julie Andrews impersonation"*: Laura Ingraham, "Ingraham: Someone Should Give Her a Lesson in Basic Administrative

Law," *The Ingraham Angle*, Fox News, April 30, 2022, https://www.youtube.com/watch?v=-gscCsvqqIo.

18 *"Everyone involved"*: Carlson, "Tucker: This the Point."

20 *"My concern"*: Paul Gigot, "What Is the Disinformation Governance Board Trying to Accomplish?," May 2, 2022, in *Potomac Watch* podcast, 04:35, https://www.wsj.com/podcasts/opinion-potomac-watch/what-is-the-disinformation-governance-board-trying-to-accomplish/e33d2c82-a3d0-4121-a702-cf4a386ff4d7.

20 *"Can you give us an idea"*: "Press Briefing by Press Secretary Jen Psaki, April 28, 2022," https:§//www.whitehouse.gov/briefing-room/press-briefings/2022/04/28/press-briefing-by-press-secretary-jen-psaki-april-28-2022/.

22 *On Fox, Bret Baier*: Alejandro Mayorkas, "Sec. Mayorkas: 'I'm Looking Forward to Testifying before the US Senate,'" *Fox News Sunday*, May 1, 2022, https://www.foxnews.com/video/6305481541112.

23 *"There has been confusion"*: Department of Homeland Security, "Fact Sheet: DHS Internal Working Group Protects Free Speech and Other Fundamental Rights When Addressing Disinformation That Threatens the Security of the United States," May 2, 2022, accessed March 22, 2024, https://www.dhs.gov/news/2022/05/02/fact-sheet-dhs-internal-working-group-protects-free-speech-other-fundamental-rights.

CHAPTER 2 A Taxonomy of Lying

25 *the definition that a lie was*: "Lie Definition & Meaning," Dictionary.com, accessed April 24, 2024, https://www.dictionary.com/browse/lie.

25 *broader definitions for the word*: Merriam-Webster offers several definitions of "lie" as a noun. In addition to "an assertion of something known or believed by the speaker or writer to be untrue with intent to deceive," it also defines "lie" as "an untrue or inaccurate statement that may or may not be believed true by the speaker or writer" and "something that misleads or deceives." "Lie," merriamwebster.com, 2024, https://www.merriamwebster.com/dictionary/lie#:~:text=lie%2C%20prevaricate%2C%20equivocate%2C%20palter,quibbling%20or%20confusing%20the%20issue.

25 *Dean Baquet told NPR*: "'New York Times' Editor: 'We Owed It to Our Readers' to Call Trump Claims Lies,'" NPR, September 22, 2016, https://www.npr.org/2016/09/22/494919548/new-york-times-editor-we-owed-it-to-our-readers-to-call-trump-claims-lies.

26 *A 2018 study*: Paul Mena, "Principles and Boundaries of Fact-Checking: Journalists' Perceptions," *Journalism Practice* 13, no. 6 (2019): 657–672, https://www.tandfonline.com/doi/abs/10.1080/17512786.2018.1547655.

26 *President Obama's promises*: PolitiFact Obameter, "Provide a Path to Citizenship for Undocumented Immigrants," PolitiFact, September 21, 2016, https://www.politifact.com/truth-o-meter/promises/obameter/promise/288/provide-a-path-to-citizenship-for-undocumented-imm/.

26 *"Fund proposals"*: PolitiFact Obameter, "Fund Proposals to Help Fish and Game Survive Climate Change," PolitiFact, November 8, 2012, https://www.politifact.com/truth-o-meter/promises/obameter/promise/283/fund-proposals-to-help-fish-and-game-survive-clima/.

28 *the impact of the border wall*: Miriam Valverde, "No, Border Barrier Did Not Drive Down Crime in El Paso, Texas," PolitiFact, February 8, 2019, https://www.politifact.com/factchecks/2019/feb/08/donald-trump/no-border-barrier-did-not-drive-down-crime-el-paso/.

28 *size of his tax cut*: Eugene Kiely and D'Angelo Gore, "FactChecking Trump's Nashville Rally," FactCheck.org, May 30, 2018, https://www.factcheck.org/2018/05/factchecking-trumps-nashville-rally/.

28 *health care policy*: Shefali Luthra, "Trump's Claim That He 'Saved' Pre-ex Conditions 'Part Fantasy, Part Delusion,'" PolitiFact, January 15, 2020, https://www.politifact.com/factchecks/2020/jan/15/donald-trump/trumps-claim-he-saved-pre-ex-conditions-part-fanta/.

28 *cherry-picking*: Dave Umhoefer, "Mary Burke Says Wages Are Declining in Wisconsin at Double the Rate of Other States," PolitiFact, March 31, 2014, https://www.politifact.com/factchecks/2014/mar/31/mary-burke/mary-burke-says-wages-are-declining-wisconsin-doub/.

29 *The Lie of the Year*: PolitiFact Staff, "They Were Whoppers: A Look Back at PolitiFact's Lies of the Year, 2009 to 2021," PolitiFact, December 13, 2021, https://www.politifact.com/article/2022/dec/13/they-were-whoppers-a-look-back-at-politifacts-lies/.

30 *Schlafly's warnings*: Phyllis Schlafly, "What's Wrong with 'Equal Rights' for Women?," *Phyllis Schlafly Report* 5, no. 7 (February 1972), https://eagleforum.org/wp-content/uploads/2017/03/PSR-Feb1972.pdf.

CHAPTER 3 The Lying Hall of Fame

33 *"20,679 physicians say"*: "Doctors Smoking," Stanford Research into the Impact of Tobacco Advertising, https://tobacco.stanford.edu/cigarettes/doctors-smoking/.

33 *The surveys mentioned*: Martha N. Gardner and Allan M. Brandt, "The Doctors' Choice Is America's Choice," *American Journal of Public Health* 96, no. 2 (February 2006): 222–232, https://doi.org/10.2105/ajph.2005.066654.

34 *Tobacco Industry Research*: Michael J. Goodman, "Tobacco's PR Campaign: The Cigarette Papers," *Los Angeles Times*, September 18, 1994, www.latimes.com/archives/la-xpm-1994-09-18-tm-40179-story.html.

34 *"For more than 300 years"*: "A Frank Statement to Cigarette Smokers." Wikisource, June 16, 2020, https://en.wikisource.org/wiki/A_Frank_Statement_to_Cigarette_Smokers.

34 *smoking and lung cancer*: Goodman, "Tobacco's PR Campaign."

34 *The approach set*: Matt Egan, "Exxon Uses Big Tobacco's Playbook to Downplay the Climate Crisis, Harvard Study Finds," CNN, May 25, 2021, https://www.cnn.com/2021/05/13/business/exxon-climate-change-harvard/index.html; "Food Industry Pursues the Strategy of Big Tobacco," Yale E360, https://e360.yale.edu/features/food_industry_pursues_the_strategy_of_big_tobacco.

34 *Henry Waxman*: Philip J. Hilts, "Tobacco Chiefs Say Cigarettes Aren't Addictive," *New York Times*, April 15, 1994, https://www.nytimes.com/1994/04/15/us/tobacco-chiefs-say-cigarettes-aren-t-addictive.html.

35 *The companies falsely denied*: "The 5 Ways Tobacco Companies Lied about the Dangers of Smoking Cigarettes," Truth Initiative, https://truthinitiative.org/research-resources/tobacco-prevention-efforts/5-ways-tobacco-companies-lied-about-dangers-smoking.

35 *"This may be the kind of opportunity"*: "1978 Exxon Memo Proposing a Worldwide Effort to Answer 'CO2 Problem,'" Climate Files, https://www.climatefiles.com/exxonmobil/1978-exxon-memo-proposing-a-worldwide-effort-to-answer-co2-problem/.

35 *A famous 1998 strategy memo*: "1998 Global Science Team Memo: Smoke, Mirrors & Hot Air: How ExxonMobil Uses Big Tobacco's Tactics to Manufacture Uncertainty on Climate Science," Union of Concerned Scientists, January 2007, Appendix D, https://www.ucsusa.org/sites/default/files/2019-09/exxon_report.pdf.

37 *An in-depth examination*: Liam Stack, "6 Takeaways from the Times's Investigation Into Rupert Murdoch and His Family," *New York Times Magazine*, April 3, 2019, https://www.nytimes.com/interactive/2019/04/03/magazine/murdoch-family-investigation.html.

37 Times *reporters*: Jonathan Mahler and Jim Rutenberg, "Planet Fox: How Rupert Murdoch's Empire of Influence Remade The World," *New York Times Magazine*, April 3, 2019, https://www.nytimes.com/interactive/2019/04/03/magazine/rupert-murdoch-fox-news-trump.html.

38 *"Watching Giuliani!"*: US Dominion, Inc., Dominion Voting Systems, Inc., and Dominion Voting Systems Corporation v. Fox Corporation (Superior Court of the State of Delaware, February 27, 2023).

39 *That channel had a mix*: Richard Johnson, "MSNBC Predecessor America's Talking Commemorated," Page Six, July 2, 2014, https://pagesix.com/2014/07/02/msnbcs-predecessor-americas-talking-commemorated/.

39 *a show hosted by Ailes himself*: "1994: Launch of America's Talking," TV Worth Watching, accessed March 24, 2024, http://www.tvworthwatching.com/post/THISDAYINTVHISTORY20200704.aspx.

39 *A study by political scientist*: Jonathan S. Morris, "Slanted Objectivity? Perceived Media Bias, Cable News Exposure, and Political Attitudes," *Social Science Quarterly* 88, no. 3 (September 2007), https://onlinelibrary.wiley.com/doi/full/10.1111/j.1540-6237.2007.00479.x.

39 *Fox became such a powerhouse*: Stefano DellaVigna and Ethan Kaplan, "The Fox News Effect: Media Bias and Voting," *Quarterly Journal of Economics* 122, no. 3 (August 1, 2007): 1187–1234, https://doi.org/10.1162/qjec.122.3.1187.

40 *In* How to Watch Television: Jeffrey P. Jones, "Fox & Friends: Political Talk," in *How to Watch Television: Media Criticism in Practice*, ed. Ethan Thompson and Jason Mittell (New York: NYU Press, 2013), 186–194.

41 *The Friends aren't fact-checked often*: "Steve Doocy Report Card," PolitiFact accessed March 26, 2024, https://www.politifact.com/personalities/steve-doocy/; "Ainsley Earhardt Report Card," PolitiFact, accessed March 26, 2024, https://www.politifact.com/personalities/ainsley-earhardt/; "Brian Kilmeade Report Card," PolitiFact, accessed March 26, 2024, https://www.politifact.com/personalities/brian-kilmeade/.

42 *In* The Chaos Machine: Max Fisher, *The Chaos Machine: The Inside Story of How Social Media Rewired Our Minds and Our World* (New York: Little Brown, 2023), P. 65.

42 *Said Yanghee Lee*: Tom Miles, "U.N. Investigators Cite Facebook Role in Myanmar Crisis," Reuters, https://www.reuters.com/article/us-myanmar-rohingya-facebook-idUKKCN1GO2PN.

43 *of immigrants*: Dominick Mastrangelo, "Critics Blast Tucker Carlson over Immigration Remarks amid Border Surge," *The Hill*, September 23, 2021, https://thehill.com/homenews/media/573690-critics-blast-tucker-carlson-over-immigration-remarks/.

43 *of government*: Bill McCarthy, "Tucker Carlson Distorts New CDC Report, Makes False Mask Claim," PolitiFact, October 15, 2020, https://www.politifact.com/factchecks/2020/oct/15/tucker-carlson/tucker-carlson-distorts-new-cdc-report-makes-false/.

43 *of election fraud*: Jon Greenberg, "Tucker Carlson Wrong about People Not Being Able to Vote in Arizona's Maricopa County," PolitiFact, November 9,

2022, https://www.politifact.com/factchecks/2022/nov/09/tucker-carlson/tucker-carlson-wrong-arizona-voting-machines-not-l/.

43 *They originated with*: Rob Farley, "Anonymous GOP Officials Claim Commerce Nominee John Bryson Endorses World Government," PolitiFact, June 9, 2011, https://www.politifact.com/factchecks/2011/jun/09/gop-critics/anonymous-gop-officials-claim-commerce-nominee-joh/; Amy Sherman, "Allen West Says EPA Wants to Hire 230,000 Workers at a Cost of $21 Billion," PolitiFact, https://www.politifact.com/factchecks/2011/nov/07/allen-west/allen-west-says-epa-wants-hire-230000-workers-cost/.

43 *Fox's lawyers contended*: McDougal v. Fox News Network, LLC, No. 1:§2019cv11161—Document 39 (S.D.N.Y. 2020), https://law.justia.com/cases/federal/district-courts/new-york/nysdce/1:2019cv11161/527808/39/.

44 *The best numbers come*: "Talkers Estimetrix," Talkers, June 2023, https://talkers.com/top-talk-audiences/.

45 *Thornton's podcast*: *The Divided Dial*, in *On the Media*, November 15–December 21, 2022, https://www.wnycstudios.org/podcasts/otm/divided-dial.

45 *Joe Rogan, whose Spotify podcast*: Joe Rogan's falsehoods have been well-documented by many media organizations. For examples, see Linda Qiu, "Fact-Checking Joe Rogan's Interview with Robert Malone That Caused an Uproar," *New York Times*, February 8, 2022, https://www.nytimes.com/2022/02/08/arts/music/fact-check-joe-rogan-robert-malone.html; BBC Reality Check Team, "Joe Rogan: Four Claims from His Spotify Podcast Fact-Checked," BBC, January 31, 2022, https://www.bbc.com/news/60199614.

45 *In college, he was known as*: Robert Caro, *The Years of Lyndon Johnson*, Vol. 1, *The Path to Power* (New York: Knopf, 1981), 156.

46 *Three days after the second attack*: Gulf of Tonkin Resolution, H.J. Res. 1145, 88th Cong. (1964).

46 *The number of troops*: "Infographic: The Vietnam War Military Statistics," The Vietnam War Military Statistics | Gilder Lehrman Institute of American History, accessed March 31, 2024, https://www.gilderlehrman.org/history-resources/teacher-resources/infographic-vietnam-war-military-statistics.

47 *"Johnson's lies had poisoned"*: Eric Alterman, *Lying in State: Why Presidents Lie—And Why Trump Is Worse* (New York: Basic Books. 2020), 119.

47 *"Nixon lied to gain love"*: Fawn Brodie, *Richard Nixon: The Shaping of His Character* (New York: Norton. 1981), 25.

47 *Nixon then declared*: John M. Crewdson, "Nixon Ordered That the F.B.I. Be Told: 'Don't Go Any Further into This Case,'" *New York Times*, August 6, 1974, https://www.nytimes.com/1974/08/06/archives/nixon-ordered-that-the-fbi-be-told-dont-go-any-further-into-this.html.

48 *"I brought myself down"*: Frank Jackman, "President Nixon to David Frost: 'I Let Down the Country,'" *Daily News* (New York), May 5, 1977, https://www.nydailynews.com/2017/05/05/president-nixon-to-david-frost-i-let-down-the-country/.

48 *"You deliberately stood"*: Julian Zelizer, "Trump Steals a Page from Newt Gingrich," *The Atlantic*, December 12, 2018, https://www.theatlantic.com/ideas/archive/2018/12/before-wall-brawl-there-was-camscam/577945/.

49 *In an* Atlantic *article*: McKay Coppins, "The Man Who Broke Politics," *The Atlantic*, October 17, 2018, https://www.theatlantic.com/magazine/archive/2018/11/newt-gingrich-says-youre-welcome/570832/.

50 *Greenberg told the* Washington Post: Kevin Merida, "Slick Willie: Nickname Proves Hard to Slip," *Washington Post*, December 20, 1998, https://www.washingtonpost.com/wp-srv/politics/special/clinton/stories/slick122098.htm.

51 *30,573 false or misleading claims*: Glenn Kessler et al., "Trump's False or Misleading Claims Total 30,573 over 4 Years," *Washington Post*, January 24, 2021, https://www.washingtonpost.com/politics/2021/01/24/trumps-false-or-misleading-claims-total-30573-over-four-years/.

51 *Press Secretary Sean Spicer*: Mahita Gajanan, "Sean Spicer 'Absolutely' Regrets Attacking Reporters over President Trump's Inauguration Crowd Size," *Time*, September 18, 2017, https://time.com/4946886/sean-spicer-inauguration-emmys-regret/.

52 *"lying is second nature to him"*: Jane Mayer, "Donald Trump's Ghostwriter Tells All," *The New Yorker*, July 18, 2016, https://www.newyorker.com/magazine/2016/07/25/donald-trumps-ghostwriter-tells-all.

CHAPTER 4 Consumed by Lies

53 *posted them on a little-noticed website*: House Select Committee to Investigate the January 6th Attack on the United States Capitol, "Select January 6th Committee Final Report and Supporting Materials Collection," U.S. Government Publishing Office, December 22, 2022, https://www.govinfo.gov/collection/january-6th-committee-final-report.

54 *I found a sad tale*: Barber's thoughts and comments in this chapter come from his committee interview, his Facebook messages with me, and a documentary about him produced by Chris Jones for The Intercept. Select Committee to Investigate the January 6th Attack on the U.S. Capitol, *Interview of: Eric Barber*, GPO-J6-TRANSCRIPT-CTRL0000055539, U.S. Government Publishing Office, 2022, https://www.govinfo.gov/content/pkg/GPO

-J6-TRANSCRIPT-CTRL0000055539/pdf/GPO-J6-TRANSCRIPT -CTRL0000055539.pdf; Christopher Jones, "What Drove a West Virginia Democrat to Storm the Capitol on January 6?," The Intercept, January 5, 2022, https://theintercept.com/2022/01/05/january-6-capitol-west-virginia -parkersburg/.

55 *He won by six votes*: Brett Dunlap, "Election Results Unchanged as Officials Canvass Ballots," *Parkersburg News and Sentinel*, November 16, 2016, https:// www.newsandsentinel.com/news/local-news/2016/11/election-results -unchanged-as-officials-canvass-ballots/.

55 *He initially joined fellow Democrats*: Jess Mancini, "Wood County Democratic Party Executive Committee Endorses Non-discrimination Ordinance," *Parkersburg News and Sentinel*, March 14, 2017, https://www.newsandsentinel .com/news/local-news/2017/03/wood-county-democratic-party-executive -committee-endorses-non-discrimination-ordinance/.

55 *"I just took the politician's road"*: Jones, "What Drove a West Virginia Democrat."

56 *"I think Mr. Barber"*: Evan Bevins, "Monday Not Parkersburg City Councilman Barber's First Arrest," *Parkersburg News and Sentinel*, July 22, 2017, https://www.newsandsentinel.com/news/local-news/2017/07/monday -not-parkersburg-city-councilman-barbers-first-arrest/.

56 *He liked his new identity*: Jones, "What Drove a West Virginia Democrat."

57 *which the Fox clips portrayed*: Gregg Re, "What Is Antifa, the Far-Left Group Tied to Violent Protests?," Fox News, June 1, 2020, https://www.foxnews. com/politics/what-is-antifa; Tucker Carlson, "Tucker Carlson: Antifa Is the Armed Militia of the Democratic Party," Fox News, January 23, 2023, https:// www.foxnews.com/opinion/tucker-carlson-antifa-armed-militia-democratic -party-back-in-force.

57 *The number of people*: Daniel Funke, "Ask PolitiFact: What Is Antifa, and Why Is It All over My Timeline?," PolitiFact, July 2, 2020, https://www .politifact.com/article/2020/jul/02/ask-politifact-what-antifa-and-why-it -all-over-my-/.

58 *"These groups are rarely militant"*: Stanislav Vysotsky, "What?—or Who?—Is Antifa?," The Conversation, September 4, 2020, https://apnews.com /article/race-and-ethnicity-the-conversation-ec8606bc075f7922c9041 f3068e4bc25.

58 *The* New York Times *documented*: Davey Alba and Ben Decker, "41 Cities, Many Sources: How False Rumors about Antifa Spread Locally," *New York Times*, June 22, 2020, https://www.nytimes.com/2020/06/22/technology /antifa-local-disinformation.html.

58 *Barber told committee investigators*: To verify this, John Lee, one of my research assistants, used the phrases that Barber mentioned in his interview with the committee's investigators and then searched for them in transcripts of Fox News programs and other conservative media. Lee found dozens of matches.

59 *lost reelection by ten points*: "68 of 68 Precincts Counted in Wood County," *Parkersburg News and Sentinel*, November 3, 2020, https://www.newsandsentinel.com/news/local-news/2020/11/68-of-68-precincts-counted-in-wood-county/.

60 *That scene*: *Gangs of New York*, directed by Martin Scorsese (2002; Miramax), https://www.youtube.com/watch?v=Len_myPvlUQ.

61 *Trump continued to rattle off false claims*: Arijeta Lajka, "More Votes Were Not Cast in Detroit in 2020 Than There Are People," Associated Press, November 18, 2020, https://apnews.com/article/fact-checking-9742674804.

62 *He got close*: U.S. Department of Justice, "Department of Justice Closes Investigation into the Death of Ashli Babbitt," U.S. Attorney's Office, District of Columbia, April 14, 2021, https://www.justice.gov/usao-dc/pr/department-justice-closes-investigation-death-ashli-babbitt.

62 *"I don't think it"*: Evan Bevins, "Parkersburg Man Shares Experience from U.S. Capitol," January 7, 2021, *Parkersburg News and Sentinel*, https://www.newsandsentinel.com/news/local-news/2021/01/parkersburg-man-shares-experience-from-u-s-capitol/.

62 *His short segment*: "Former Parkersburg City Councilman Recounts Wednesday's Protests," WTAP, January 6, 2021, https://www.wtap.com/video/2021/01/07/wtap-news-eric-barber/.

62 *He was charged with*: Andrew Cooper, "Affidavit in Support of a Criminal Complaint," United States v. Eric Gene Barber, 1:21-mj-00235 (D.D.C. February 16, 2021) ECF No. 1.

63 *He was sentenced to*: "Signed Plea Agreement," United States v. Eric Gene Barber, 1:21-mj-00235 (D.D.C. February 16, 2021) ECF No. 1.

63 *"It's troubling"*: Brad McElhinny, "Former Parkersburg Councilman Is Sentenced to 45 Days after Jan. 6 Riot," MetroNews, June 14, 2022, https://wvmetronews.com/2022/06/14/former-parkersburg-councilman-is-sentenced-to-45-days-after-jan-6-riot/.

63 *"A stolen phone charger"*: Evan Bevins, "Barber Sentenced to 45 Days for Role in Capitol Riot," *Parkersburg News and Sentinel*, June 17, 2022, https://www.newsandsentinel.com/uncategorized/2022/06/barber-sentenced-to-45-days-for-role-in-capitol-riot-2/.

67 *Here are some of the big reasons*: This summary is based on interviews with researchers David Markowitz, Brendan Nyhan, and Jon Roozenbeek. For

a helpful summary of the research, see Brendan Nyhan, "Facts and Myths about Misperceptions," *Journal of Economic Perspectives* 34, no. 3 (Summer 2020): 220–236.

67 *Barber, like all of us*: Timothy Levine, "Truth-Default Theory and the Psychology of Lying and Deception Detection," *Current Opinion in Psychology* 47 (October 2022), https://doi.org/10.1016/j.copsyc.2022.101380.

67 *"Our preferred position"*: "Why Do We Assume That Everyone's Telling the Truth?," *Oprah's Super Soul Sunday*, September 15, 2019, https://www.oprah.com/own-super-soul-sunday/why-do-we-assume-that-everyones-telling-the-truth.

67 *A study of more than*: Benjamin Lyons et al., "Overconfidence in News Judgments Is Associated with False News Susceptibility," *Proceedings of the National Academy of Sciences* 118, no. 21 (May 2021), https://doi.org/10.1073/pnas.2019527118.

68 *network comparisons by PolitiFact*: The network's hosts and guests consistently earn more False and Pants on Fire ratings than other networks. For examples, see "PunditFact," PolitiFact, accessed March 19, 2024, https://www.politifact.com/punditfact/.

68 *A 2023 study*: Raunak Pillai et al., "All the President's Lies: Repeated False Claims and Public Opinion," *Public Opinion Quarterly* 87, no. 3 (Fall 2023): 764–802, https://doi.org/10.1093/poq/nfad032.

CHAPTER 5 Catching the Liars

73 *"No ducking and hiding"*: David Broder, "Five Ways to Put Some Sanity Back in Elections," *Washington Post*, January 14, 1990, https://www.washingtonpost.com/archive/opinions/1990/01/14/five-ways-to-put-some-sanity-back-in-elections/c6d98e0b-25fc-413d-8724-73e1a5f170c3/.

74 *A typical ad watch*: Mark Sherman, "Coverdell Steps up Attacks on Fowler Commercial Faults Senator for Raises," *Atlanta Journal-Constitution*, October 13, 1992, E4.

74 *A study examining*: Courtney Bennett, "Assessing the Impact of Ad Watches on the Strategic Decision-Making Process: A Comparative Analysis of Ad Watches in the 1992 and 1996 Presidential Elections," *American Behavioral Scientist* 40, no. 8 (August 1997): 1161–1182, https://doi.org/10.1177/0002764297040008014.

75 *He launched FactCheck.org*: Brooks Jackson, "Is This a Great Job, or What?," FactCheck.org, December 5, 2003, https://www.factcheck.org/2003/12/is-this-a-great-job-or-what/.

75 *headlines such as*: FactCheck.org Staff, "Latest FactCheck Articles," FactCheck .org, January 24, 2004, https://web.archive.org/web/20040124203914/ http:/factcheck.org/.

76 *I wasn't the first*: We liked it so much we obtained trademarks for Truth-O-Meter and the Pants on Fire rating. See U.S. Trademark Registrations 3855782/77835123 and 5011920/8683071.

78 *"So far we like what we've seen"*: Brooks Jackson, "We Have Company!," FactCheck .org, August 28, 2007, https://www.factcheck.org/2007/08/we-have -company/.

CHAPTER 6 The Ministry of Truth, Part 2

81 *"Executive Director Nina Jankowicz"*: Ben Shapiro, "Joe Biden's Ministry of Truth," May 2, 2022, in *The Ben Shapiro Show*, produced by The Daily Wire, podcast, 18:15, https://podcasts.apple.com/us/podcast/the-ben-shapiro -show/id1047335260.

82 *"By the way, she's eight months pregnant"*: Lis Power (@LisPower1), "Fox News Host Brian Kilmeade Lashes Out at Biden DHS Appointee for Being Pregnant," Twitter, April 29, 2022, 9:44 a.m., https://twitter.com/lispower1 /status/1520036342243246080?s=61&t=UEeuiEPNGl_oxk-UzNuYLQ.

83 *"The American people"*: "Lauren Boebert – House Session May 10, 2022," C-SPAN video, May 10, 2022, https://www.c-span.org/video/?c5044659 /user-clip-lauren-boebert-house-session-10-2022.

85 *Sen. Josh Hawley of Missouri sent*: Josh Hawley, email message, May 5, 2022, archived by Archive of Political Emails, accessed March 29, 2024, https:// politicalemails.org/messages/655884.

85 *Rep. Mike Johnson of Louisiana*: Mike Johnson, email message, May 4, 2022, archived by Archive of Political Emails, accessed March 29, 2024, https:// politicalemails.org/messages/655098.

85 *"DHS hasn't adequately explained"*: ACLU (@ACLU), "DHS hasn't adequately explained the need for or scope of its eerily named Disinformation Governance Board [...]," Twitter, May 5, 2022, https://twitter.com/ACLU /status/1522377607324520448.

85 *"The Department has a history"*: "Re: Significant Concerns regarding the 'Disinformation Governance Board,'" May 3, 2022, https://s3.document cloud.org/documents/21850086/letter-to-mayorkas-re-disinformation -governance-board_may-3-2022.pdf.

85 *In her letter to Mayorkas*: Nina Jankowicz, "Nina Jankowicz Resignation Letter," U.S. Department of Homeland Security, May 18, 2022, https://www

.dhs.gov/sites/default/files/2023-06/Nina%20Jankowicz%20resignation%20 letter.pdf.

90 *DHS also made a late and feeble effort*: Taylor Lorenz, "How the Biden Administration Let Right-Wing Attacks Derail Its Disinformation Efforts," *Washington Post*, May 18, 2022, https://www.washingtonpost.com/technology/2022/05/18/disinformation-board-dhs-nina-jankowicz/.

90 *Now that she was free*: Nomaan Merchant and Amanda Seitz, "New 'disinformation' board paused amid free speech questions," Associated Press, May 18, 2022, accessed at *Portland Press Herald*, https://www.pressherald.com/2022/05/18/new-disinformation-board-paused-amid-free-speech-questions/.

90 *When we put pressure*: Lauren Boebert (@LaurenBoebert) "When we put pressure on this administration, they fold like a house of cards. The so-called Disinformation Governance Board is done. Hopefully Nina figures out another way to get famous. Watch out for that!," Twitter, May 18, 2022, https://twitter.com/laurenboebert/status/1526955619755900928.

90 "*We have done it*": Benny Johnson, "Breaking: Joe Biden's Ministry of Truth Will Be Shut Down, Nina Jankowicz Resigned—We Did It, America!," Facebook, May 18, 2022, https://www.facebook.com/bennyjohnson/videos/518851766563400/.

91 *Overall, the letter just plucked*: Charles Grassley and Josh Hawley, Letter to Alejandro Mayorkas, June 7, 2022, https://www.grassley.senate.gov/imo/media/doc/grassley_hawley_to_deptofhomelandsecuritydisinformation governanceboard.pdf. It's conceivable the whistle-blower could have provided more evidence that prompted the senators' concerns. But it seems likely they would have included that in the letter and attachments.

CHAPTER 7 Why They Lie (and the Tale of Mike Pence)

96 *They often sat with*: Indiana Democratic Party, "A Timeline of Mike Pence's Discrimination against the LGBT Community," INDEMS, July 16, 2016, https://indems.org/press-release/a-timeline-of-mike-pences-discrimination-against-the-lgbt-community/.

96 *His slogans were*: Brian Slodysko, "Running Mate Mike Pence: Conservative but Not Angry about it," Associated Press, July 16, 2016, https://apnews.com/article/ee95b629a1ba47bab829d696c8c1d170.

96 *He partnered with*: "Federal Shield Law Introduced in House Once More," Reporters Committee for Freedom of the Press, September 29, 2011, https://www.rcfp.org/federal-shield-law-introduced-house-once-more/.

96 *He was the lead*: Jim VandeHei and Charles Babbington, "Immigration Bill Aims to Bridge Republican Divide," *Washington Post*, July 25, 2006, https://www.washingtonpost.com/archive/politics/2006/07/25/immigration-bill-aims-to-bridge-republican-divide/bd152d79-a7a3-4290-8d85-bca737897f83/.

97 *He joined other Republicans*: Angie Drobnic Holan, "No Money in the Stimulus for San Francisco Mice," PolitiFact, February 13, 2009, https://www.politifact.com/factchecks/2009/feb/13/mike-pence/no-money-stimulus-san-francisco-mice/; Angie Drobnic Holan, "Stimulus Has Money to Help Fish, Off-roaders," PolitiFact, February 4, 2009, https://www.politifact.com/factchecks/2009/feb/04/mike-pence/stimulus-has-money-help-fish-roaders/.

97 *He ended 2009*: "Mike Pence Report Card," PolitiFact, https://www.politifact.com/factchecks/list/?page=3&speaker=mike-pence.

97 *In 2015, investigative journalist*: Andrew Kaczynski, "'Smoking Doesn't Kill' and Other Great Old Op-Eds from Mike Pence," BuzzFeed, March 31, 2015, https://www.buzzfeednews.com/article/andrewkaczynski/smoking-doesnt-kill-and-other-great-old-op-eds-from-mike-pen.

98 *he earned False ratings*: Angie Drobnic Holan, "Mike Pence Said Republican Medicare Proposal Gives Seniors the Same Health Care as Congress," PolitiFact, April 13, 2011, https://www.politifact.com/factchecks/2011/apr/13/mike-pence/mike-pence-said-republican-medicare-proposal-will-/; Angie Drobnic Holan, "Mike Pence Says Raising Taxes Lowers Tax Revenues," PolitiFact, November 9, 2010, https://www.politifact.com/factchecks/2010/nov/09/mike-pence/mike-pence-says-raising-taxes-lowers-tax-revenues/.

98 *Mike is famous*: Mike Pence, "Confessions of a Negative Campaigner," archived by Craig Fehrman, 1991, https://craigfehrman.com/2013/01/06/mike-pences-confessions-of-a-negative-campaigner/.

98 The Atlantic*'s McKay Coppins*: McKay Coppins, "God's Plan for Mike Pence," *The Atlantic*, January/February 2018, https://www.theatlantic.com/magazine/archive/2018/01/gods-plan-for-mike-pence/546569/.

99 *Mike squeaked by*: "2012 Indiana Governor Results," *Politico*, November 19, 2012, https://www.politico.com/2012-election/results/governor/indiana/.

99 *He signed bills*: Tom Davies and Brian Slodysko, "Pence's Indiana Record More Complicated Than Campaign Claims," Associated Press, July 20, 2016, https://www.pbs.org/newshour/politics/pences-indiana-record-complicated-campaign-claims; Emily Crockett, "Indiana Crammed as Many Anti-abortion Bills as It Could into This Horrifying New Law," Vox, March 26, 2016, https://www.vox.com/2016/3/26/11308890/indiana-abortion-law-miscarriage.

99 *But critics said*: Tom LoBianco, "State-Run News Outlet Will Compete with Media," *Indianapolis Star*, January 26, 2015, https://www.usatoday.com/story/news/politics/2015/01/26/state-run-news-outlet-will-compete-with-media/22379417/; Joe Archambault, "Mike Pence's Indiana Medicaid Expansion: Rhetoric vs. Reality," *Forbes*, May 28, 2014, https://www.forbes.com/sites/theapothecary/2014/05/28/rhetoric-vs-reality-the-mike-pence-medicaid-expansion/?sh=4c55e672ec9c.

99 *Mike made a clumsy*: Dwight Adams, "Why the 'Religious Freedom Law' Signed by Mike Pence Is So Controversial," *Indianapolis Star*, April 25, 2018, https://www.indystar.com/story/news/2018/04/25/rfra-indiana-why-law-signed-mike-pence-so-controversial/546411002/.

99 *Facing a huge*: Tony Cook et al., "Gov. Mike Pence Signs RFRA Fix," *Indianapolis Star*, April 1, 2015, https://web.archive.org/web/20200531004610/https://eu.indystar.com/story/news/politics/2015/04/01/indiana-rfra-deal-sets-limited-protections-for-lgbt/70766920/.

99 *"some of the victories"*: Tom LoBianco, "Fact Check: Pence Stretches Bounds with Claims," Associated Press, May 18, 2014, https://www.goshennews.com/news/fact-check-pence-stretches-bounds-with-claims/article_70059579-f5e4-5bc7-a2a1-516e194cb638.html.

99 *PolitiFact gave him*: Katie Sanders, "Did Barack Obama Vote for Religious Freedom Restoration Act with 'Very Same' Wording as Indiana's?," PolitiFact, March 29, 2015, https://www.politifact.com/factchecks/2015/mar/29/mike-pence/did-barack-obama-vote-religious-freedom-restoratio/.

100 *They met a few times*: Maggie Haberman and Alexander Burns, "How Donald Trump Settled on Mike Pence," *New York Times*, July 15, 2016, https://www.nytimes.com/2016/07/16/us/politics/mike-pence-donald-trump-vice-president.html.

100 *unknown to nine*: Sarah Dutton et al., "Poll: Mike Pence Is Unknown to Most Voters," CBS News, July 14, 2016, https://www.cbsnews.com/news/poll-mike-pence-trump-vice-president-is-unknown-to-most-voters/.

100 *In the summer that*: "PolitiFact Scorecard: Mike Pence," PolitiFact, https://www.politifact.com/personalities/mike-pence/; "Person: Mike Pence," FactCheck.org, https://www.factcheck.org/person/mike-pence/.

101 *President Donald Trump's*: Louis Jacobson, "Discussing Health Care, Mike Pence Is Wrong about How Car Insurance Works," PolitiFact, March 23, 2017, https://www.politifact.com/factchecks/2017/mar/23/mike-pence/discussing-health-care-mike-pence-wrong-about/

101 *"Along the southern border"*: W. Gardner Selby, "VP Mike Pence Says Government Nabbing 7 Terrorists or Suspected Terrorists a Day on Southern

Border," PolitiFact, February 21, 2018, https://www.politifact.com/factchecks/2018/feb/21/mike-pence/pants-fire-mike-pences-claim-about-nabbing-7-terro/.

101 *"The reality of voter"*: Glenn Kessler, "Pence's Hyped-Up Claims of 'Voter Fraud' in Indiana," *Washington Post*, August 5, 2020, https://www.washingtonpost.com/politics/2020/08/05/pences-hyped-up-claims-voter-fraud-that-took-place-indiana/.

101 *To help spread*: Michael Pence, "There Isn't a Coronavirus 'Second Wave,'" *Wall Street Journal*, June 16, 2020, https://www.wsj.com/articles/there-isnt-a-coronavirus-second-wave-11592327890.

101 *"Nowhere does he"*: Glenn Kessler, Twitter, June 16, 2020, https://twitter.com/GlennKesslerWP/status/1272968436218507265.

101 *A week and a half*: Linda Qiu, "As Cases Surge, Pence Misleads on Coronavirus Pandemic," *New York Times*, June 26, 2020, https://www.nytimes.com/2020/06/26/us/politics/coronavirus-pence-fact-check.html; Daniel Dale, "Fact Check: As Pandemic Situation Worsens, Pence Paints a Deceptively Rosy Picture," CNN, June 26, 2020, https://www.cnn.com/2020/06/26/politics/fact-check-pence-briefing-coronavirus-june/index.html.

102 *"After an election"*: Mike Pence, "Election Integrity Is a National Imperative," The Daily Signal, March 3, 2021, https://www.dailysignal.com/2021/03/03/election-integrity-is-a-national-imperative.

104 *A 2018 profile*: Coppins, "God's Plan for Mike Pence."

105 *he filed the disclosures*: Liz Essley White, "A Senator Couldn't Find Fauci Financial Info. But We Did," Center for Public Integrity, January 12, 2022, https://publicintegrity.org/health/coronavirus-and-inequality/senator-couldnt-find-fauci-financial-disclosure/.

108 *At PolitiFact, we*: "Obama Birth Certificate Scorecard," PolitiFact, https://www.politifact.com/obama-birth-certificate/.

108 *Some related falsehoods*: Bill Adair, "Photo Was Taken during Anthem, Not Pledge," PolitiFact, November 8, 2007, https://www.politifact.com/factchecks/2007/nov/08/chain-email/photo-was-taken-during-anthem-not-pledge/.

108 *"he turns his back"*: Bill Adair, "A New Twist on an Old Distortion," PolitiFact, February 8, 2008, https://www.politifact.com/factchecks/2008/feb/08/chain-email/a-new-twist-on-an-old-distortion/.

108 *"Mr. and Mrs. Barack"*: "Barack Obama Birth Announcement," *Honolulu Advertiser*, https://www.newspapers.com/article/the-honolulu-advertiser-barack-obama-bir/18503640/. An identical announcement ran in the *Honolulu Star-Bulletin*.

109 *"What we learned"*: Valerie Jarrett, *Finding My Voice: My Journey to the West Wing and the Path Forward* (New York: Viking, 2019).

109 *"You guys know I'm Black"*: This account comes from a lengthy interview with my Duke class on February 1, 2021. He gave a similar account in an interview: Michael Steele and William Kristol, America at a Crossroads," June 17, 2021, YouTube video, June 17, 2021, https://youtube.com/watch?v=QQh6zZE9cFA.

CHAPTER 8 Orca and the Teacher Who Wouldn't Lie

112 *Orcas eat narwhals*: "Narwhal Fast Facts," Milwaukee Public Museum, accessed March 25, 2024, https://www.mpm.edu/sites/default/files/files%20and%20dox/education/Summer-2022/Narwhal_FastFacts.pdf.

112 *Spokeswoman Gail Gitcho*: Margaret Warner, "Romney Campaign Enlists Help of Killer Whale Project to Get Out the Vote," *PBS NewsHour*, November 12, 2012, www.pbs.org/newshour/politics/romney-campaign-enlists-help-of-killer-whale-project-to-get-out-thvote.

112 *"You'll be the key link"*: Maggie Haberman and Alexander Burns, "Romney's ORCA Program Sank," *Politico*, November 9, 2012, https://www.politico.com/story/2012/11/romneys-orca-program-cant-stay-afloat-083653.

113 Politico *reporter Steve Friess pursued the tips*: Steve Friess, "Romney Poll App Reportedly Glitchy," *Politico*, November 6, 2012, https://www.politico.com/story/2012/11/romney-poll-watching-app-reportedly-glitchy-083439.

114 *Paul Boyer's office*: Unless noted otherwise, this account of Paul Boyer's vote and the aftermath is based on interviews with him from January to June 2022.

116 *At seventeen lines, the bill's brevity*: "A Resolution Declaring the Maricopa County Board of Supervisors in Contempt of the Arizona Senate," S.R. 1005, 55th Leg., 1st Sess. (Az, 2021).

119 *All key figures in fighting the election lie*: Editorial Board of the *Arizona Republic*, "It Wasn't Easy to Stand Up to Arizona's Election Audit Madness. These 6 Did," *Arizona Republic*, December 30, 2021, www.azcentral.com/story/opinion/editorial/2021/12/30/arizonans-year-risked-destruction-buck-election-audit/9025932002/.

120 *"I made up my mind that I would run the risk"*: Plato, *The Apology of Socrates*, Center for Hellenic Studies, March 2, 2021, accessed July 1, 2022, chs.harvard.edu/primary-source/plato-the-apology-of-socrates-sb/.

120 *"Death is something"*: Plato, *The Apology*, https://www2.hawaii.edu/~freeman/courses/phil100/04.%20Apology.pdf, 158.

CHAPTER 9 Patterns of Lying

123 *Researchers at George Mason University*: "Study: Media Fact-Checker Says Republicans Lie More," Center for Media and Public Affairs at George Mason University, May 28, 2013, https://cmpa.gmu.edu/study-media-fact-checker-says-republicans-lie-more/.

123 *found a similar ratio*: Eric Ostermeier, "Selection Bias? PolitiFact Rates Republican Statements as False at 3 Times the Rate of Democrats," Smart Politics, February 10, 2011, https://smartpolitics.lib.umn.edu/2011/02/10/selection-bias-politifact-rate/.

124 *Republicans were slightly worse*: Glenn Kessler, "One Year of Fact Checking: An Accounting," *Washington Post*, December 27, 2011, https://www.washingtonpost.com/blogs/fact-checker/post/one-year-of-fact-checking--an-accounting/2011/12/27/gIQAR1taOP_blog.html.

129 *Democrat got $30 million in tax money*: Paul Specht, "Budd Falsely Accuses Manning of Getting $30M in Taxpayer Money," PolitiFact, October 23, 2018, https://www.politifact.com/factchecks/2018/oct/23/ted-budd/budd-falsely-accuses-manning-getting-30m-taxpayer-/.

129 *a false claim from Democratic Sen. Cory Booker*: Jon Greenberg, "On Expanded Medicare, Booker Cites Nonexistent CBO Study," PolitiFact, February 8, 2019, https://www.politifact.com/factchecks/2019/feb/08/cory-booker/medicare-booker-cites-non-existent-cbo-study/.

129 *a Texas official's Pants on Fire claim*: W. Gardner Selby, "Ken Paxton Draws on Debunked Figures, Says 'Illegals' Committed 600,000 Crimes in Texas since 2011," PolitiFact, September 7, 2018, https://www.politifact.com/factchecks/2018/sep/07/ken-paxton/ken-paxton-draws-debunked-figures-says-illegals-co/.

129 *"amnesty" for immigrants*: Maria Ramirez Uribe, 'Ron DeSantis' Claim That Trump Wanted to Grant 'Amnesty' to 2 Million People Needs Context," PolitiFact, June 5, 2023, https://www.politifact.com/factchecks/2023/jun/05/ron-desantis/ron-desantis-claim-that-trump-wanted-to-grant-amne/.

129 *"to stop illegal immigrants from voting"*: Miriam Valverde, "Did Brian Kemp Fight Obama Twice 'to Stop Illegal Immigrants from Voting'?," PolitiFact, March 21, 2018, http://www.politifact.com/factchecks/2018/mar/21/brian-kemp/Did-Brian-Kemp-fight-Obama-twice-to-stop-illegal/.

129 *portray Democrats as immigrant-cuddling softies*: Bill McCarthy, "Corey Stewart Falsely Claims Sen. Tim Kaine Wants to Do Away with ICE, Border Patrol," PolitiFact, July 3, 2018, http://www.politifact.com/factchecks/2018/jul/03/corey-stewart/corey-stewart-falsely-claims-sen-tim-kaine-wants-d/.

130 *PolitiFact chose "Republicans voted to end Medicare"*: Bill Adair and Angie Holan, "Lie of the Year 2011: Republicans Voted to End Medicare," PolitiFact, December 20, 2011, https://www.politifact.com/article/2011/dec/20/lie-year-democrats-claims-republicans-voted-end-me/.

130 *he was "morbidly obese"*: Emily Venezky, "Donald Trump Doesn't Meet the Definition of Morbidly Obese," PolitiFact, May 19, 2020, https://www.politifact.com/factchecks/2020/may/19/nancy-pelosi/no-he-not-morbidly-obese/.

130 *his administration was "raiding money"*: Chris Nichols, "Kamala Harris Is Wrong, Trump Isn't 'Raiding Money' from Military Pensions," PolitiFact, March 28, 2019, https://www.politifact.com/factchecks/2019/mar/28/kamala-harris/kamala-harris-wrong-trump-isnt-raiding-money-milit/.

131 *"the president is cutting the CDC's budget"*: Paul Specht, "NC Democrat Says Trump Is Cutting the CDC Budget by 80 Percent," PolitiFact, February 16, 2018, https://www.politifact.com/factchecks/2018/feb/16/bobbie-richardson/nc-democrat-says-trumps-cutting-cdc-budget-80-perc/.

131 *"to walk right into a school zone with a loaded weapon"*: John Kruzel, "No, the GOP Concealed Carry Bill Does Not Block States from Keeping Guns out of Schools," PolitiFact, December 7, 2017, https://www.politifact.com/factchecks/2017/dec/07/brendan-boyle/no-gop-concealed-carry-bill-does-not-block-states-/.

131 *"Hedge fund managers"*: Sarah Hauer, "Testing Tammy Baldwin Claim on Taxes for Hedge Fund Managers vs. Truck Drivers," PolitiFact, April 13, 2016, http://www.politifact.com/factchecks/2016/apr/13/tammy-baldwin/testing-tammy-baldwin-claim-taxes-hedge-fund-manag/.

131 *"There are 43 states"*: Louis Jacobson, "James Clyburn Misspeaks in Saying 43 States Have Passed Voting Restrictions," PolitiFact,, March 29, 2021, https://www.politifact.com/factchecks/2021/mar/29/james-clyburn/james-clyburn-misspeaks-saying-43-states-have-pass/.

131 *A few of his big ones*: John Greenberg, "Biden Wrong That McDonald's Workers Can't Jump to Competing Chains," PolitiFact, July 28, 2020, https://www.politifact.com/factchecks/2020/jul/28/joe-biden/biden-wrong-mcdonalds-workers-cant-jump-competing-/; Amy Sherman, "Joe Biden's Pants on Fire Claim about His Arrest in South Africa," PolitiFact, March 4, 2020, https://www.politifact.com/factchecks/2020/mar/04/joe-biden/joe-bidens-pants-fire-claim-about-his-arrest-south/; Glenn Kessler, "Biden's False Claim That the 2nd Amendment Bans Cannon Ownership," *Washington Post*, June 28, 2021, https://www.washingtonpost.com/politics/2021/06/28/bidens-false-claim-that-2nd-amendment-bans-cannon-ownership/.

131 *Writing in* The Atlantic: Molly Ball, "Donald Trump and the Politics of Fear," *The Atlantic*, September 2, 2016, https://www.theatlantic.com/politics/archive/2016/09/donald-trump-and-the-politics-of-fear/498116/.

132 *A 2015 review*: "Fear-Based Appeals Effective at Changing Attitudes, Behaviors after All," American Psychological Association, October 2015, https://www.apa.org/news/press/releases/2015/10/fear-based-appeals.

134 *we more often fact-check*: Angie Holan, "The Principles of the Truth-O-Meter: PolitiFact's Methodology for Independent Fact-Checking," PolitiFact, July 12, 2023, https://www.politifact.com/article/2018/feb/12/principles-truth-o-meter-politifacts-methodology-i/#How%20we%20choose%20claims.

135 *claimed a PolitiFact Virginia reporter was biased*: Bill McMorris, "Fisking Fiske's Record," *Washington Free Beacon*, August 7, 2012, https://freebeacon.com/politics/fisking-fiskes-record/.

135 *"Despite the media's admirably tough-minded stance"*: Dan Kennedy, "Fact-Checking in the Age of Trump: Why False Equivalence Is Harming Democracy," WGBH, September 18, 2019, https://www.wgbh.org/news/commentary/2019-09-18/fact-checking-in-the-age-of-trump-why-false-equivalence-is-harming-democracy.

135 New York Times *columnist Paul Krugman said*: Paul Krugman, "Politifact, R.I.P.," *New York Times*, December 20, 2011, https://archive.nytimes.com/krugman.blogs.nytimes.com/2011/12/20/politifact-r-i-p/.

136 *The Associated Press checked the claim*: Sophia Tulp, "Old Comments by Disinformation Board Director Misrepresented Online," Associated Press, May 14, 2022, https://apnews.com/article/fact-check-disinformation-board-director-twitter-049631150022.

136 *PolitiFact published a Q&A*: Jeff Cercone and Maria Ramirez Uribe, "What Exactly Will New DHS 'Disinformation Governance Board' Do?," PolitiFact, May 10, 2022, https://www.politifact.com/article/2022/may/10/what-exactly-will-new-dhs-disinformation-governanc/.

137 *only a small percentage*: In 2022, only 33 of 435 U.S. representatives got checked on any claim. Mark Stencel and Erica Ryan, "From Fact Deserts to Fact Streams," Duke Reporters' Lab, March 2023, https://reporterslab.org/wp-content/uploads/2023/03/From-Fact-Deserts-to-Fact-Streams.pdf.

CHAPTER 10 The Jeep Lie

139 *"I saw a story today"*: "Mitt Romney Campaign Rally in Ohio," October 25, 2012, ElectAd, YouTube, https://www.youtube.com/watch?v=7U-en3jwb5U.

140 *The Bloomberg story*: Craig Trudell, "Fiat Says China May Build All Jeeps as SUV Demand Increases," Bloomberg News, October 21, 2012, https://www.bloomberg.com/news/articles/2012-10-21/fiat-says-china-may-build-all-jeep-models-as-suv-demand-climbs.

140 *"In another potential blow"*: Paul Bedard, "Jeep, an Obama Favorite, Looks to Shift Production to China," *Washington Examiner*, October 25, 2016, https://www.washingtonexaminer.com/jeep-an-obama-favorite-looks-to-shift-production-to-china#.UL-XlmejhAN.

140 *It got amplified*: Drudge Report Archives, October 25, 2012, https://www.drudgereportarchives.com/data/2012/10/25/20121025_174238.htm.

141 *"Let's set the record straight*: Gualberto Ranieri, "Jeep in China," Chrysler corporate blog, October 25, 2012, accessed via the Wayback Machine, https://web.archive.org/web/20121026045354/http://blog.chryslerllc.com/blog.do?id=1932&p=entry.

141 *"Romney Repeats False Claim"*: Nathan Bomey and Brent Snavely, "Romney Repeats False Claim of Jeep Outsourcing to China; Chrysler Refutes Story," *Detroit Free Press*, October 25, 2012, https://www.dailyitem.com/archives/romney-repeats-false-claim-of-jeep-outsourcing-to-china-chrysler-refutes-story/article_9c6b8197-70b7-515e-bc20-24f983ea"806.html.

142 *"In what many in the campaign"*: Mike Allen and Jim Vande Hei, "Inside the Campaign: How Mitt Romney Stumbled," *Politico*, September 18, 2012, https://web.archive.org/web/20120918081809/http://dyn.politico.com/printstory.cfm?uuid=B6BEB452-8AF1-45FC-8831-9FCFF5CE1576.

143 *nuanced argument for a managed bankruptcy*: Jon Greenberg, "Jennifer Granholm Says Romney's Response to the Auto Crisis Was 'Let Detroit Go Bankrupt,'" PolitiFact, September 7, 2012, https://www.politifact.com/factchecks/2012/sep/07/jennifer-granholm/granholm-says-romneys-response-auto-crisis-was-let/.

144 *Stevens held his ground*: This account comes from Madden. Stevens said he didn't recall details of the conversation but didn't dispute Madden's account. Stevens said he would have countered with the points he makes at this conclusion of this chapter about new jobs still going to China instead of the United States.

145 *He had anchorman good looks*: Betsy Rothstein, "Sighting: Kevin Madden at the Ritz-Carlton," *The Hill*, December 13, 2006, https://thehill.com/capital-living/in-the-know/17845-julia-carson-lingers-in-nougatocity/.

146 *Glenn Kessler, the* Washington Post: Glenn Kessler, "4 Pinocchios for Mitt Romney's Misleading Ad on Chrysler and China," *Washington Post*, October 29, 2012, https://www.washingtonpost.com/blogs/fact-checker/post

/4-pinocchios-for-mitt-romneys-misleading-ad-on-chrysler-and-china/2012/10/29/2a153a04-21d7-11e2-ac85-e669876c6a24_blog.html.

146 *Michael Tomasky in The Daily Beast*: Michael Tomasky, "Romney and Jeeps: F-you Dishonest," Daily Beast, October 29, 2012, https://www.thedailybeast.com/f-you-dishonesty-romney-and-jeep.

146 *PolitiFact*: *"The ad ignores"*: Jon Greenberg, "Mitt Romney Says Obama's Chrysler Deal Undermined U.S. Workers," PolitiFact, October 30, 2012, https://www.politifact.com/factchecks/2012/oct/30/mitt-romney/mitt-romney-obama-chrysler-sold-italians-china-ame/.

146 *Of course, this kind of deception*: Jonathan Cohn, "A Desperate, Deceptive Gambit for Romney in Ohio," *The New Republic*, October 28, 2012, https://newrepublic.com/article/109256/romney-uses-debunked-story-about-chrysler-undermine-obamas-story-auto-industry-rescue.

147 *The editorial board of the* Cleveland Plain Dealer: "Flailing in Ohio, Romney Rolls Out Jeep Ploy," *Cleveland Plain Dealer*, October 30, 2012, https://www.cleveland.com/opinion/2012/10/flailing_in_ohio_romney_rolls.html.

147 *"I feel obliged to unambiguously restate"*: Sergio Marchionne, "Message from Sergio Marchionne regarding Jeep Production," Chrysler corporate blog, October 30, 2012, https://web.archive.org/web/20121102191823/http://blog.chryslergroupllc.com/entry/1950/message_from_sergio_marchionne_regarding__jeep_production.

147 *Donald Trump got*: Bernie Woodall, "Chrysler Exec Has Rough Words for Trump," Reuters, November 1, 2012, https://www.reuters.com/article/2012/11/01/chrysler-trump-idUSL1E8M1G2G20121101/.

147 *"Ladies and gentlemen, have they no shame?"*: Matthew Daly, "Buddy Act: Clinton, Biden Gave Fiery Ohio Speeches," Associated Press, October 30, 2012, https://www.the-review.com/story/news/2012/10/30/buddy-act-clinton-biden-gave/19259869007/.

148 *"The ad makes the point"*: Devin Dwyer, "Misleading Romney Ad on Jeeps Draws Obama Retorts," ABC News, October 29, 2012, https://abcnews.go.com/blogs/politics/2012/10/misleading-romney-ad-on-jeeps-draws-obama-retort.

148 *University of Akron*: Stephen Koff, "Mitt Romney Didn't Win Ohio, yet GOP Margins in White House Race Improved," Cleveland.com, November 8, 2012, https://www.cleveland.com/politics/2012/11/post_6.html.

149 *"People often say"*: Angie Drobnic Holan, "Lie of the Year: The Romney Campaign's Ad on Jeeps Made in China," PolitiFact, December 12, 2012, https://www.politifact.com/article/2012/dec/12/lie-year-2012-Romney-Jeeps-China/.

149 *FactCheck.org included*: Glenn Kessler, "The Biggest Pinocchios of 2012," *Washington Post*, December 21, 2012, https://www.washingtonpost.com/blogs/fact-checker/post/the-biggest-pinocchios-of-2012/2012/12/20/27b69404-4ae7-11e2-b709-667035ff9029_blog.html.

149 *Managing Editor Lori Robertson*: Lori Robertson, "Whoppers of 2012: Final Edition," FactCheck.org, December 10, 2012, https://www.factcheck.org/2012/10/whoppers-of-2012-final-edition/.

CHAPTER 11 Working the Refs

153 *"work the refs"*: Lloyd Grove, "Media to the Left! Media to the Right! The GOP, Shooting the Messengers," *Washington Post*, August 20, 1992, https://www.washingtonpost.com/archive/lifestyle/1992/08/20/media-to-the-left-media-to-the-right-the-gop-shooting-the-messengers/d140cc5b-ec9b-47f3-8afd-df10beebce8d/.

155 *"accurate representation of the facts"*: Nicole Hemmer, *Messengers of the Right: Conservative Media and the Transformation of American Politics* (Philadelphia: University of Pennsylvania Press, 2016).

156 *But for Nixon*: Ibid., 222.

156 *"an oppressed minority"*: Ibid., xiv.

156 *That coziness between*: King Williams, "The History of Conservative Media with Nicole Hemmer, Author of Messengers of the Right," July 23, 2022, in *The Breakdown*, podcast, https://podcastaddict.com/?id=https%3A%2F%2Fanchor.fm%2Fs%2Ff77be24%2Fpodcast%2Fplay%2F55213163%2Fhttps%253A%252F%252Fd3ctxlq1ktw2nl.cloudfront.net%252Fstaging%252F2022-6-23%252Fda8e0fca-c290-36b2-b992-5fcfd9bc17a9.mp3&podcastId=4040913.

156 *"The press is the enemy"*: Jonathan Aitken, *Charles Colson: A Life Redeemed* (New York: Random House, 2010), 143.

156 *He said on-screen graphics*: Gabriel Sherman, *The Loudest Voice in the Room: How the Brilliant, Bombastic Roger Ailes Built Fox News—and Divided a Country* (New York: Random House, 2014).

158 *Two well-respected academic centers*: The EIP also included Graphika, a social media analytics company, and the Atlantic Council's Digital Forensic Research Lab. See "The Long Fuse," Election Integrity Partnership, July 1, 2021, https://www.eipartnership.net/report.

159 *In November 2023*: Interim Staff Report of the Committee on the Judiciary and the Select Subcommittee on the Weaponization of the Federal Government, "The Weaponization of 'Disinformation' Pseudo-experts

and Bureaucrats: How the Federal Government Partnered with Universities to Censor Americans' Political Speech," U.S. House of Representatives, November 2023, https://judiciary.house.gov/sites/evo-subsites/republicans-judiciary.house.gov/files/evo-media-document/EIP_Jira_Ticket_Staff_Report_11-6-23_Clean.pdf.

159 *The Gateway Pundit*: Jim Hoft, "The Weaponization of 'Disinformation' Pseudo-experts and Bureaucrats: How the Federal Government Partnered with Universities to Censor Americans'" Political Speech," The Gateway Pundit, May 2, 2023, https://www.thegatewaypundit.com/2023/05/breaking-attorneys-gateway-pundit-including-america-first-legal/.

160 *Naismith College Player of the Year*: "NCAA Women's Basketball's Finest," Women's Basketball's Finest, March 2007, http://fs.ncaa.org/Docs/stats/w_basketball_RB/misc/wbbfinest.pdf, 68.

161 *In real life*: "Vaccines, Misinformation, and the Internet (Part 2)," February 27, 2020, in *Short Wave,* produced by NPR, podcast, https://www.npr.org/transcripts/809601288.

164 *"flock of birds"*: There's a fascinating theory that flocks of birds help explain human political behavior. Kate Starbird described it as "collective intelligence that explains how birds and other groups of animals coordinate their behavior by taking physical cues (and sometimes cues left behind in the environment) from each other. They don't explicitly chat and say, 'Here's our plan for how we're going to find food and avoid danger today.' They make choices based on the behavior of others, and if a few birds start to go investigate something in one direction, often the whole group follows." Renée DiResta wrote about this in "How Online Mobs Act Like Flocks of Birds," *NOĒMA*, November 3, 2022, https://www.noemamag.com/how-online-mobs-act-like-flocks-of-birds/.

165 *The case was initiated*: Ian Millhiser, "The Supreme Court Showdown over Social Media 'Censorship,' Explained," Vox, September 29, 2023, https://www.vox.com/scotus/2023/9/22/23883888/supreme-court-social-media-first-amendment-netchoice-paxton-murthy-missouri-twitter-facebook.

165 *Jim Hoft, the owner*: Jason Hancock, "Missouri AG Aligns with St. Louis Conspiracy Theorist in Social Media Lawsuit," *Missouri Independent*, November 21, 2022, https://missouriindependent.com/2022/11/21/missouri-ag-aligns-with-st-louis-conspiracy-theorist-in-social-media-lawsuit/.

165 *But Starbird was defiant*: Kate Starbird, "UW Misinformation Researchers Will Not Buckle under Political Attacks," *Seattle Times*, October 6, 2023, https://www.seattletimes.com/opinion/uw-misinformation-researchers-will-not-buckle-under-political-attacks/.

166 *"In Republican circles"*: Miles Parks and Shannon Bond, "Why the Fight to Counter False Election Claims May Be Harder in 2024," NPR, November 10, 2023, https://www.npr.org/2023/11/10/1211929764/election-false-claims-social-media-cisa-trump.

166 *Texas attorney general Ken Paxton*: "Complaint for Declaratory and Injunctive Relief," The Daily Wire, LLC v. Department of State, December 2023, https://dw-wp-production.imgix.net/2023/12/DailyWire-v-State-final.pdf.

167 *In a 2024 paper*: Napoli presented the paper at the annual meeting of the Southern Political Science Association in January 2024. Philip M. Napoli, "Agnotology, Free Speech and the Precarious Politics of Media Research," SSRN, January 2024, https://papers.ssrn.com/sol3/papers.cfm?abstract_id=4695907.

167 *Meta kicked him off Facebook*: Twitter, "Permanent Suspension of @realDonaldTrump," January 8, 2021, https://blog.twitter.com/en_us/topics/company/2020/suspension.

168 *Meta allowed him back*: Nick Clegg, "Ending Suspension of Trump's Accounts with New Guardrails to Deter Repeat Offenses," Meta, January 25, 2023, https://about.fb.com/news/2023/01/trump-facebook-instagram-account-suspension/.

CHAPTER 12 The Ministry of Truth, Part 3

170 *The Department of Homeland Security issued a statement*: "Following HSAC Recommendation, DHS Terminates Disinformation Governance Board: Homeland Security," U.S. Department of Homeland Security, August 24, 2022, https://www.dhs.gov/news/2022/08/24/following-hsac-recommendation-dhs-terminates-disinformation-governance-board.

171 *On BlazeTV*: BlazeTV, "Disgraced 'Disinformation Czar' Is Now a Foreign Agent | @patgray," YouTube, November 28, 2022, https://www.youtube.com/watch?v=nffOJfzW1pI.

172 *"I just never saw"*: John Dickerson, "Former House Speaker John Boehner Accuses Some in Congress of Being 'Political Terrorists,'" CBS News, April 9, 2021, https://www.cbsnews.com/news/former-house-speaker-john-boehner-accuses-some-in-congress-of-being-political-terrorists/.

172 *He complained she hadn't*: The letter is posted at https://judiciary.house.gov/sites/evo-subsites/republicans-judiciary.house.gov/files/legacy_files/wp-content/uploads/2022/12/2022-12-01-JDJ-to-Jankowicz-v2.pdf.

174 *"We know where you sleep"*: Andrew Rice, "The Women Rudy Giuliani Tried to Destroy Ruby Freeman and Shaye Moss Testify How a Smear Campaign Turned Their Lives to Hell," *New York*, December 15, 2023, https://nymag

.com/intelligencer/2023/12/ruby-freeman-shaye-moss-describe-smears-by-rudy-giuliani.html.

174 *Dominion needed to prove*: Coverage in the *New York Times* and on NPR explained the significant burden Dominion was facing. See Jeremy Peters, "Defamation Suit against Fox Grows More Contentious," *New York Times*, December 4, 2022, https://www.nytimes.com/2022/12/04/business/media/fox-dominion-lawsuit.html?searchResultPosition=12; David Folkenflik, "Fox News Stands in Legal Peril. It Says Defamation Loss Would Harm All Media," NPR, March 6, 2023, https://www.npr.org/2023/03/06/1161221798/if-fox-news-loses-defamation-dominion-media.

176 *"Good riddance, Tucker"*: Nina Jankowicz, "Good Riddance, Tucker. You Have Contributed More to the Degradation of Our Democracy and the Hell My Family Has Endured for the Past Year than Anyone Else," Twitter, April 24, 2023, https://twitter.com/wiczipedia/status/1650535148612403200?s=61&t=qce2hOlHkJEvtDuMP3OKAA.

183 *Sharyl Attkisson, a video journalist*: Sharyl Attkisson, "Censored," *Full Measure with Sheryl Attkisson*, October 1, 2023, https://sharylattkisson.com/2023/12/watch-censored-2/.

184 *Writing about the video*: Nina Jankowicz, "I Shouldn't Have to Accept Being in Deepfake Porn," *The Atlantic*, June 25, 2023, https://www.theatlantic.com/ideas/archive/2023/06/deepfake-porn-ai-misinformation/674475/.

184 *He even appeared on the show*: "Jake the Dog Comes to NPR, Howls Along with All Things Considered Theme," NPR, November 22, 2019, https://www.npr.org/2019/11/22/782130884/jake-the-dog-comes-to-npr-howls-along-with-all-things-considered-theme.

185 *Connolly was a former*: Craig Whitlock, "Capano Found Guilty in Lovers Slaying," *Washington Post*, January 18, 1999, https://www.washingtonpost.com/archive/local/1999/01/18/capano-found-guilty-in-lovers-slaying/1b73fd2e-9dec-4ea7-8dd9-34915d3b148c/.

CHAPTER 13 How Can We Stop the Lying?

189 *"The fact-checkers are basically just a P.R. arm of the Democrats"*: Laura Ingraham said this in an exchange with Rep. Tom Tiffany. *The Ingraham Angle*, September 7, 2022, 7:29 PM PDT, https://archive.org/details/FOXNEWSW_20220908_020000_The_Ingraham_Angle/start/1792/end/1852?q=politifact+democrats.

190 *Many people were fooled by falsehoods*: Daniel Funke, "Fact-Checking False Claims about the Election," PolitiFact, November 19, 2020, https://www

.politifact.com/article/2020/nov/20/fact-checking-false-claims-about-2020-election/.

190 *more than one-third of Americans*: Martin Pengelly, "More than a Third of US Adults Say Biden's 2020 victory Was Not Legitimate," *The Guardian*, January 6, 2024, https://www.theguardian.com/us-news/2024/jan/02/poll-biden-2020-election-illegitimate.

190 *more than one-fourth of Americans*: "Many Americans Believe That Climate Change Is Mostly Caused by Human Activity, but Few Report Making Changes to Help Limit It," Ipsos, May 4, 2023, https://www.ipsos.com/sites/default/files/ct/news/documents/2023-05/Extreme%20Weather%20Topline_0.pdf.

191 *He cites promising signs*: Brian Stelter, *Network of Lies* (New York: One Signal, 2023).

191 *But still, changes happen*: Ibid.

191 *2017 study that I co-authored*: Rebecca Iannucci and Bill Adair, "Heroes or Hacks: The Partisan Divide over Fact-Checking," Duke Reporters' Lab, June 2017, https://drive.google.com/file/d/1sK35viB_7F8T6JZ7CFq3tm5wKjNY9Qxn/view.

192 *The most famous fact-checking study*: Nyhan discussed the original study and the subsequent research in his article. Brendan Nyhan, "Why the Backfire Effect Does Not Explain the Durability of Political Misperceptions," *PNAS*, April 9, 2021, https://www.pnas.org/doi/10.1073/pnas.1912440117.

193 *91 percent of Americans believe*: John Gramlich, "Partisans Agree Political Leaders Should Be Honest and Ethical, Disagree Whether Trump Fits the Bill," Pew Research Center, January 30, 2019, https://www.pewresearch.org/short-reads/2019/01/30/partisans-agree-political-leaders-should-be-honest-and-ethical-disagree-whether-trump-fits-the-bill/.

193 *people are more affected by an aggregate report card*: Brendan Nyhan et al., "Counting the Pinocchios: The Effect of Summary Fact-Checking Data on Perceived Accuracy and Favorability of Politicians," *Research & Politics* 6, no. 3 (July–September, 2019).

193 *politicians who were reminded*: David Leonhardt, "Study Suggests Fact-Checking Influences Political Behavior," *New York Times*, October 8, 2013, https://archive.nytimes.com/thecaucus.blogs.nytimes.com/2013/10/08/study-suggests-fact-checking-influences-political-behavior/?searchResultPosition=2.

193 "Taxpayer Protection Pledge," Americans for Tax Reform, https:§//www.atr.org/take-the-pledge/.

195 *under the ownership of Elon Musk*: Jennifer Szalai, "The Problem of Misinformation in an Era without Trust," *New York Times*, December 31, 2023,

https://www.nytimes.com/2023/12/31/books/review/elon-musk-trust-misinformation-disinformation.html.

196 *candidates with the worst records*: Most of the student papers that proposed bonus or reduced time during debates relied on instant fact-checking. Some outlets, including PolitiFact, have tried to provide that kind of live journalism, but it's not practical on the scale that the students proposed, so my proposal here is based on the aggregate records of the candidates over the course of a campaign.

196 *found there was so little scrutiny*: Mark Stencel and Erica Ryan et al., "Duke Reporters' Lab: Vast Gaps in Fact-Checking across the U.S. Allow Politicians to Elude Scrutiny," March 2023, https://reporterslab.org/wp-content/uploads/2023/03/From-Fact-Deserts-to-Fact-Streams.pdf.

197 *has experimented with a debate format*: You can watch the Vox debates on YouTube. Cannabis: "A Fact-Checked Debate about Legal Weed," Vox, December 14, 2022, YouTube video, 11:31, https://www.youtube.com/watch?v=8TPaCsQVwA8; euthanasia: "A Fact-Checked Debate about Euthanasia in Canada," Vox, July 27, 2023, YouTube video, 20:51, https://www.youtube.com/watch?v=TJAklSh_rjk.

199 *segments are rarely collected*: Our team at the Duke Reporters' Lab has noticed this over the years, particularly when they conduct our annual census of fact-checking. Local stations post their segments on the web but make little effort to collect them so viewers can review them by candidate or race. See Mark Stencel and Rebecca Iannucci, "Plenty of Fact-Checking Is Taking Place, but Finding It Is Another Issue," Poynter, October 16, 2017, https://www.poynter.org/fact-checking/2017/plenty-of-fact-checking-is-taking-place-but-finding-it-is-another-issue/.

203 *gloomy report about the risks facing the planet*: "Global Risks Report 2024," World Economic Forum, January 10, 2024, https://www.weforum.org/publications/global-risks-report-2024/. Previous reports are archived at https://www.weforum.org/publications/series/global-risks-report/.

203 *"Humanity faces a perilous future"*: Hanna Ziady, "The People Paid to Spot Risks See High Chance of 'Global Catastrophe' within 10 Years," CNN, January 10, 2024, https://www.cnn.com/2024/01/10/business/wef-global-risks-report/index.html.

203 *Conservatives reacted predictably*: James Bovard, "The Elites' Absurd Davos Crusade: Destroy Freedom to Save Humanity," *New York Post*, January 17, 2024, https://nypost.com/2024/01/17/opinion/the-elites-absurd-davos-crusade-destroy-freedom-to-save-humanity/; Tom Olohan, "WEF Flunky Calls for Censorship of Greatest Risk 'Mis- and Disinformation,'" *NewsBusters*, January

12, 2024, https://www.newsbusters.org/blogs/free-speech/tom-olohan/2024/01/12/wef-flunky-calls-censorship-greatest-risk-mis-and.

204 *Hawley, who replied in just ninety minutes*: Josh Hawley (@HawleyMO), "The Biden Admin lied about their censorship board for months. Only when a patriotic whistleblower came forward [. . .]," Twitter, July 18, 2022, https://x.com/HawleyMO/status/1549066076805541888?s=20.

EPILOGUE

207 *Judge Christopher Cooper wasn't buying it*: United States v. Eric Gene Barber, 1:21-cr-00228-CRC-1 (Washington D.C., March 2021), May 30 and June 1, 2023.

212 *joined the chorus of Republicans*: Mike Pence, "Election Integrity Is a National Imperative," The Daily Signal, March 3, 2021, https://www.dailysignal.com/2021/03/03/election-integrity-is-a-national-imperative.

212 *"There are some Trump supporters who think he's the Antichrist"*: David Siders, "Pence Flatlines as 2024 Field Takes Shape," *Politico*, July 19, 2023, https://www.politico.com/news/2021/07/19/pence-flatlines-2024-499919.

212 *included in an indictment against Trump*: Shane Goldmacher et al., "From Right-Hand Man to Critical Witness: Pence at Heart of Trump Prosecution," *New York Times*, August 2, 2023, https://www.nytimes.com/2023/08/02/us/politics/mike-pence-trump-indictment.html.

213 *joined Jeb Bush as communications director*: Timothy Miller, LinkedIn, https://www.linkedin.com/in/timmillernola/.

213 *ended the interview*: Timothy Miller, "Steve Bannon Says 'Kari Lake Is the Future,'" *The Circus on SHOWTIME,* November 14, 2022, YouTube video, 0:58, https://www.youtube.com/watch?v=TLpIBSxQHvs.

Index

About the Author

Bill Adair is an award-winning journalist and educator. He is the creator of PolitiFact and the co-founder of the International Fact-Checking Network. He is the Knight Professor of the Practice of Journalism and Public Policy at Duke University. His awards include the Pulitzer Prize for National Reporting (with the PolitiFact staff), the Manship Prize for New Media in Democratic Discourse, and the Everett Dirksen Award for Distinguished Coverage of Congress.